WILLIAM WELLS BROWN

The Negro
IN THE
American Rebellion

Introduced and annotated by
WILLIAM EDWARD FARRISON

New York: THE CITADEL PRESS

Introduction copyright © 1971 by William Edward Farrison
Published by Citadel Press, Inc.
A subsidiary of Lyle Stuart, Inc.
222 Park Avenue South, New York, N. Y. 10003
In Canada: George J. McLeod Limited
73 Bathurst St., Toronto 2B, Ontario
Manufactured in the United States of America
Library of Congress catalog card number: 76-147828
ISBN 0-8065-0232-0 (clothbound)
ISBN 0-8065-0238-X (paperbound)

INTRODUCTION

On its second page the *National Anti-Slavery Standard* for October 6, 1866, informed its readers as follows: "William Wells Brown, who has, for the past two or three years, given himself mainly to his profession as a physician, is engaged upon a new book, to be entitled, 'The Negro in the Great Rebellion.' " By the end of the year Brown had the work ready for the press and had copyrighted it under the title *The Negro in the American Rebellion: His Heroism and His Fidelity*. It was first published by Lee and Shepard in Boston in the spring of 1867.

In four earlier works Brown had proved himself a pioneering Negro author. This he had done in his *Three Years in Europe* (London, 1852), a book of travels; *Clotel; Or, The President's Daughter* (London, 1852), a novel; *Experience; Or, How to Give a Northern Man a Backbone* (1856), a drama which seems never to have been published; and *The Escape; Or, A Leap for Freedom: A Drama in Five Acts* (Boston, 1858). With the new book Brown again became a pioneer, in this instance in the writing of the military history of the American Negro.[1] Accounts of the part

1. All five of these works are discussed at length in William Edward Farrison's *William Wells Brown: Author and Reformer* (Chicago: The University of Chicago Press, 1969). *Clotel* has also been edited by an introduction and notes by Farrison and published by The Citadel Press (New York, 1969).

Negroes had played in the American Revolution and the War of 1812 had been included in previously published works. Foremost among these was William C. Nell's monumental *The Colored Patriots of the American Revolution* (Boston, 1855). This was an enlargement of the same author's *Services of Colored Americans, in the Wars of 1776 and 1812,* a pamphlet which had been published in Boston in 1852. Another of these works, one distinguished by rare scholarship, was George Livermore's *An Historical Research Respecting the Opinions of the Founders of the Republic on Negroes as Slaves, as Citizens, and as Soldiers* (Boston, 1862). Brown's, nevertheless, was the first attempt to write a history of the Negro's part in the Civil War and the first attempt to encompass in one work the history of the Negro's part in all three of these wars.

Although in this volume Brown did not refer to Nell's book, he was certainly familiar with it. He and Nell had long been closely associated in the Massachusetts Anti-Slavery Society, at various times he had been a boarder in Nell's home, and Nell had acknowledged indebtedness to him for "interesting facts and testimonies" for use in the book.[2] In his Preface, Brown referred to Livermore's work as his source of information concerning the services of Negroes in the American Revolution. He was also indebted to the same work, as he did not explain, for what he recounted concerning the part Negroes had in the War of 1812.

2. See the listings of Brown and Nell in *The Boston Directory* for 1856 and 1857. See also the prospectus for *The Colored Patriots of the American Revolution* in *The Liberator* for May 25 and June 1, 1855, pp. 83 and 87 respectively.

Brown's somewhat petulant statement at the end of his Preface that he had waited patiently but in vain "before beginning this work, with the hope that some one more competent would take the subject in hand" strained the quality of accuracy as well as good taste. When his book appeared, the Civil War had been over only two years. This period was hardly long enough to tax the patience of anyone who wanted to see written a thorough history of the part played by Negroes in the war.

Considering the fact that *The Negro in the American Rebellion* was a very good pioneering work, the first edition of it received much less attention than it merited. The only review of it which I have found appeared belatedly on the third page of the *National Anti-Slavery Standard* for September 21, 1867. That review briefly complimented both the book and its author.

According to an advertisement on an end leaf in the third edition of Brown's *My Southern Home,* which was published in Boston in 1882, almost all of the first edition of *The Negro in the American Rebellion* "was burnt in the great Boston fire, so that but few copies were sold." Presumably the fire referred to was the conflagration of November 9, 1872, which devastated sixty-five acres in the business section of the city, including the area in which Lee and Shepard's publishing house was located.[3] The book having been on the market five years before that fire, however, there had been sufficient time for an appreciable number of copies of it to have been sold. In the same advertisement favor-

3. Moses King, *King's Handbook of Boston,* Seventh Edition (Cambridge, Massachusetts, 1885), p. 18.

able comments on the book were quoted from the *National Monitor* of Brooklyn, New York, William Lloyd Garrison, the *New York Daily Tribune*, and the *New York Evening Post*. A "New Edition," which was in fact only a new printing, of the book had been published in 1880 with the imprint of A. G. Brown and Company of Boston. A. G. Brown was Mrs. Annie (Gray) Brown, the author's second wife. Most probably all of the comments just referred to except the one by Garrison pertained to this edition. Garrison had died on May 24, 1879. The "New Edition" was last reprinted by A. G. Brown and Company in 1885 within a year after Brown died.

Although Brown eulogized especially the Negro soldiers who fought for the Union in the Civil War, he was possessed of no grand illusions concerning war. Ever devoted to the cause of peace as he was, he considered war exactly what Sherman said it was. He did not consider it an agency of civilization nor a necessary evil nor a matter of historical necessity, but the predictable effect of recognizable and remediable causes which would always lead to war wherever they were permitted to operate. Accordingly he was convinced that peace congresses and compromises, like the Missouri Compromise of 1820, the Compromise of 1850, and those proffered at the end of James Buchanan's administration, which failed to remove these causes would never prevent war. To him the Civil War was obviously the effect of an equally obvious cause, namely, the irrepressible conflict between freedom and slavery, the worst of crimes against humanity. It was the logical end of a long period of tyranny, immorality, and hypocrisy. Having deliberately sown the wind,

America had inevitably reaped the whirlwind, as Henry Wadsworth Longfellow had predicted on the day of John Brown's execution (December 2, 1859) that it would do.[4]

Brown hoped, of course, that his book would contribute to a great lesson America needed and still needs to learn from history. That lesson was and still is that to be worthwhile, democracy must be practiced as well as idealized.

The present edition of *The Negro in the American Rebellion* is a reproduction of the original edition of 1867.

WILLIAM EDWARD FARRISON

Durham, North Carolina

4. Samuel Longfellow, *Life of Henry Wadsworth Longfellow* (Boston, 1886), II, 347.

THE NEGRO

IN THE

AMERICAN REBELLION

His Heroism and his Fidelity

BY

WILLIAM WELLS BROWN

AUTHOR OF "SKETCHES OF PLACES AND PEOPLE ABROAD," "THE BLACK MAN," ETC

BOSTON

LEE & SHEPARD, 149 WASHINGTON STREET

1867

TO

WENDELL PHILLIPS, ESQ.,

AS A TOKEN OF

𝕬𝖉𝖒𝖎𝖗𝖆𝖙𝖎𝖔𝖓 𝖆𝖓𝖉 𝕲𝖗𝖆𝖙𝖎𝖙𝖚𝖉𝖊

FOR HIS

LONG DEVOTION TO THE CAUSE OF FREEDOM,

AND HIS UNTIRING ADVOCACY OF

THE EQUALITY OF THE NEGRO,

THIS VOLUME

IS MOST RESPECTFULLY INSCRIBED

BY THE AUTHOR.

PREFACE.

FEELING anxious to preserve for future reference an account of the part which the Negro took in suppressing the Slaveholders' Rebellion, I have been induced to write this work. In doing so, it occurred to me that a sketch of the condition of the race previous to the commencement of the war would not be uninteresting to the reader.

For the information concerning the services which the blacks rendered to the Government in the Revolutionary War, I am indebted to the late George Livermore, Esq., whose "Historical Research" is the ablest work ever published on the early history of the negroes of this country.

In collecting facts connected with the Rebellion, I have availed myself of the most reliable information that could be obtained from newspaper correspondents, as well as from those who were on the battle-field. To officers and privates of several of the colored regiments I am under many obligations for detailed accounts of engagements.

No doubt, errors in fact and in judgment will be discovered, which I shall be ready to acknowledge, and
correct in subsequent editions. The work might have
been swelled to double its present size; but I did
not feel bound to introduce an account of every little
skirmish in which colored men were engaged.

I waited patiently, before beginning this work, with
the hope that some one more competent would take
the subject in hand; but, up to the present, it has not
been done, although many books have been written
upon the Rebellion.

WILLIAM WELLS BROWN.

CAMBRIDGEPORT, MASS., Jan. 1, 1867.

CONTENTS.

CHAPTER I.

BLACKS IN THE REVOLUTIONARY WAR AND IN 1812.

CHAPTER II.

THE SOUTH-CAROLINA FRIGHT.

CHAPTER III.

THE NAT TURNER INSURRECTION.

CHAPTER IV.

SLAVE REVOLT AT SEA.

CHAPTER V.

GROWTH OF THE SLAVE-POWER.

CHAPTER VI.

THE JOHN BROWN RAID.

CHAPTER VII.

THE FIRST GUN OF THE REBELLION.

CHAPTER VIII.

THE UNION AND SLAVERY BOTH TO BE PRESERVED.

CHAPTER IX.

INTELLIGENT CONTRABANDS.

CHAPTER X.

PROCLAMATIONS OF FREMONT AND HUNTER.

CHAPTER XI.

HEROISM OF NEGROES ON THE HIGH SEAS.

CHAPTER XII.

GENERAL BUTLER AT NEW ORLEANS.

CHAPTER XIII.

THE DISTRICT OF COLUMBIA FREE.

CHAPTER XIV.

THE BLACK BRIGADE OF CINCINNATI.

CHAPTER XV.

PROCLAMATION OF FREEDOM.

CHAPTER XVI.

THE NEW POLICY.

CHAPTER XVII.

ARMING THE BLACKS.

CHAPTER XVIII.

BATTLE OF MILLIKEN'S BEND.

CHAPTER XIX.

RAISING BLACK REGIMENTS AT THE NORTH.

CHAPTER XXV.

HONORS TO THE NOBLE DEAD.

CHAPTER XXVI.

THE NORTHERN WING OF THE REBELLION.

CHAPTER XXVII.

ASSAULT ON FORT WAGNER.

CHAPTER XXVIII.

THE SLAVE-MARTYR.

CHAPTER XXIX.

BATTLE OF OLUSTEE, FLORIDA.

CHAPTER XXX.

BATTLE OF POISON SPRINGS, ARKANSAS.

CHAPTER XXXI.

THE MASSACRE AT FORT PILLOW.

CHAPTER XXXII.

INJUSTICE TO COLORED TROOPS.

CHAPTER XXXIII.

BATTLE OF HONEY HILL, SOUTH CAROLINA.

CHAPTER XXXIV.

BEFORE PETERSBURG AND RICHMOND.

CHAPTER XXXV.

WIT AND HUMOR OF THE WAR.

CHAPTER XXXVI.

A THRILLING INCIDENT OF THE WAR.

CHAPTER XXXVII.

PROGRESS AND JUSTICE.

CHAPTER XXXVIII.

FOURTH-OF-JULY CELEBRATION AT THE HOME OF JEFF. DAVIS.

CHAPTER XXXIX.

GALLANTRY, LOYALTY, AND KINDNESS OF THE NEGRO.

CHAPTER XL.

FALL OF THE CONFEDERACY, AND DEATH OF PRESIDENT LINCOLN.

CHAPTER XLI.

PRESIDENT ANDREW JOHNSON.

CHAPTER XLII.

ILL TREATMENT OF COLORED PEOPLE SOUTH.

CHAPTER XLIII.

PROTECTION FOR THE COLORED PEOPLE.

CHAPTER XLIV.

CASTE.

CHAPTER XLV.

SIXTH REGIMENT UNITED-STATES VOLUNTEERS.

THE NEGRO

IN THE

AMERICAN REBELLION.

CHAPTER I [1]

BLACKS IN THE REVOLUTIONARY WAR AND IN 1812.

The First Cargo of Slaves landed in the Colonies in 1620. — Slave Repre-
sentation in Congress. — Opposition to the Slave-Trade. — Crispus
Attucks, the First Victim of the Revolutionary War. — Bancroft's
Testimony. — Capture of Gen. Prescott. — Colored Men in the War
of 1812. — Gen. Andrew Jackson on Negro Soldiers.

I NOW undertake to write a history of the part which
the colored men took in the great American Rebellion.
Previous to entering upon that subject, however, I may
be pardoned for bringing before the reader the condition
of the blacks previous to the breaking out of the war.

The Declaration of American Independence, made
July 4, 1776, had scarcely been enunciated, and an
organization of the government commenced, ere the
people found themselves surrounded by new and trying
difficulties, which, for a time, threatened to wreck the
ship of state.

The forty-five slaves landed on the banks of the James

River, in the colony of Virginia, from the coast of Africa, in 1620, had multiplied to several thousands, and were influencing the political, social, and religious institutions of the country.[2] Brought into the colonies against their will; made the " hewers of wood and the drawers of water;" considered, in the light of law and public opinion, as mere chattels, — things to be bought and sold at the will of the owner; driven to their unrequited toil by unfeeling men, picked for the purpose from the lowest and most degraded of the uneducated whites, whose moral, social, and political degradation, by slavery, was equal to that of the slave, — the condition of the negro was indeed a sad one.

The history of this people, full of sorrow, blood, and tears, is full also of instruction for mankind. God has so ordered it that one class shall not degrade another, without becoming themselves contaminated. So with slavery in America. The institution bred in the master insulting arrogance, deteriorating sloth, pampered the loathsome lust it inflamed, until licentious luxury sapped the strength and rottened the virtue of the slave-owners of the South. Never were the institutions of a people, or the principles of liberty, put to such a severe test as those of the American Republic. The convention to frame the Constitution for the government of the United States had not organized before the slave-masters began to press the claims of their system upon the delegates. They wanted their property represented in the national Congress, and undue guarantees thrown around it; they wanted the African slave-trade made lawful, and their victims returned if they should attempt to escape; they begged that an article might be inserted in the Constitution, making it the duty of the General Government to put down the slaves if they should imitate their masters in striking a blow for freedom. They seemed afraid of the very evil they were clinging so closely to. "Thus conscience doth make cowards of us all."

In all this early difficulty, South Carolina took the lead against humanity, her delegates ever showing themselves the foes of freedom. Both in the Federal Convention to frame the Constitution, and in the State Conventions to ratify the same, it was admitted that the blacks had fought bravely against the British, and in favor of the American Republic; for the fact that a black man (Crispus Attucks) was the first to give his life at the commencement of the Revolution was still fresh in their minds. Eighteen years previous to the breaking out of the war, Attucks was held as a slave by Mr. William Brown of Framingham, Mass., and from whom he escaped about that time, taking up his residence in Boston. The Boston Massacre, March 5, 1770, may be regarded as the first act in the great drama of the American Revolution. "From that moment," said Daniel Webster, "we may date the severance of the British Empire." The presence of the British soldiers in King Street excited the patriotic indignation of the people. The whole community was stirred, and sage counsellors were deliberating and writing and talking about the public grievances. But it was not for "the wise and prudent" to be the first to *act* against the encroachments of arbitrary power. "A motley rabble of saucy boys, negroes and mulattoes, Irish Teagues, and outlandish Jack tars" (as John Adams described them in his plea in defence of the soldiers) could not restrain their emotion, or stop to inquire if what they *must do* was according to the letter of any law. Led by Crispus Attucks,

the mulatto slave, and shouting, " The way to get rid of
these soldiers is to attack the main guard ; strike at the
root ; this is the nest," with more valor than discretion,
they rushed to King Street, and were fired upon by
Capt. Preston's Company.   Crispus Attucks was the first
to fall : he and Samuel Gray and Jonas Caldwell were
killed on the spot.   Samuel Maverick and Patrick Carr
were mortally wounded.

The excitement which followed was intense.   The
bells of the town were rung.   An impromptu town-
meeting was held, and an immense assembly was gathered.

Three days after, on the 8th, a public funeral of the
martyrs took place.   The shops in Boston were closed ;
and all the bells of Boston and the neighboring towns
were rung.   It is said that a greater number of persons
assembled on this occasion than were ever before gathered on this continent for a similar purpose.   The body
of Crispus Attucks, the mulatto slave, had been placed
in Faneuil Hall, with that of Caldwell, both being
strangers in the city.   Maverick was buried from his
mother's house, in Union Street ; and Gray from his
brother's, in Royal Exchange Lane.   The four hearses
formed a junction in King Street ; and there the procession marched in columns six deep, with a long file of
coaches belonging to the most distinguished citizens, to
the Middle Burying-ground, where the four victims were
deposited in one grave, over which a stone was placed
with this inscription : —

> " Long as in Freedom's cause the wise contend,
>   Dear to your country shall your fame extend ;
>   While to the world the lettered stone shall tell
>   Where Caldwell, Attucks, Gray, and Maverick fell."

The anniversary of this event was publicly commemorated in Boston, by an oration and other exercises, every year until after our national independence was achieved, when the Fourth of July was substituted for the Fifth of March as the more proper day for a general celebration. Not only was the event commemorated, but the martyrs who then gave up their lives were remembered and honored.

For half a century after the close of the war, the name of Crispus Attucks was honorably mentioned by the most noted men of the country who were not blinded by foolish prejudice. At the battle of Bunker Hill, Peter Salem, a negro, distinguished himself by shooting Major Pitcairn, who, in the midst of the battle, having passed the storm of fire without, mounting the redoubt, and waving his sword, cried to the "rebels" to surrender. The fall of Pitcairn ended the battle in favor of liberty.

A single passage from Mr. Bancroft's history will give a succinct and clear account of the condition of the army, in respect to colored soldiers, at the time of the battle of Bunker Hill: —

"Nor should history forget to record, that, as in the army at Cambridge, so also in this gallant band, the free negroes of the colony had their representatives. For the right of free negroes to bear arms in the public defence was, at that day, as little disputed in New England as their other rights. They took their place, not in a separate corps, but in the ranks with the white man; and their names may be read on the pension-rolls of the country, side by side with those of other soldiers of the Revolution." — *Bancroft's History of the United States,* vol. vii. p. 421.

The capture of Major-Gen. Prescott, of the British army, on the 9th of July, 1777, was an occasion of great joy throughout the country. Prince, the valiant negro who seized that officer, ought always to be remembered with honor for his important service. The exploit was much commended at the time, as its results were highly important; and Col. Barton, very properly, received from Congress the compliment of a sword for his ingenuity and bravery. It seems, however, that it took more than one head to plan and to execute the undertaking. The following account of the capture is historical : —

" They landed about five miles from Newport, and three-quarters of a mile from the house, which they approached cautiously, avoiding the main guard, which was at some distance. *The colonel went foremost, with a stout, active negro close behind him, and another at a small distance : the rest followed so as to be near, but not seen.*

" A single sentinel at the door saw and hailed the colonel: he answered by exclaiming against, and inquiring for, rebel prisoners, but kept slowly advancing. The· sentinel again challenged him, and required the countersign. He said he had not the countersign, but amused the sentry by talking about rebel prisoners, and still advancing till he came within reach of the bayonet, which, he presenting, the colonel suddenly struck aside, and seized him. He was immediately secured, and ordered to be silent on pain of instant death. *Meanwhile, the rest of the men surrounding the house, the negro, with his head. at the second stroke, forced a passage into it, and then into the landlord's apartment. The landlord at first refused to give the necessary in-*

telligence; but, on the prospect of present death, he pointed to the general's chamber, which being instantly opened by the negro's head, the colonel, calling the general by name, told him he was a prisoner." — *Pennsylvania Evening Post,* Aug. 7, 1777 (in Frank Moore's "Diary of the American Revolution," vol. i. p. 468).

There is abundant evidence of the fidelity and bravery of the colored patriots of Rhode Island during the whole war. Before they had been formed into a separate regiment, they had fought valiantly with the white soldiers at Red Bank and elsewhere. Their conduct at the "Battle of Rhode Island," on the 29th of August, 1778, entitles them to perpetual honor. That battle has been pronounced by military authorities to have been one of the best-fought battles of the Revolutionary War. Its success was owing, in a great degree, to the good fighting of the negro soldiers. Mr. Arnold, in his "History of Rhode Island," thus closes his account of it : —

" A third time the enemy, with desperate courage and increased strength, attempted to assail the redoubt, and would have carried it, but for the timely aid of two Continental battalions despatched by Sullivan to support his almost exhausted troops. It was in repelling these furious onsets, that the newly raised black regiment, under Col. Greene, distinguished itself by deeds of desperate valor. Posted behind a thicket in the valley, they three times drove back the Hessians, who charged repeatedly down the hill to dislodge them ; and so determined were the enemy in these successive charges, that, the day after the battle, the Hessian colonel, upon whom this duty had devolved, applied to exchange his command, and go to New York, because he dared not

lead his regiment again to battle; lest his men should
shoot him for having caused them so much loss." — *Arnold's History of Rhode Island*, vol. ii. pp. 427, 428.

Three years later, these soldiers are thus mentioned
by the Marquis de Chastellux : —

" The 5th [of January, 1781] I did not set out till
eleven, although I had thirty miles' journey to Lebanon.
At the passage to the ferry, I met with a detachment
of the Rhode-Island regiment, — the same corps we had
with us all the last summer; but they have since been
recruited and clothed. The greatest part of them are
negroes or mulattoes : they are strong, robust men; and
those I have seen had a very good appearance." —
Chastellux's Travels, vol. i. p. 454 ; London, 1789.

When Col. Greene was surprised and murdered, near
Points Bridge, New York, on the 14th of May, 1781,
his colored soldiers heroically defended him till they
were cut to pieces; and the enemy reached him over
the dead bodies of his faithful negroes.

That large numbers of negroes were enrolled in the
army, and served faithfully as soldiers during the whole
period of the war of the Revolution, may be regarded
as a well-established historical fact. And it should be
borne in mind, that the enlistment was not confined, by
any means, to those who had before enjoyed the privileges of free citizens. Very many slaves were offered
to, and received by, the army, on the condition that
they were to be emancipated, either at the time of enlisting, or when they had served out the term of their
enlistment. The inconsistency of keeping in slavery
any person who had taken up arms for the defence of
our national liberty had led to the passing of an order
forbidding " slaves," as such, to be received as soldiers.

That colored men were equally serviceable in the last war with Great Britain is true, as the following historical document will show : —

GENERAL JACKSON'S PROCLAMATION TO THE NEGROES.

HEADQUARTERS, SEVENTH MILITARY DISTRICT,
MOBILE, Sept. 21, 1814.

To the Free Colored Inhabitants of Louisiana.

Through a mistaken policy, you have heretofore been deprived of a participation in the glorious struggle for national rights in which our country is engaged.   This no longer shall exist.

As sons of freedom, you are now called upon to defend our most inestimable blessing.   As Americans, your country looks with confidence to her adopted children for a valorous support, as a faithful return for the advantages enjoyed under her mild and equitable government. As fathers, husbands, and brothers, you are summoned to rally around the standard of the Eagle to defend all which is dear in existence.

Your country, although calling for your exertions, does not wish you to engage in her cause without amply remunerating you for the services rendered.   Your intelligent minds are not to be led away by false representations.   Your love of honor would cause you to despise the man who should attempt to deceive you. In the sincerity of a soldier, and the language of truth, I address you.

To every noble-hearted, generous freeman of color, volunteering to serve during the present contest with Great Britain, and no longer, there will be paid the same bounty, in money and lands, now received by the white soldiers of the United States ; viz., one hundred and twenty dollars in money, and one hundred and sixty acres of land. The non-commissioned officers and privates will also be entitled to the same monthly pay, and daily rations, and clothes, furnished to any American soldier.

On enrolling yourselves in companies, the Major-General Commanding will select officers for your government from your white fellow-citizens. Your non-commissioned officers will be appointed from among yourselves.

Due regard will be paid to the feelings of freemen and soldiers. You will not, by being associated with white men in the same corps, be exposed to improper comparisons or unjust sarcasm. As a distinct, independent battalion or regiment, pursuing the path of glory, you will, undivided, receive the applause and gratitude of your countrymen.

To assure you of the sincerity of my intentions, and my anxiety to engage your invaluable services to our country, I have communicated my wishes to the Governor of Louisiana, who is fully informed as to the manner of enrollment, and will give you every necessary information on the subject of this address.

ANDREW JACKSON,
Major-General Commanding.
[Niles's Register, vol. vii. p. 205.]

Three months later, Gen. Jackson addressed the same troops as follows : —

" To the Men of Color. Soldiers ! From the shores of Mobile I collected you to arms. I invited you to share in the perils and to divide the glory of your white countrymen. I expected much from you ; for I was not uninformed of those qualities which must render you so formidable to an invading foe. I knew that you could endure hunger and thirst, and all the hardships of war. I knew that you loved the land of your nativity, and that, like ourselves, you had to defend all that is most dear to man. But you surpass my hopes. I have found in you, united to these qualities, that noble enthusiasm which impels to great deeds.

" Soldiers ! The President of the United States shall be informed of your conduct on the present occasion ; and the voice of the Representatives of the American nation shall applaud your valor, as your general now praises your ardor. The enemy is near. His sails cover the lakes. But the brave are united; and, if he finds us contending with ourselves, it will be for the prize of valor, and fame its noblest reward."—*Niles's Register*, vol. vii. pp. 345, 346.

Black men served in the navy with great credit to themselves, receiving the commendation of Com. Perry and other brave officers.

Extract of a Letter from Nathaniel Shaler, Commander of the private-armed Schooner Gen. Tompkins, to his Agent in New York, dated, —

"At Sea, Jan. 1, 1813.

.   .   .   .   .   .

" Before I could get our light sails in, and almost before I could turn round, I was under the guns, not of a transport, but of a large *frigate !* and not more than a quarter of a mile from her. . . . . Her first broadside killed two men, and wounded six others. . . . . My officers conducted themselves in a way that would have done honor to a more permanent service. . . . .

The name of one of my poor fellows who was killed
ought to be registered in the book of fame, and remembered with reverence as long as bravery is considered a
virtue.   He was a black man, by the name of John
Johnson.   A twenty-four pound shot struck him in the
hip, and took away all the lower part of his body.   In
this state, the poor brave fellow lay on the deck, and
several times exclaimed to his shipmates, '*Fire away,
my boy : no haul a color down.*'   The other was also a
black man, by the name of John Davis, and was struck
in much the same way.   He fell near me, and several
times requested to be thrown overboard, saying he was
only in the way of others.

" When America has such tars, she has little to fear
from the tyrants of the ocean." — *Niles's Weekly Register,
Saturday, Feb.* 26, 1814.

CHAPTER II.[1]

THE SOUTH-CAROLINA FRIGHT.

Denmark Vesey, Peter Poyas, and their Companions. — The deep-laid Plans. — Religious Fanaticism. — The Discovery. — The Trials. — Convictions. — Executions.

HUMAN bondage is ever fruitful of insurrection, wherever it exists, and under whatever circumstances it may be found.

An undeveloped discontent always pervaded the black population of the South, bond and free. Many attempts at revolt were made : two only, however, proved of a serious and alarming character. The first was in 1812, the leader of which was Denmark Vesey, a free colored man, who had purchased his liberty in the year 1800, and who resided in Charleston, S.C. A carpenter by trade, working among the blacks, Denmark gained influence with them, and laid a plan of insurrection which showed considerable generalship. Like most men who take the lead in revolts, he was deeply imbued with a religious duty ; and his friends claimed that he had " a magnetism in his eye, of which his confederates stood in great awe : if he once got his eye on a man, there was no resisting it."

After resolving to incite the slaves to rebellion, Denmark began taking into his confidence such persons as he could trust, and instructing them to gain adherents from among the more reliable of both bond and free.

13

Peter Poyas, a slave of more than ordinary foresight and ability, was selected by him as his lieutenant; and to him was committed the arduous duty of arranging the mode of attack, and of acting as the military leader. Poyas voluntarily undertook the management of the most difficult part of the enterprise, the capture of the main guard-house, and had pledged himself to advance alone, and surprise the sentinel. Gullah Jack, Tom Russell, and Ned Bennett, — the last two were not less valuable than Peter Poyas; for Tom was an ingenious mechanic, and made battle-axes, pikes, and other instruments of death with which to carry on the war, — all of the above were to be generals of brigades, and were let into every secret of the intended rising. It had long been the custom in Charleston for the country slaves to visit the city in great numbers on Sunday, and return to their homes in time to commence work on the following morning. It was, therefore, determined by Vesey to have the rising take place on Sunday. The slaves of nearly every plantation in the neighborhood were enlisted, and were to take part. The details of the plan, however, were not rashly committed to the mass of the confederates: they were known only to a few, and were finally to have been announced after the evening prayer-meeting on the appointed Sunday. But each leader had his own company enlisted, and his own work marked out. When the clock struck twelve, all were to move. Poyas was to lead a party ordered to assemble at South Bay, and to be joined by a force from James' Island: he was then to march up and seize the arsenal and guard-house opposite St. Michael's Church, and detach a sufficient number to cut off all white citizens who should appear at the alarm-posts. A second body of blacks, from the country and the Neck, headed by Ned Bennett, was to assemble on the Neck, and seize the arsenal there. A third was to meet at Governor Bennett's Mills under the command of Rolla, another leader, and, after putting the governor and intendant to death, to march through the city, or be posted at Cannon's Bridge, thus preventing the inhabitants of Cannonsborough from entering the city.

A fourth, partly from the country and partly from the neighboring localities in the city, was to rendezvous on Gadsden's Wharf, and attack the upper guard-house. A fifth, composed of country and Neck blacks, was to assemble at Bulkley's Farm, two miles and a half from the city, seize the upper powder magazine, and then march down; and a sixth was to assemble at Vesey's, and obey his orders. A seventh detachment, under Gullah Jack, was to come together in Boundry Street, at the head of King Street, to capture the arms of the Neck company of militia, and to take an additional supply from Mr. Duguercron's shop. The naval stores on Meg's Wharf were also to be attacked. Meanwhile a horse company, consisting of many draymen, hostlers, and butcher boys, was to meet at Lightwood's Alley, and then scour the streets to prevent the whites from assembling.

Every white man coming out of his own door was to be killed, and, if necessary, the city was to be fired in several places; a slow match for this purpose having been purloined from the public arsenal, and placed in an accessible position. The secret and plan of attack, however, were incautiously divulged to a slave named Devany, belonging to Col. Prioleau; and he at once informed his master's family. The mayor, on getting possession of the facts, called the city council together for consultation. The investigation elicited nothing new, for the slaves persisted in their ignorance of the matter; and the authorities began to feel that they had been imposed upon by Devany and his informants, when another of the conspirators, being bribed, revealed what he knew. Arrest after arrest was made, and the mayor's court held daily examinations for weeks. After several weeks of incarceration, the accused, one hundred and twenty in number, were brought to trial: thirty-four were sentenced to transportation, twenty-seven acquitted by the court, twenty-five discharged without trial, and thirty-five condemned to death. With but two or three exceptions, all of the conspirators went to the gallows feeling that they had acted right, and died like men giving their lives for the cause of freedom. A report of the trial, written soon after, says of Denmark Vesey, " For several years before he disclosed his intentions to any one, he appears to have been constantly and assiduously engaged in endeavoring to imbitter the minds of the colored population against the whites. He rendered himself perfectly familiar with those parts of the Scriptures which he could use to show that slavery was contrary to the laws of God; that slaves were bound to attempt their emancipation, however shocking and bloody might be the consequences; and that such efforts would not only be pleasing to the Almighty, but were absolutely enjoined, and their success predicted, in the Scriptures.

" His favorite texts, when he addressed those of his own color, were Zech. xiv. 1–3, and Joshua vi. 21; and, in all his conversations, he identified their situation with that of the Israelites. Even while walking through the streets in company with another, he was not idle; for, if his companion bowed to a white person, he would rebuke him, and observe that all men were born equal, and that he was surprised that any one would degrade himself by such conduct; that he would never cringe to the whites, nor ought any one who had the feelings of a man. When answered, 'We are slaves,' he would sarcastically and indignantly reply, 'You deserve to remain slaves;' and if he were further asked, 'What can we do?' he would remark, 'Go and buy a spelling-book, and read the fable of Hercules and the wagoner,' which he would then repeat, and apply it to their situation.

" He sought every opportunity of entering into conversation with white persons, when they could be overheard by slaves near by, especially in grog-shops, during which conversation, he would artfully introduce some bold remark on slavery; and sometimes, when from the character of the person he was conversing with he found he might be still bolder, he would go so far, that, had not his declarations in such situations been clearly proved, they would scarcely have been credited. He continued this course till some time after the commencement of the last winter; by which time he had not only obtained incredible influence amongst persons of color, but many feared him more than they did their masters, and one of them declared, even more than his God."

The excitement which the revelations of the trial occasioned, and the continual fanning of the flame by the newspapers, was beyond description. Double guard in the city, the country patrol on horseback and on foot, the watchfulness that was observed on all plantations, showed the deep feeling of fear pervading the hearts of the slave-holders, not only in South Carolina, but the fever extended to the other Southern States, and all seemed to feel that a great crisis had been passed. And indeed, their fears appear not to have been without ground ; for a more complicated plan for an insurrection could scarcely have been conceived.

Many were of opinion, that, the rising once begun, they would have taken the city, and held it, and might have sealed the fate of slavery in the South. The best account of this whole matter is to be found in an able article in the " Atlantic Monthly " for June, 1861, from the pen of Col. T. W. Higginson, and to which I am indebted for the extracts contained in this sketch.

CHAPTER III.[1]

THE NAT TURNER INSURRECTION.

Nat Turner. — His Associates. — Their Meetings. — Nat's Religious Enthusiasm. — Bloodshed. — Wide-spread Terror. — The Trials and Executions.

The slave insurrection which occurred in Southampton County, Va., in the year 1831, although not as well planned as the one portrayed in the preceding chapter, was, nevertheless, more widely felt in the South. Its leader was Nat Turner, a slave.

On one of the oldest and largest plantations in Southampton County, Va., owned by Benjamin Turner, Esq., Nat was born a slave, on the 2d of October, 1800. His parents were of unmixed African descent. Surrounded as he was by the superstition of the slave-quarters, and being taught by his mother that he was born for a prophet, a preacher, and a deliverer of his race, it was not strange that the child should have imbibed the principles which were afterwards developed in his career. Early impressed with the belief that he had seen visions, and received communications direct from God, he, like Napoleon, regarded himself as a being of destiny. In his childhood, Nat was of an amiable disposition; but circumstances in which he was placed as a slave brought out incidents that created a change in his disposition, and turned his kind and docile feeling into the most intense hatred to the white race.

19

The ill-treatment he experienced at the hands of the whites, and the visions he claimed to have seen, caused Nat to avoid, as far as he could, all intercourse with his fellow-slaves, and threw around him a gloom and melancholy that disappeared only with his life.

Both the young slave and his friends averred that a full knowledge of the alphabet came to him in a single night. Impressed with the belief that his mission was a religious one, and this impression strengthened by the advice of his grandmother, a pious but ignorant woman, Nat commenced preaching when about twenty-five years of age, but never went beyond his own master's locality. In stature, he was under the middle size, long-armed, round-shouldered, and strongly marked with the African features. A gloomy fire burned in his looks, and he had a melancholy expression of countenance. He never tasted a drop of ardent spirits in his life, and was never known to smile. In the year 1828, new visions appeared to Nat; and he claimed to have direct communication with God. Unlike most of those born under the influence of slavery, he had no faith in conjuring, fortune-telling, or dreams, and always spoke with contempt of such things. Being hired out to a cruel master, he ran away, and remained in the woods thirty days, and could have easily escaped to the Free States, as did his father some years before; but he received, as he says in his confession, a communication from the Spirit, which said, " Return to your earthly master; for he who knoweth his Master's will, and doeth it not, shall be beaten with many stripes." It was not the will of his earthly but his heavenly Master that he felt bound to do; and therefore Nat returned. His fellow-slaves were greatly incensed at him for coming back; for they knew well his ability to reach Canada, or some other land of freedom, if he was so inclined. He says further, " About this time I had a vision, and saw white spirits and black spirits engaged in battle ; and the sun was darkened, the thunder rolled in the heavens, and blood flowed in streams; and I heard a voice saying, ' Such is your luck, such are you called on to see ; and let it come, rough or smooth, you must surely bear it ! ' " Some time after this, Nat had, as he says, another vision, in which the spirit appeared and said, " The Serpent is loosened, and Christ has laid down the yoke he has borne for the sins of men ; and you must take it up, and fight against the Serpent, for the time is fast approaching when the first shall be last, and the last shall be first." There is no doubt but that this last sentence filled Nat with enthusiastic feeling in favor of the liberty of his race, that he had so long dreamed of. " The last shall be first, and the first shall be last," seemed to him to mean something. He saw in it the overthrow of the whites, and the establishing of the blacks in their stead; and to this end he bent the energies of his mind. In February, 1831, Nat received his last communication, and beheld his last vision. He said, " I was told I should arise and prepare myself, and slay my enemies with their own weapons."

The plan of an insurrection was now formed in his own mind, and the time had arrived for him to take others into the secret; and he at once communicated his ideas to four of his friends, in whom he had implicit confidence. Hark Travis, Nelson Williams, Sam Edwards, and Henry Porter were slaves like himself, and, like him, had taken their names from their masters. A meeting must be held with these, and it must take place in some secluded place where the whites would not disturb them; and a meeting was appointed. The spot where they assembled was as wild and romantic as were the visions that had been impressed upon the mind of their leader.

Three miles from where Nat lived was a dark swamp, filled with reptiles, in the middle of which was a dry spot, reached by a narrow, winding path, and upon which human feet seldom ever trod, on account of its having been the place where a slave had been tortured to death by a slow fire, for the crime of having flogged his cruel and inhuman master. The night for the meeting arrived, and they came together. Hark brought a pig, Sam bread, Nelson sweet potatoes, and Henry brandy; and the gathering was turned into a feast. Others were taken in, and joined the conspiracy. All partook heartily of the food, and drank freely, except Nat. He fasted and prayed. It was agreed that the revolt should commence that night, and in their own masters' households, and that each slave should give his oppressor the death-blow. Before they left the swamp, Nat made a speech, in which he said, "Friends and brothers! We are to commence a great work to-night. Our race is to be delivered from slavery, and God has appointed us as the men to do his bidding; and let us be worthy of our calling. I am told to slay all the whites we encounter, without regard to age or sex. We have no arms or ammunition, but we will find these in the houses of our oppressors; and, as we go on, others can join us. Remember that we do not go forth for the sake of blood and carnage; but it is necessary, that, in the commencement of this revolution, all the whites we meet should die, until we have an army strong enough to carry on the war upon a Christian basis. Remember that ours is not a war for robbery, and to satisfy our passions: it is a struggle for freedom. Ours must be deeds, and not words. Then let's away to the scene of action."

Among those who had joined the conspirators was Will, a slave, who scorned the idea of taking his master's name. Though his soul longed to be free, he evidently became one of the party as much to satisfy revenge as for the liberty that he saw in the dim distance. Will had seen a dear and beloved wife sold to the negro-trader, and taken away, never to be beheld by him again in this life. His own back was covered with scars, from his shoulders to his feet. A large scar, running from his right eye down to his chin, showed that he had lived with a cruel master. Nearly six feet in height, and one of the strongest and most athletic of his race, he proved to be the most unfeeling of all the insurrectionists. His only weapon was a broad-axe, sharp and heavy.

Nat and his accomplices at once started for the plantation of Joseph Travis, with whom the four lived; and there the first blow was struck. In his confession, just before his execution, Nat said,—

"On returning to the house, Hark went to the door with an axe, for the purpose of breaking it open,— as we knew we were strong enough to murder the family should they be awakened by the noise ; but, reflecting that it might create an alarm in the neighborhood, we determined to enter the house secretly, and murder them whilst sleeping. Hark got a ladder, and set it against the chimney, on which I ascended, and, hoisting a window, entered and came down stairs, unbarred the doors, and removed the guns from their places. It was then observed that I must spill the first blood. On which, armed with a hatchet, and accompanied by Will, I entered my master's chamber. It being dark, I could not give a death-blow. The hatchet glanced from his head: he sprang from the bed, and called his wife. It was his last word. Will laid him dead with a blow of his axe."

They went from plantation to plantation, until the whole neighborhood was aroused; and the whites turned out in large numbers to suppress the rebellion. Nat and his accomplices fought bravely, but to no purpose.

Reinforcements came to the whites; and the blacks were overpowered and defeated by the superior numbers of the enemy. In this battle, many were slain on both sides. Will, the blood-thirsty and revengeful slave, fell with his broad-axe uplifted, after having laid three of the whites dead at his feet with his own strong arm and his terrible weapon. His last words were, "Bury my axe with me." For he religiously believed, that, in the next world, the blacks would have a contest with the whites, and that he would need his axe. Nat Turner, after fighting to the last with his short sword, escaped with some others to the woods near by, and was not captured for nearly two months. When brought to trial, he pleaded "not guilty," feeling, as he said, that it was always right for one to strike for his own liberty. After going through a mere form of trial, he was convicted and executed at Jerusalem, the county-seat for Southampton County, Va. Not a limb trembled, or a muscle was observed to move. Thus died Nat Turner, at the early age of thirty-one years, a martyr to the freedom of his race, and a victim to his own fanaticism. He meditated upon the wrongs of his oppressed and injured people till the idea of their deliverance excluded all other ideas from his mind; and he devoted his life to its realization. Every thing appeared to him a vision, and all favorable omens were signs from God. He foretold, that, at his death, the sun would refuse to shine, and that there would be signs of disapprobation given from Heaven. And it is true that the sun was darkened, a storm gathered, and more boisterous weather had never appeared in Southampton County than on the day of Nat's execution. The sheriff, warned by the prisoner, refused to cut the cord that held the trap. No black man would touch the rope. A poor old white man, long besotted by drink, was brought forty miles to be the executioner.

Fifty-five whites and seventy-three blacks lost their lives in the Southampton Rebellion. On the fatal night, when Nat and his companions were dealing death to all they found, Capt. Harris, a wealthy planter, had his life saved by the devotion and timely warning of his slave Jim, said to have been half-brother to his master. After the revolt had been put down, and parties of whites were out hunting the suspected blacks, Capt. Harris, with his faithful slave, went into the woods in search of the negroes. In saving his master's life, Jim felt that he had done his duty, and could not consent to become a betrayer of his race; and, on reaching the woods, he handed his pistol to his master, and said, " I cannot help you hunt down these men: they, like myself, want to be free. Sir, I am tired of the life of a slave: please give me my freedom, or shoot me on the spot." Capt. Harris took the weapon, and pointed it at the slave. Jim, putting his right hand upon his heart, said, " This is the spot; aim here." The captain fired, and the slave fell dead at his feet.

CHAPTER IV.

SLAVE REVOLT AT SEA.

Madison Washington. — His Escape from the South. — His Love of Liberty. — His Return. — His Capture. — The Brig "Creole." — The Slave-traders. — Capture of the Vessel. — Freedom of the Oppressed.

THE revolt on board of the brig "Creole," on the high seas, by a number of slaves who had been shipped for the Southern market, in the year 1841, created at the time a profound sensation throughout the country. Before entering upon it, however, I will introduce to the reader the hero of the occasion.

Among the great number of fugitive slaves who arrived in Canada towards the close of the year 1840, was one whose tall figure, firm step, and piercing eye attracted at once the attention of all who beheld him. Nature had treated him as a favorite. His expressive countenance painted and reflected every emotion of his soul. There was a fascination in the gaze of his finely cut eyes that no one could withstand. Born of African parentage, with no mixture in his blood, he was one of the handsomest of his race. His dignified, calm, and unaffected features announced at a glance that he was endowed with genius, and created to guide his fellow-men. He called himself Madison Washington, and said that his birthplace was in the "Old Dominion." He might have been twenty-five years; but very few slaves have any correct idea of their age. Madison was not poorly

26

dressed, and had some money at the end of his journey, which showed that he was not from amongst the worst-used slaves of the South. He immediately sought employment at a neighboring farm, where he remained some months. A strong, able-bodied man, and a good worker, and apparently satisfied with his situation, his employer felt that he had a servant who would stay with him a long while. The farmer would occasionally raise a conversation, and try to draw from Madison some account of his former life, but in this he failed; for the fugitive was a man of few words, and kept his own secrets. His leisure hours were spent in learning to read and write; and in this he seemed to take the utmost interest. He appeared to take no interest in the sports and amusements that occupied the attention of others. Six months had not passed ere Madison began to show signs of discontent. In vain his employer tried to discover the cause.

"Do I not pay you enough, and treat you in a becoming manner?" asked Mr. Dickson one day when the fugitive seemed in a very desponding mood.

"Yes, sir," replied Madison.

"Then why do you appear so dissatisfied of late?"

"Well, sir," said the fugitive, "since you have treated me with such kindness, and seem to take so much interest in me, I will tell you the reason why I have changed, and appear to you to be dissatisfied. I was born in slavery, in the State of Virginia. From my earliest recollections I hated slavery, and determined to be free. I have never yet called any man master, though I have been held by three different men who claimed me as their property. The birds in the trees and the wild beasts of the forest made me feel that I, like them, ought to be free. My feelings were all thus centred in the one idea of liberty, of which I thought by day and dreamed by night. I had scarcely reached my twentieth year, when I became acquainted with the angelic being who has since become my wife. It was my intention to have escaped with her before we were married, but circumstances prevented.

"I took her to my bosom as my wife, and then resolved to make the attempt. But, unfortunately, my plans were discovered; and, to save myself from being caught and sold off to the far South, I escaped to the woods, where I remained during many weary months. As I could not bring my wife away, I would not come without her. Another reason for remaining was that I hoped to get up an insurrection of the slaves, and thereby be the means of their liberation. In this, too, I failed. At last it was agreed, between my wife and I, that I should escape to Canada, get employment, save my earnings, and with it purchase her freedom. With the hope of attaining this end, I came into your service. I am now satisfied, that, with the wages I can command here, it will take me not less than five years to obtain by my labor the amount sufficient to purchase the liberty of my dear Susan. Five years will be too long for me to wait; for she may die, or be sold away, ere I can raise the money. This, sir, makes me feel low spirited; and I have come to the rash determination to return to Virginia for my wife."

The recital of the story had already brought tears to the eyes of the farmer, ere the fugitive had concluded. In vain did Mr. Dickson try to persuade Madison to give up the idea of going back into the very grasp of the tyrant, and risking the loss of his own freedom without

securing that of his wife. The heroic man had made up
his mind, and nothing could move him. Receiving the
amount of wages due him from his employer, Madison
turned his face once more towards the South. Supplied with papers purporting to have been made out in
Virginia, and certifying to his being a freeman, the fugitive had no difficulty in reaching the neighborhood of
his wife. But these "free papers" were only calculated
to serve him where he was not known. Madison had
also provided himself with files, saws, and other implements, with which to cut his way out of any prison into
which he might be cast. These instruments were so
small as to be easily concealed in the lining of his clothing; and, armed with them, the fugitive felt sure he
should escape again were he ever captured. On his return, Madison met, in the State of Ohio, many of those
whom he had seen on his journey to Canada; and all
tried to prevail upon him to give up the rash attempt.
But to every one he would reply, "Liberty is worth
nothing to me while my wife is a slave." When near
his former home, and unable to travel in open day without being detected, Madison betook himself to the woods
during the day, and travelled by night. At last he arrived at the old farm at night, and hid away in the nearest forest. Here he remained several days, filled with
hope and fear, without being able to obtain any information about his wife. One evening, during this sus-
pense, Madison heard the singing of a company of
slaves, the sound of which appeared nearer and nearer,
until he became convinced that it was a gang going to a
corn-shucking; and the fugitive resolved that he would
join it, and see if he could get any intelligence of his wife.
   In Virginia, as well as in most of the other corn-rais-

ing slave-States, there is a custom of having what is termed "a corn-shucking," to which slaves from the neighboring plantations, with the consent of their masters, are invited. At the conclusion of the shucking, a supper is provided by the owner of the corn; and thus, together with the bad whiskey which is freely circulated on such occasions, the slaves are made to feel very happy. Four or five companies of men may be heard in different directions, and at the same time, approaching the place of rendezvous; slaves joining the gangs along the roads as they pass their masters' farms.[2] Madison came out upon the highway; and, as the company came along singing, he fell into the ranks, and joined in the song. Through the darkness of the night he was able to keep from being recognized by the remainder of the company, while he learned from the general conversation the most important news of the day.

Although hungry and thirsty, the fugitive dared not go to the supper-table for fear of recognition. However, before he left the company that night, he gained information enough to satisfy him that his wife was still with her old master; and he hoped to see her, if possible, on the following night. The sun had scarcely set the next evening, ere Madison was wending his way out of the forest, and going towards the home of his loved one, if the slave can be said to have a home. Susan, the object of his affections, was indeed a woman every way worthy of his love. Madison knew well where to find the room usually occupied by his wife, and to that spot he made his way on arriving at the plantation; but, in his zeal and enthusiasm, and his being too confident of success, he committed a blunder which nearly cost him his life. Fearful that if he waited until a late hour,

Susan would be asleep, and in awakening her she would in her fright alarm the household, Madison ventured to her room too early in the evening, before the whites in the " great house " had retired. Observed by the overseer, a sufficient number of whites were called in, and the fugitive secured ere he could escape with his wife ; but the heroic slave did not yield until he with a club had laid three of his assailants upon the ground with his manly blows ; and not then until weakened by loss of blood. Madison was at once taken to Richmond, and sold to a slave-trader, then making up a gang of slaves for the New-Orleans market.

The brig " Creole," owned by Johnson & Eperson of Richmond, and commanded by Capt. Enson, lay at the Richmond dock, waiting for her cargo, which usually consisted of tobacco, hemp, flax, and slaves. There were two cabins for the slaves, — one for the men, the other for the women. The men were generally kept in chains while on the voyage ; but the women were usually unchained, and allowed to roam at pleasure in their own cabin. On the 27th of October, 1841, " The Creole " sailed from Hampton Roads, bound for New Orleans, with her full load of freight, a hundred and thirty-five slaves, and three passengers, besides the crew. Forty of the slaves were owned by Thomas McCargo, nine belonged to Henry Hewell, and the remainder were held by Johnson & Eperson. Hewell had once been an overseer for McCargo, and on this occasion was acting as his agent.

Among the slaves owned by Johnson & Eperson, was Madison Washington. He was heavily ironed, and chained down to the floor of the cabin occupied by the men, which was in the forward hold. As it was known

by Madison's purchasers that he had once escaped, and
had been in Canada, they kept a watchful eye over him.
The two cabins were separated, so that the men and
women had no communication whatever during the
passage.

Although rather gloomy at times, Madison on this occasion seemed very cheerful, and his owners thought
that he had repented of the experience he had undergone as a runaway, and in the future would prove a
more easily-governed chattel. But, from the first hour
that he had entered the cabin of " The Creole," Madison
had been busily engaged in the selection of men who
were to act parts in the great drama. He picked out
each one as if by intuition. Every thing was done at
night and in the dark, as far as the preparation was concerned. The miniature saws and files were faithfully
used when the whites were asleep.

In the other cabin, among the slave-women, was one
whose beauty at once attracted attention. Though not
tall, she yet had a majestic figure. Her well-moulded
shoulders, prominent bust, black hair which hung in
ringlets, mild blue eyes, finely-chiselled mouth, with a
splendid set of teeth, a turned and well-rounded chin,
skin marbled with the animation of life, and veined by
blood given to her by her master, she stood as the representative of two races. With only one-eighth of African
blood, she was what is called at the South an "octoroon."
It was said that her grandfather had served his country
in the Revolutionary War, as well as in both Houses of
Congress. This was Susan, the wife of Madison. Few
slaves, even among the best-used house-servants, had so
good an opportunity to gain general information as she.

Accustomed to travel with her mistress, Susan had often been to Richmond, Norfolk, White-Sulphur Springs, and other places of resort for the aristocracy of the Old Dominion. Her language was far more correct than that of most slaves in her position. Susan was as devoted to Madison as she was beautiful and accomplished.

After the arrest of her husband, and his confinement in Richmond jail, it was suspected that Susan had long been in possession of the knowledge of his whereabouts when in Canada, and knew of his being in the neighborhood; and for this crime it was resolved that she should be sold, and sent off to a Southern plantation, where all hope of escape would be at an end. Each was not aware that the other was on board " The Creole ; " for Madison and Susan were taken to their respective cabins at different times. On the ninth day out, " The Creole" encountered a rough sea, and most of the slaves were sick, and therefore were not watched with that vigilance that they had been since she first sailed. This was the time for Madison and his accomplices to work, and nobly did they perform their duty. Night came on, the first watch had just been summoned, the wind blowing high, when Madison succeeded in reaching the quarter-deck, followed by eighteen others, all of whom sprang to different parts of the vessel, seizing whatever they could wield as weapons. The crew were nearly all on deck. Capt. Enson and Mr. Merritt, the first mate, were standing together, while Hewell was seated on the companion, smoking a cigar. The appearance of the slaves all at once, and the loud voice and commanding attitude of their leader, so completely surprised the whites, that —

> " They spake not a word ;
> But, like dumb statues or breathless stones,
> Stared at each other, and looked deadly pale."

The officers were all armed ; but so swift were the motions of Madison that they had nearly lost command of the vessel before they attempted to use them.

Hewell, the greater part of whose life had been spent on the plantation in the capacity of a negro-driver, and who knew that the defiant looks of these men meant something, was the first to start. Drawing his old horse-pistol from under his coat, he fired at one of the blacks, and killed him. The next moment Hewell lay dead upon the deck, for Madison had struck him with a capstan bar. The fight now became general, the white passengers, as well as all the crew, taking part. The battle was Madison's element, and he plunged into it without any care for his own preservation or safety. He was an instrument of enthusiasm, whose value and whose place was in his inspiration. " If the fire of heaven was in my hands, I would throw it at those cowardly whites," said he to his companions, before leaving their cabin. But in this he did not mean revenge, only the possession of his freedom and that of his fellow-slaves. Merritt and Gifford, the first and second mates of the vessel, both attacked the heroic slave at the same time. Both were stretched out upon the deck with a single blow each, but were merely wounded : they were disabled, and that was all that Madison cared for for the time being. The sailors ran up the rigging for safety, and a moment more he that had worn the fetters an hour before was master of the brig "Creole." His commanding attitude and daring orders, now that he was free, and his perfect preparation for the grand alternative of liberty or death which stood before him, are splendid exemplifications of the true heroic. After his accomplices had covered the slaver's deck, Madison forbade the shedding of more blood, and ordered the sailors to come down, which they did, and with his own hands dressed their wounds. A guard was placed over all except Merritt, who was retained to navigate the vessel. With a musket doubly charged, and pointed at Merritt's breast, the slaves made him swear that he would safely take the brig into a British port. All things now secure, and the white men in chains or under guard, Madison ordered that the fetters should be severed from the limbs of those slaves who still wore them. The next morning "Capt. Washington" (for such was the name he now bore) ordered the cook to provide the best breakfast that the store-room could furnish, intending to surprise his fellow-slaves, and especially the females, whom he had not yet seen. But little did he think that the woman for whom he had risked his liberty and life would meet him at the breakfast-table. The meeting of the hero and his beautiful and accomplished wife, the tears of joy shed, and the hurrahs that followed from the men, can better be imagined than described. Madison's cup of joy was filled to the brim. He had not only gained his own liberty, and that of one hundred and thirty-four others, but his dear Susan was safe. Only one man, Hewell, had been killed. Capt. Enson, and others who were wounded, soon recovered, and were kindly treated by Madison, and for which they proved ungrateful; for, on the second night, Capt. Enson, Mr. Gifford, and Merritt, took advantage of the absence of Madison from the deck, and attempted to retake the vessel. The slaves, exasperated at this treachery, fell upon the whites with deadly weapons. The captain and his men fled to the cabin, pursued by the blacks. Nothing but the heroism of the negro leader saved the lives of the white men on this occasion; for, as the slaves were rushing into the cabin,

Madison threw himself between them and their victims, exclaiming, "Stop! no more blood. My life, that was perilled for your liberty, I will lay down for the protection of these men. They have proved themselves unworthy of life which we granted them; still let us be magnanimous." By the kind heart and noble bearing of Madison, the vile slave-traders were again permitted to go unwhipped of justice. This act of humanity raised the uncouth son of Africa far above his Anglo-Saxon oppressors.

The next morning "The Creole" landed at Nassau, New Providence, where the noble and heroic slaves were warmly greeted by the inhabitants, who at once offered protection, and extended hospitality to them.

But the noble heroism of Madison Washington and his companions found no applause from the Government, then in the hands of the slaveholders. Daniel Webster, then Secretary of State, demanded of the British authorities the surrender of these men, claiming that they were murderers and pirates: the English, however, could not see the point.

Had the "Creole" revolters been white, and committed their noble act of heroism in another land, the people of the United States would have been the first to recognize their claims. The efforts of Denmark Vesey, Nat Turner, and Madison Washington to strike the chains of slavery from the limbs of their enslaved race will live in history, and will warn all tyrants to beware of the wrath of God and the strong arm of man.

Every iniquity that society allows to subsist for the benefit of the oppressor is a sword with which she herself arms the oppressed. Right is the most dangerous of weapons: woe to him who leaves it to his enemies.

CHAPTER V.

THE introduction of the cotton-gin into the South, by
Whitney of Connecticut, had materially enhanced the
value of slave property; the emancipation societies of
Virginia and Maryland had ceased to petition their Leg-
islatures for the " Gradual Emancipation " of the slaves;
and the above two States had begun to make slave-rais-
ing a profitable business, when the American Antislavery Society was formed in the city of Philadelphia, in
the year 1833. The agitation of the question in Congress, the mobbing of William Lloyd Garrison in Boston,
the murder of the Rev. E. P. Lovejoy in Illinois, and the
attempt to put down free speech throughout the country, only hastened the downfall of the institution.

In the earlier days of the Antislavery movement, not
a year, sometimes hardly a month, passed that did not
bear upon its record the report of mobs, almost always
ferocious in spirit, and sometimes cruel and blood-stained
in act. It was the first instinctive and brutal response
of a proslavery people convicted of guilt and called to
repentance; and it was almost universal. Wherever anti-
slavery was preached, honestly, and effectually, there
the mobocratic spirit followed it; so that, in those times,

he who escaped this ordeal was, with some justice, held to be either inefficient or unfaithful. Hardly a town or city, from Alton to Portland, where much antislavery labor was bestowed, in the first fifteen years of this enterprise, that was not the scene of one of these attempts to crush all free discussion of the subject of slavery by violence or bloodshed. Hardly one of the earlier public advocates of the cause that was not made to suffer, either in person or in property, or in both, from popular violence, — the penalty of obedience to the dictates of his own conscience. Nor was this all: official countenance was often given to the mad proceedings of the mob; or, if not given, its protection was withheld from those who were the objects of popular hatred; and, as if this were not enough, legislation was invoked to the same end. It was suggested to the Legislature of one of the Southern States, that a large reward be offered for the head of a citizen of Massachusetts who was the pioneer in the modern antislavery movement. A similar reward was offered for the head of a citizen of New York. Yet so foul an insult excited neither the popular indignation nor legislative resentment in either of those States.

Great damage was done to the cause of Christianity by the position assumed on the question of slavery by the American churches, and especially those in the Southern States. Think of a religious kidnapper! a Christian slave-breeder! a slave-trader, loving his neighbor as himself, receiving the " sacraments " in some Protestant church from the hand of a Christian apostle, then the next day selling babies by the dozen, and tearing young women from the arms of their husbands to feed the lust of lecherous New Orleans! Imagine a

religious man selling his own children into eternal bondage ! Think of a Christian defending slavery out of the
Bible, and declaring there is no higher law, but atheism
is the first principle of Republican Government !

Yet this was the stand taken, and maintained, by the
churches in the slave States down to the day that Lee
surrendered to Grant.

One of the bitterest fruits of slavery in our land is the
cruel spirit of caste, which makes the complexion even
of the free negro a badge of social inferiority, exposing
him to insult in the steamboat and the railcar, and in all
places of public resort, not even excepting the church ;
banishing him from remunerative occupations ; expell-
ing him from the legislative hall, the magistrate's bench,
and the jury-box ; and crushing his noblest aspirations
under a weight of prejudice and proscription which he
struggles in vain to throw off. Against this unchristian
and hateful spirit, every lover of liberty should enter his
solemn protest. This hateful prejudice caused the
breaking up of the school of Miss Prudence Crandall, in
the State of Connecticut, in the early days of the anti-
slavery agitation.

Next came the burning of Pennsylvania Hall, one of
the most beautiful edifices in the City of Brotherly Love,
simply because colored persons were permitted to occupy seats by the side of whites.

The enactment by Congress of the Fugitive Slave
Law caused the friends of freedom, both at home and
abroad, to feel that the General Government was fast
becoming the bulwark of slavery. The rendition of
Thomas Sims, and still later that of Anthony Burns, was,
indeed, humiliating in the extreme to the people of the
Northern States.

On that occasion, the sons of free, enlightened, and Christian Massachusetts, descendants of the Pilgrim Fathers, bowed submissively to the behests of a tyranny more cruel than Austrian despotism ; yielded up their dignity and self-respect ; became the allies of slave-catchers, the associates and companions of bloodhounds. At the bidding of slaveholders and serviles, they seized the image of God, bound their fellow-man with chains, and consigned him to torture and premature death under the lash of a piratical overseer. God's law and man's rights were trampled upon ; the self-respect, the consti-tutional privileges, of the free States, were ignominiously surrendered. A people who resisted a paltry tax upon tea, at the cannon's mouth, basely submitted to an impo-sition tenfold greater, in favor of brutalizing their fellow-men. Soil which had been moistened with the blood of American patriots was polluted by the footsteps of slave-catchers and their allies.

The Boston Court House in chains, two hundred row-dies and thieves sworn in as special policemen, respect-able citizens shoved off the side-walks by these slave-catchers ; all for the purpose of satisfying " our brethren of the South." But this act did not appease the feel-ings, or satisfy the demands, of the slave-holders, while it still further inflamed the fire of abolitionism.

The " Dred Scott Decision " added fresh combustibles to the smouldering heap. Dred Scott, a slave, taken by his master into free Illinois, and then beyond the line of 36° 30', and then back into Missouri, sued for and ob-tained his freedom on the ground, that, having been taken where by the Constitution slavery was illegal, his master had lost all claim. But the Supreme Court, on appeal, reversed the judgment ; and Dred Scott, with his wife and children, was taken back into slavery. By this decision in the highest court of American law, it was affirmed that no free negro could claim to be a citizen of the United States, but was only under the jurisdiction of the separate State in which he resided; that the prohibition of slavery in any Territory of the Union was unconstitutional; and that the slave-owner might go where he pleased with his property, throughout the United States, and retain his right.

This decision created much discussion, both in America and in Europe, and materially injured the otherwise good name of our country abroad.

The Constitution, thus interpreted by Judge Taney, became the emblem of the tyrants and the winding sheet of liberty, and gave a boldness to the people of the South, which soon showed itself, while good men at the North felt ashamed of the Government under which they lived.

The slave-holders in the cotton, sugar, and rice growing States began to urge the re-opening of the African slave-trade, and the driving out from the Southern States of all free colored persons.

In the Southern Rights' Convention, which assembled at Baltimore, June 8, 1860, a resolution was adopted, calling on the Legislature to pass a law driving the free colored people out of the State. Nearly every speaker took the ground that the free colored people must be driven out to make the slave's obedience more secure. Judge Mason, in his speech, said, "It is the thrifty and well-to-do free negroes, that are seen by our slaves, that make them dissatisfied." A similar appeal was made to the Legislature of Tennessee. Judge Catron, of the Supreme Court of the United States, in a long and able letter to " The Nashville Union," opposed the driving out of the colored people. He said they were among the best mechanics, the best artisans, and the most indus- trious laborers in the State, and that to drive them out would be an injury to the State itself. This is certainly good evidence in their behalf.

The State of Arkansas passed a law driving the free colored people out of the State, and they were driven out three years ago. The Democratic press howled upon the heels of the free blacks until they had all been expa- triated; but, after they had been driven out, "The Little Rock Gazette" — a Democratic paper — made a candid acknowledgment with regard to the character of the free colored people. It said, "Most of the exiled free negroes are industrious and respectable. One of them, Henry King, we have known from our boyhood, and take the greatest pleasure in testifying to his good character. The community in which he casts his lot will be blessed with that noblest work of God, an honest man."

Yet these free colored people were driven out of the State, and those who were unable to go, as many of the women and children were, were reduced to slavery.

"The New Orleans True Delta" opposed the passage of a similar law by the State of Louisiana. Among other things, it said, "There are a large free colored popu- lation here, correct in their general deportment, honor- able in their intercourse with society, and free from re- proach so far as the laws are concerned; not surpassed in the inoffensiveness of their lives by any equal number of persons in any place, North or South."

And yet these free colored persons were not permitted by law to school their children, or to read books that treated against the institution of slavery. The Rev. Samuel Green, a colored Methodist preacher, was convicted and sent to the Maryland penitentiary, in 1858, for the offence of being found reading " Uncle Tom's Cabin."

The growth of the " Free-Soil " party, which had taken the place of the " Liberty " party; and then the rapid increase of the " Republican " party; the struggle in Kansas; the " Oberlin Rescue Trials;" and, lastly, the " John Brown Raid," carried the discussion of slavery to its highest point.

All efforts, in Congress, in the proslavery political conventions, and in the churches, only added fuel to the flame that was fast making inroads upon the vitals of the monster.

CHAPTER VI.

THE JOHN BROWN RAID.

John Brown. — His Religious Zeal. — His Hatred to Slavery. — Organization of his Army. — Attack on Harper's Ferry. — His Execution. — John Brown's Companions, Green and Copeland. — The Executions.

THE year 1859 will long be memorable for the bold attempt of John Brown and his companions to burst the bolted door of the Southern house of bondage, and lead out the captives by a more effectual way than they had yet known: an attempt in which, it is true, the little band of heroes dashed themselves to bloody death, but, at the same time, shook the prison-walls from summit to foundation, and shot wild alarm into every tyrant-heart in all the slave-land. What were the plans and purposes of the noble old man is not precisely known, and perhaps will never be; but, whatever they were, there is reason to believe they had been long maturing, — brooded over silently and secretly, with much earnest thought, and under a solemn sense of religious duty. As early as the fall of 1857, he began to organize his band, chiefly from among the companions of his warfare against the "Border Ruffians" in Kansas. Nine or ten of these spent the winter of 1857–8 in Iowa, where a Col. Forbes was to have given them military instruction; but he, having fallen out with Brown, did not join them, and Aaron D. Stevens, one of the company, took his place.

About the middle of April, 1858, they left Iowa, and went to Chatham, Canada, where, on the 8th of May, was

44

held a convention, called by a written circular, which was sent to such persons only as could be trusted. The convention was composed mostly of colored men, a few of whom were from the States, but the greater part residents in Canada, with no white men but the organized band already mentioned. A "Provisional Constitution," which Brown had previously prepared, was adopted; and the members of the convention took an oath to support it. Its manifest purpose was to insure a perfect organization of all who should join the expedition, whether free men or insurgent slaves, and to hold them under such strict control as to restrain them from every act of wanton or vindictive violence, all waste or needless destruction of life or property, all indignity or unnecessary severity to prisoners, and all immoral practices; in short, to keep the meditated movement free from every possibly avoidable evil ordinarily incident to the armed uprising of a long-oppressed and degraded people.

And let no one who glories in the revolutionary struggles of our fathers for their freedom deny the right of the American bondsman to imitate their high example. And those who rejoice in the deeds of a Wallace or a Tell, a Washington or a Warren; who cherish with unbounded gratitude the name of Lafayette for volunteering his aid in behalf of an oppressed people in a desperate crisis, and at the darkest hour of their fate, — cannot refuse equal merit to this strong, free, heroic man, who freely consecrated all his powers, and the labors of his whole life, to the help of the most needy, friendless, and unfortunate of mankind.

The picture of the Good Samaritan will live to all future ages, as the model of human excellence, for helping one whom he chanced to find in need.

John Brown did more: he went to *seek* those who were lost that he might save them.

On Sunday night, Oct. 16, John Brown, with twenty followers (five. of them colored), entered the town of Harper's Ferry, in the State of Virginia; captured the place, making the United-States Armory his headquarters; sent his men in various directions in search of slaves with which to increase his force.

The whole thing, though premature in its commencement, struck a blow that rang on the fetters of the enslaved in every Southern State, and caused the oppressor to tremble for his own safety, as well as for that of the accursed institution.

John Brown's trial, heroism, and execution, an excellent history of which has been given to the public by Mr. James Redpath, saves me from making any lengthened statement here.[1] His life and acts are matters of history, which will live with the language in which it is written. But little can be said of his companions in the raid on slavery. They were nearly all young men, unknown to fame, enthusiastic admirers of the old Puritan, entering heartily into all of his plans, obeying his orders, and dying bravely, with no reproach against their leader.

Of the five colored men, two only were captured alive,— Shields Green and John A. Copeland. The former was a native of South Carolina, having been born in the city of Charleston in the year 1832. Escaping to the North in 1857, he resided in Rochester, N.Y., until attracted by the unadorned eloquence and native magnetism of the hero of Harper's Ferry. The latter was from North Carolina, and was a mulatto of superior abilities, and a genuine lover of liberty and justice. The following letter, written a short time before his execution, needs no explanation: —

"CHARLESTOWN, VA., Dec. 10, 1859.

" MY DEAR BROTHER, — I now take my pen to write you a few lines to let you know how I am, and in answer to your kind letter of the 5th inst. Dear brother, I am, it is true, so situated at present as scarcely to know how to commence writing : not that my mind is filled with fear, or that it has become shattered in view of my near approach to death ; not that I am terrified by the gallows which I see staring me in the face, and upon which I am so soon to stand and suffer death for doing what George Washington, the so-called father of this great but slavery-cursed country, was made a hero for doing while he lived, and when dead his name was immortalized, and his great and noble deeds in behalf of freedom taught by parents to their children. And now, brother, for having lent my aid to a general no less brave, and engaged in a cause no less honorable and glorious, I am to suffer death. Washington entered the field to fight for the freedom of the American people, — not for the white man alone, but for both black and white. Nor were they white men alone who fought for the freedom of this country. The blood of black men flowed as freely as that of white men. Yes, the *very first* blood that was spilt was that of a negro. It was the blood of that heroic man (though black he was), Crispus Attucks. And some of the *very last* blood shed was that of black men. To the truth of this, history, though prejudiced, is compelled to attest. *It is true* that black men did an equal share of the fighting for American independence ; and they were assured by the whites that they should share equal benefits for so doing. But, after having performed their part honorably, they were by the whites most treacherously deceived, — they refusing to fulfil their part of the contract. But this you know as well as I do; and I will therefore say no more in reference to the claims which we, as colored men, have on the American people. . . .

"It was a sense of the wrongs which we have suffered that prompted the noble but unfortunate Capt. Brown and his associates to attempt to give freedom to a small number, at least, of those who are now held by cruel and unjust laws, and by no less cruel and unjust men. To this freedom they were entitled by every known principle of justice and humanity; and, for the enjoyment of it, God created them. And now, dear brother, could I die in a more noble cause? Could I, brother, die in a manner and for a cause which would induce true and honest men more to honor me, and the angels more readily to receive me to their happy home of everlasting jcy above? I imagine that I hear you, and all of you, mother, father, sisters and brothers, say, "No, there is not a cause for which we, with less sorrow, could see you die!"

"Your affectionate brother,

"JOHN A. COPELAND."

"The Baltimore Sun" says, "A few moments before leaving the jail, Copeland said, 'If I am dying for freedom, I could not die for a better cause. *I had rather die than be a slave!*' A military officer in charge on the day of the execution says, 'I had a position near the gallows, and carefully observed all. I can truly say I never witnessed more firm and unwavering fortitude, more perfect composure, or more beautiful propriety, than were manifested by young Copeland to the very last.' "

Shields Green behaved with equal heroism, ascending the scaffold with a firm and unwavering step, and died, as he had lived, a brave man, and expressing to the last his eternal hatred to human bondage, prophesying that slavery would soon come to a bloody end.

CHAPTER VII.

THE FIRST GUN OF THE REBELLION.

Nomination of Fremont. — Nomination of Lincoln. — The Mob Spirit. — Spirit of Slavery. — The Democracy. — Cotton. — Northern Promises to the Rebels. — Assault on Fort Sumter. — Call for 75,000 Men. — Response of the Colored Men.

THE nomination of John C. Fremont by the Republican party in 1856, and the large vote given him at the election that autumn, cleared away all doubts, if any existed, as to the future action of the Federal Government on the spread and power of slavery. The Democratic party, which had ruled the nation so long and so badly, saw that it had been weighed, and found wanting; that it must prepare to give up the Government into the hands of better men.

But the party determined to make the most of Mr. Buchanan's administration, both in the profuse expenditure of money among themselves, and in getting ready to take the Southern States out of the Union.

Surrounded by the men who believed that the Government was made for them, and that their mission was to rule the people of the United States, Mr. Buchanan was nothing more than a tool, — clay in the hands of the potters; and he permitted them to prepare leisurely for disunion, which culminated, in 1860, in the nomination of Abraham Lincoln for the presidency.

The proslavery Democracy became furious at the

prospect of losing the control of the situation, and their hatred of free speech was revived. From the nomination of Mr. Lincoln to his inauguration, mob-law ruled in most of the cities and large villages. These disgraceful scenes, the first of which commenced at the anti-slavery meeting at the Tremont Temple, Boston, was always gotten up by members of the Democratic party, who usually passed a series of resolutions in favor of slavery. New York, Philadelphia, Albany, Buffalo, Troy, Cincinnati, and Chicago, all followed the example set by Boston.

These demonstrations were caused more by sympathy with the South, and the long-accustomed subserviency of the Northern people to slaveholding dictation, than to any real hatred to the negro.

During all this time the Abolitionists were laboring faithfully to widen the gulf between the North and South.

Towards the close of the year 1860, the spirit of compromise began to show itself in such unmistakable terms as to cause serious apprehension on the part of the friends of freedom for the future of American liberty. The subdued tone of the liberal portion of the press, the humiliating offers of Northern political leaders of compromises, and the numerous cases of fugitive slaves being returned to their masters, sent a thrill of fear to all colored men in the land for their safety, and nearly every train going North found more or less negroes fleeing to Canada.

At the South, the people were in earnest, and would listen to no proposals whatever in favor of their continuance in the Union.

The vast wealth realized by the slave-holder had

made him feel that the South was independent of the rest of the world.

Prosperity had made him giddy. Cotton was not merely king: it was God. Moral considerations were nothing. The sentiment of right, he argued, would have no influence over starving operatives; and England and France, as well as the Eastern States of the Union, would stand aghast, and yield to the masterstroke which should deprive them of the material of their labor. Millions were dependent on it in all the great centres of civilization; and the ramifications of its power extended into all ranks of society and all departments of industry and commerce. It was only necessary to wave this imperial sceptre over the nations; and all of them would fall prostrate, and acknowledge the supremacy of the power which wielded it. Nothing could be more plausible than this delusion. Satan himself, when about to wage war in heaven, could not have invented one better calculated to marshal his hosts, and give promise of success in rebellion against the authority of the Most High. But, alas! the supreme error of this anticipation lay in omitting from the calculation all power of principle. The right still has authority over the minds of men and in the counsels of nations. Factories may cease their din; men and women may be thrown out of employment; the marts of commerce may be silent and deserted: but truth and justice still command some respect among men; and God yet remains the object of their adoration.

Drunk with power, and dazzled with prosperity, monopolizing cotton, and raising it to the influence of a veritable fetich, the authors of the Rebellion did not admit a doubt of the success of their attack on the Fed-

eral Government. They dreamed of perpetuating slavery, though all history shows the decline of the system
as industry, commerce, and knowledge advance. The
slave-holders proposed nothing less than to reverse the
currents of humanity, and to make barbarism flourish in
the bosom of civilization.

Weak as were the Southern people in point of numbers and political power, compared with those of the
opposite section, the haughty slave-holders easily persuaded themselves and their dependents that they could
successfully cope in arms with the Northern adversary,
whom they affected to despise for his cowardly and mer-
cenary disposition. Proud and confident, they indulged
the belief that their great political prestige would continue to serve them among their late party associates in
the North, and that the counsels of the adversary would
be distracted, and his power weakened, by the fatal
effects of dissension.

The proslavery men in the North are very much to
blame for the encouragement that they gave the rebels
before the breaking out of the war. The Southerners
had promises from their Northern friends, that, in the
event of a rebellion, civil war should reign in the free
States, — that men would not be permitted to leave the
North to go South to put down their rebellious brethren.

All legitimate revolutions are occasioned by the
growth of society beyond the growth of government;
and they will be peaceful or violent just in proportion
as the people and government shall be wise and virtu-
ous or vicious and ignorant. Such revolutions or re-
forms are generally of a peaceful nature in communities
in which the government has made provision for the
gradual expansion of its institutions to suit the onward

march of society. No government is wise in overlook
ing, whatever may be the strength of its own traditions,
or however glorious its history, that human institutions
which have been adapted for a barbarous age or state
of society will cease to be adapted for more civilized
and intelligent times; and, unless government makes a
provision for the gradual expansion, nothing can prevent a storm, either of an intellectual or a physical
nature. Slavery was always the barbarous institution
of America; and the Rebellion was the result of this
incongruity between it and freedom.[1]

The assault on Fort Sumter on the 12th of April,
1861, was the dawn of a new era for the negro. The
proclamation of President Lincoln, calling for the first
75,000 men to put down the Rebellion, was responded to
by the colored people throughout the country. In Boston, at a public meeting of the blacks, a large number
came forward, put their names to an agreement to form
a brigade, and march at once to the seat of war. A
committee waited on the Governor three days later,
and offered the services of these men. His Excellency
replied that he had no power to receive them. This
was the first wet blanket thrown over the negro's enthusiasm. "This is a white man's war," said most of
the public journals. "I will never fight by the side of a
nigger," was heard in every quarter where men were
seen in Uncle Sam's uniform.

Wherever recruiting offices were opened, black men
offered themselves, and were rejected. Yet these people, feeling conscious that right would eventually prevail, waited patiently for the coming time, pledging
themselves to go at their country's call, as the following
will show : —

" Resolved, That our feelings urge us to say to our countrymen that we are ready to stand by and defend the Government as the equals of its white defenders ; to do so with " our lives, our fortunes, and our sacred honor," for the sake of freedom and as good citizens; and we ask you to modify your laws, that we may enlist, — that full scope may be given to the patriotic feelings burning in the colored man's breast." — *Colored Men's Meeting, Boston.*" [2]

CHAPTER VIII.

THE UNION AND SLAVERY BOTH TO BE PRESERVED.

Union Generals offer to suppress Slave Insurrections. — Return of Slaves coming into our Army.

AT the very commencement of the Rebellion, the pro-slavery generals in the field took the earliest opportunity of offering their services, together with those under their commands, to suppress any slave insurrection that might grow out of the unsettled condition of the country. Major-Gen. B. F. Butler led off, by tendering his services to Gov. Hicks of Maryland. About the same time, Major-Gen. Geo. B. McClellan issued the following, " *To the Union Men of Western Virginia,*" on entering that portion of the State with his troops : —

"The General Government cannot close its ears to the demands you have made for assistance. I have ordered troops to cross the river. They come as your friends and brothers, — as enemies only to the armed rebels who are preying upon you. Your homes, your families, your property, are safe under our protection. All your rights shall be religiously respected. Notwithstanding all that has been said by the traitors to induce you to believe our advent among you will be signalled by an interference with your slaves, understand one thing clearly: not only will we abstain from all such interference, but we shall, on the contrary, WITH AN IRON HAND, crush any attempt at insurrection on their part."

Slaves escaping from their masters were promptly returned by the officers of the army. Gen. W. S. Harney, commanding in Missouri, in responding to the claims of slave-holders for their blacks, said, —

" Already, since the commencement of these unhappy disturbances, slaves have escaped from their owners, and have sought refuge in the camps of United-States troops from the Northern States, and commanded by a Northern general. *They were carefully sent back to their owners.*

The correspondent of " The New-York Herald " gave publicity to the following : —

" The guard on the bridge across the Anacostia arrested a negro who attempted to pass the sentries on the Maryland side. He seemed to feel confident that he was among friends, for he made no concealment of his character and purpose. He said he had walked sixty miles, and was going North. He was very much surprised and disappointed when he was taken into custody, and informed that he would be sent back to his master. He is now in the guard-house, and answers freely all questions relating to his weary march. Of course, such an arrest excites much comment among the men. Nearly all are restive under the thought of acting as slave-catchers. The Seventy-first made a forced march, and the privations they endured have been honorably mentioned in the country's history. This poor negro made a forced march, twice the length — in perils often, in fasting, — hurrying toward the North for his liberty ! And the Seventy-first catches him at the end of his painful journey, — the goal

in sight, — and sends him back to the master who even
now may be in arms against us, or may take the slave,
sell him for a rifle, and use it on his friends in the Seventy-first New-York Regiment. Humanity speaks louder
here than it does in a large city ; and the men who in
New York would dismiss the subject with a few words
about ' constitutional obligations ' are now the loudest
in denouncing the abuse of power which changes a regiment of gentlemen into a regiment of negro-catchers."

At Pensacola, Slemmer did even more, putting in irons
fugitives who fled to him for protection, and returning
them to their masters to be scourged to death. Col. Dim-
mick, at Fortress Monroe, told the rebel Virginians that
he had not an Abolitionist in his command, and that no
molestation of their slave-system would be suffered.

Gen. D. C. Buell, commanding in Tennessee, said,
in reply to a committee of slave-holders demanding the
return of their fugitives, —

" It has come to my knowledge that slaves sometimes
make their way improperly into our lines, and in some
instances they may be enticed there ; but I think the
number has been magnified by report. *Several applica-
tions have been made to me by persons whose servants have
been found in our camps ; and, in every instance that I
know of, the master has removed his servant, and taken
him away.*

" I need hardly remind you that there will always be
found some lawless and mischievous persons in every
army ; but I assure you that the mass of this army is
law-abiding, and that it is neither its disposition nor its
policy to violate law or the rights of individuals in any
particular."

Yet, while Union soldiers were returning escaped

slaves to rebels, it was a notorious fact that the enemy were using negroes to build fortifications, drive teams, and raise food for the army.

Black hands piled up the sand-bags, and raised the batteries, which drove Anderson out of Sumter. At Montgomery, the capital of the confederacy, negroes were being drilled and armed for military duty.

CHAPTER IX.

INTELLIGENT CONTRABANDS.

James Lawson. — His Bravery. — Rescue of his Wife and Children. — He is sent out on Important Business. — He fights his Way Back. — He is Admired by Gens. Hooker and Sickles. — Rhett's Servant. — "Foraging for Butter and Eggs."

I SPENT three weeks at Liverpool Point, the outpost of Hooker's Division, almost directly opposite Aquia Creek, waiting patiently for the advance of our left wing to follow up the army, becoming, if not a participator against the dying struggles of rebeldom, at least a chronicler of the triumphs in the march of the Union army.

During this time I was the guest of Col. Graham, of Mathias-Point memory, who had brought over from that place (last November) some thirty valuable chattels. A part of the camp was assigned to them. They built log huts, and obtained from the soldiers many comforts, making their quarters equal to any in the camp.

They had friends and relatives. Negroes feel as much sympathy for their friends and kin as the whites; and, from November to the present time, many a man in Virginia has lost a very likely slave, for the camp contains now upwards of a hundred fat and healthy negroes, in addition to its original number from Mathias Point.

One of the number deserves more honor than that accorded to Toussaint L'Ouverture in the brilliant lecture delivered by Wendell Phillips.[1] He is unquestionably the hero of the Potomac, and deserves to be placed by the side of his most renowned black brethren.

The name of this negro is James Lawson,[2] born near Hempstead, Virginia, and he belonged to a Mr. Taylor. He made his escape last December. On hearing his praises spoken by the captains of the gunboats on the Potomac, I was rather indisposed to admit the possession of all the qualities they give him credit for, and thought possibly his exploits had been exaggerated. His heroic courage, truthfulness, and exalted Christian character seemed too romantic for their realization. However, my doubts on that score were dispelled; and I am a witness of his last crowning act.

Jim, after making his escape from Virginia, shipped on board of "The Freeborn," flag-gunboat, Lieut. Samuel Magaw commanding. He furnished Capt. Magaw with much valuable intelligence concerning the rebel movements, and, from his quiet, every-day behavior, soon won the esteem of the commanding officer.

Capt. Magaw, shortly after Jim's arrival on board "The Freeborn," sent him upon a scouting tour through the rebel fortifications, more to test his reliability than anything else; and the mission, although fraught with great danger, was executed by Jim in the most faithful manner. Again Jim was sent into Virginia, landing at the White House, below Mount Vernon, and going into the interior for several miles; encountering the fire of picket-guards and posted sentries; returned in safety to the shore; and was brought off in the captain's gig, under the fire of the rebel musketry.

Jim had a wife and four children at that time still in Virginia. They belonged to the same man as Jim did. He was anxious to get them; yet it seemed impossible.

One day in January, Jim came to the captain's room, and asked for permission to be landed that evening on the Virginia side, as he wished to bring off his family. " Why, Jim," said Capt. Magaw, " how will you be able to pass the pickets ? "

" I want to try, captain: I think I can get 'em over safely," meekly replied Jim.

" Well, you have my permission ; " and Capt. Magaw ordered one of the gunboats to land Jim that night on whatever part of the shore he designated, and return for him the following evening.

True to his appointment, Jim was at the spot with his wife and family, and was taken on board the gunboat, and brought over to Liverpool Point, where Col. Graham had given them a log-house to live in, just back of his own quarters. Jim ran the gauntlet of the sentries unharmed, never taking to the roads, but keeping in the woods, every foot-path of which, and almost every tree, he knew from his boyhood up.

Several weeks afterwards another reconnoissance was planned, and Jim sent on it. He returned in safety, and was highly complimented by Gens. Hooker, Sickles, and the entire flotilla.

On Thursday, week ago, it became necessary to obtain correct information of the enemy's movements. Since then, batteries at Shipping and Cockpit Points had been evacuated, and their troops moved to Fredericksburg. Jim was the man picked out for the occasion, by Gen. Sickles and Capt. Magaw. The general came down to Col. Graham's quarters, about nine in the evening, and sent for Jim. There were present, the general, Col. Graham, and myself. Jim came into the colonel's.

" Jim," said the general, " I want you to go over to

Virginia to-night, and find out what forces they have at
Aquia Creek and Fredericksburg. If you want any men
to accompany you, pick them out."

" I know *two* men that would like to go," Jim answered.

" Well, get them, and be back as soon as possible."

Away went Jim over to the contraband camp, and,
returning almost immediately, brought into our presence
two very intelligent-looking darkies.

" Are you all ready ? " inquired the general.

" All ready, sir," the trio responded.

" Well, here, Jim, you take my pistol," said Gen.
Sickles, unbuckling it from his belt; " and, if you are
successful, I will give you $100."

Jim hoped he would be, and, bidding us good-by,
started off for the gunboat " Satellite," Capt. Foster, who
landed them a short distance below the Potomac-Creek
Batteries. They were to return early in the morning,
but were unable, from the great distance they went in
the interior. Long before daylight on Saturday morning, the gunboat was lying off at the appointed place.
As the day dawned, Capt. Foster discovered a mounted
picket-guard near the beach, and almost at the same
instant saw Jim to the left of them, in the woods, sight-
ing his gun at the rebel cavalry. He ordered the " gig "
to be manned, and rowed to the shore. The rebels
moved along slowly, thinking to intercept the boat, when
Foster gave them a shell, which scattered them. Jim,
with only one of his original companions, and two fresh
contrabands, came on board. Jim had *lost the other*. He
had been challenged by a picket when some distance in
advance of Jim, and the negro, instead of answering the
summons, fired the contents of Sickles's revolver at the

picket. It was an unfortunate occurrence; for at that time the entire picket-guard rushed out of a small house near the spot, and fired the contents of their muskets at Jim's companion, killing him instantly. Jim and the other three hid themselves in a hollow, near a fence, and, after the pickets gave up pursuit, crept through the woods to the shore. From the close proximity of the rebel pickets, Jim could not display a light, which was the signal for Capt. Foster to send a boat.

Capt. Foster, after hearing Jim's story of the shooting of his companion, determined to avenge his death; so, steaming his vessel close in to the shore, he sighted his guns for a barn, where the rebel cavalry were hiding behind. He fired two shells: one went right through the barn, killing four of the rebels, and seven of their horses. Capt. Foster, seeing the effect of his shot, said to Jim, who stood by, "Well, Jim, I've avenged the death of poor Cornelius" (the name of Jim's lost companion).

Gen. Hooker has transmitted to the War Department an account of Jim's reconnoissance to Fredericksburg, and unites with the army and navy stationed on the left wing of the Potomac, in the hope that the Government will present Jim with a fitting recompense for his gallant services. — *War Correspondent of the New-York Times.*

·   ·   ·   ·   ·   ·   ·   ·   ·   ·

On Thursday, beyond Charlestown, our pickets descried a solitary horseman, with a bucket on his arm, jogging soberly towards them. He proved to be a dark mulatto, of about thirty-five. As he approached, they ordered a halt.

"Where are you from?"

"Southern Army, cap'n," giving the military salute.

" Where are you going ? "

" Coming to yous all."

" What do you want ? "

" Protection, boss.   You won't send me back, will you ? "

" No : come in.   Whose servant are you ? "

" Cap'n Rhett's, of South Carliny : you's heard of Mr. Barnwell Rhett, editor of ' The Charleston Mercury ' ? His brother commands a battery."

" How did you get away ? "

" Cap'n gove me fifteen dollars this morning, and said, ' John, go out, and forage for butter and eggs.'   So you see, boss (with a broad grin), I'se out foraging !   I pulled my hat over my eyes, and jogged along on the cap'n's horse (see the brand S.C. on him ?) with this basket on my arm, right by our guards and pickets. They never challenged me once.   If they had, though, I brought the cap'n's pass."   And the new comer pro- duced this document from his pocket-book, written in pencil, and carefully folded.   I send you the original : —

" Pass my servant, John, on horseback, anywhere between Winchester and Martinsburg, in search of butter, &c., &c.

" A. BURNETT RHETT, *Capt. Light Artillery, Lee's Battalion*."

"Are there many negroes in the rebel corps ? "

" Heaps, boss."

" Would the most of them come to us if they could? "

" All of them, cap'n.   There isn't a little pickanniny so high (waving his hand two feet from the ground) that wouldn't."

" Why did *you* expect protection ? "

" Heard so in Maryland, before the Proclamation."

" Where did you hear about the Proclamation ? "

" Read it, sir, in a Richmond paper."

" What is it ? "

" That every slave is to be emancipated on and after the thirteenth day of January. I can't state it, boss."

" Something like it. When did you learn to read ? "

" In '49, sir. I was head waiter at Mrs. Nevitt's boarding-house in Savannah, and Miss Walcott, a New-York lady, who was stopping there, taught me."

" Does your master know it ? "

" Capt. Rhett doesn't know it, sir; but he isn't my master. He thinks I'm free, and hired me at twenty five dollars a month; but he never paid me any of it. I belong to Mrs. John Spring. She used to hire me out summers, and have me wait on her every winter, when she came South. After the war, she couldn't come, and they were going to sell me for Government because I belonged to a Northerner. Sold a great many negroes in that way. But I slipped away to the army. Have tried to come to you twice before in Maryland, but couldn't pass our pickets."

" Were you at Antietam ? "

" Yes, boss. Mighty hard battle ! "

" Who whipped ? "

" Yous all, massa. They say you didn't; but I saw it, and know. If you had fought us that next day, — Thursday, — you would have captured our whole army. They say so themselves."

" Who ? "

" Our officers, sir."

" Did you ever hear of old John Brown ? "

" Hear of *him?* Lord bless you, yes, boss: I've read his life, and have it now in my trunk in Charleston; sent to New York by the steward of ' The James Adger,' and got it. I've read it to heaps of the colored folks. Lord, they think John Brown was almost a god. Just say you was a friend of his, and any slave will almost kiss your feet, if you let him. They say, if he was only alive now, he would be king. How it did frighten the white folks when he raised the insurrection! It was Sunday when we heard of it. They wouldn't let a negro go into the streets. I was waiter at the Mills House in Charleston. There was a lady from Massachusetts, who came down to breakfast that morning at my table. 'John,' she says, 'I want to see a negro church; where is the principal one?' 'Not any open to-day, mistress,' I told her. 'Why not?' 'Because a Mr. John Brown has raised an insurrection in Virginny.' 'Ah!' she says; 'well, they'd better look out, or they'll get the white churches shut up in that way some of these days, too!' Mr. Nicholson, one of the proprietors, was listening from the office to hear what she said. Wasn't that lady watched after that? I have a History of San Domingo, too, and a Life of Fred. Douglass, in my trunk, that I got in the same way."

" What do the slaves think about the war?"

" Well, boss, they all wish the Yankee army would come. The white folks tell them all sorts of bad stories about you all; but they don't believe them."

John was taken to Gen. McClellan, to whom he gave all the information he possessed about the position, numbers, and organization of the rebel army. His knowledge was full and valuable, and is corroborated by all the facts we have learned from other sources. The principal features of it I have already transmitted to you by telegraph. At the close of the interview, he asked anxiously, —

" General, you won't send me back, will you ? "

" Yes," replied the general, with a smile, "I believe I will."

" I hope you won't, general.   If you say so, I know I will have to go; but I come to yous all for protection, and I hope you won't."

" Well, then, I suppose we will not.   No, John, you are at liberty to go where you please.   Stay with the army, if you like.   No one can ever take you against your will."

" May the Lord bless you, general.   I *thought* you wouldn't drive me out.   You's the best friend I ever had; I shall never forget you till I die."   And John made the salute, re-mounted his horse, and rode back to the rear, his dusky face almost white with radiance.

An hour later, he was on duty as the servant of Capt. Batchelor, Quartermaster of Couch's Second Division; and I do not believe there was another heart in our corps so light as his in the unwonted joy of freedom. — *New-York Tribune.*

CHAPTER X.

PROCLAMATIONS OF FREMONT AND HUNTER.

Gen. Fremont's Proclamation, and its Effect on the Public Mind. — Gen. Hunter's Proclamation ; the Feeling it created.

WHILE the country seemed drifting to destruction, and the Administration without a policy, the heart of every loyal man was made glad by the appearance of the proclamation of Major-Gen. John C. Fremont, then in command at the West. The following extract from that document, which at the time caused so much discussion, will bear insertion here : —

" All persons who shall be taken with arms in their hands within these lines shall be tried by court martial, and, if found guilty, will be shot. The property, real and personal, of all persons in the State of Missouri, who shall take up arms against the United States, or who shall be directly proven to have taken active part with their enemies in the field, is declared to be confiscated to the public use, and their slaves, if any they have, are hereby declared free men."

The above was the first official paper issued after the commencement of the war, that appeared to have the ring of the right kind of mettle. But while the public mind was being agitated upon its probable effect upon the Rebellion, a gloom was thrown over the whole community by the President's removal of Gen. Fremont, and the annulling of the proclamation. This act of Mr. Lincoln gave unintentional "aid and comfort" to the enemy, and was another retrograde movement in the way of crushing out the Rebellion.

Gen. Fremont, before the arrival of the President's letter, had given freedom to a number of slaves, in accordance with his proclamation. His mode of action may be seen in the following deed of manumission : —

"Whereas, Thomas L. Snead, of the city and county of St. Louis, State of Missouri, has been taking an active part with the enemies of the United States, in the present insurrectionary movement against the Government of the United States ; now, therefore, I, John Charles Fremont, Major-General commanding the Western Department of the Army of the United States, by authority of law, and the power vested in me as such commanding general, declare Hiram Reed, heretofore held to service or labor by Thomas L. Snead, to be FREE, and forever discharged from the bonds of servitude, giving him full right and authority to have, use, and control his own labor or service as to him may seem proper, without any accountability whatever to said Thomas L. Snead, or any one to claim by, through, or under him.

"And this deed of manumission shall be respected and treated by all persons, and in all courts of justice, as the full and complete evidence of the freedom of said Hiram Reed.

"In testimony whereof, this act is done at headquarters of the Western Department of the Army of the United States, in the city of St. Louis, State of Missouri, on this twelfth day of September, A.D. eighteen hundred and sixty-one, as is evidenced by the Departmental Seal hereto affixed by my order.

"J. C. FREMONT,
"*Major-General Commanding.*"

" Done at the office of the Provost-Marshal, in the city of St. Louis, the twelfth day of September, A.D. eighteen hundred and sixty-one, at nine o'clock in the evening of said day.

" Witness my hand and seal of office hereto affixed.

J. McKINSTRY,

" *Brigadier-General, Provost-Marshal.*"

The agitation in the public mind on account of the proclamation and its annulment, great as it was, was soon surpassed by one still more bold and sweeping from Major-Gen. David Hunter, in the following language, issued from his headquarters, at Hilton Head, S.C., on the 9th of May : —

" HEADQUARTERS DEPARTMENT OF THE SOUTH,

HILTON HEAD, S.C., May 9, 1862.

" GENERAL ORDERS, No. 11:

" The three States of Georgia, Florida, and South Carolina, comprising the Military Department of the South, having deliberately declared themselves no longer under the protection of the United States of America, and having taken up arms against the said United States, it became a military necessity to declare them under martial law. This was accordingly done on the 25th day of April, 1862. Slavery and martial law in a free country are altogether incompatible. The persons in these three States, Georgia, Florida, and South Carolina, heretofore held as slaves, are therefore declared forever free.

" DAVID HUNTER,

" *Major-General Commanding.*

" [Official.]

" ED. W. SMITH, *Acting Assistant Adjutant-General.*"

But, before Mr. Lincoln was officially informed of the

issuing of the above order, he made haste to annul it in the terms following: "That neither Gen. Hunter nor any other commander or person has been authorized by the Government of the United States to make proclamation declaring the slaves of any State free; and that the supposed proclamation now in question, whether genuine or false, is altogether void, so far as respects such declaration.

"I further make known, that, whether it be competent for me, as Commander-in-Chief of the Army and Navy, to declare the slaves of any State or States free, and whether at any time or in any case it shall have become a necessity indispensable to the maintenance of the Government to exercise such supposed power, are questions which, under my responsibility, I reserve to myself, and which I cannot feel justified in leaving to the decision of commanders in the field."

These words of the President were hailed with cheers by the proslavery press of the North, and carried comfort to the hearts of the rebels; although the Chief-Magistrate did not intend either. However, before the President's proclamation reached Carolina, Gen. Hunter was furnishing slaves with free papers, of which the succeeding is a copy: —

"DEED OF EMANCIPATION.

"It having been proven, to the entire satisfaction of the general commanding the Department of the South, that the bearer, named ——— ———, heretofore held in involuntary servitude, has been directly employed to aid and assist those in rebellion against the United States of America;

"Now, be it known to all, that, agreeably to the laws, I declare the said person free, and forever absolved from all claims to his services. Both he and his wife and children have full right to go North, East, or West, as they may decide.

"Given under my hand, at the Headquarters of the Department of the South, this nineteenth day of April, 1862.

"D. HUNTER,
"*Major-General Commanding.*"

The words, "forever free," sounded like a charm upon the ears of the oppressed, and seemed to give hopes of a policy that would put down the Rebellion, and leave the people untrammelled with slavery.

"God's law of compensation worketh sure,
So we may know the right shall aye endure!
'Forever free!' God! how the pulse doth bound
At the high, glorious, Heaven-prompted sound
That greets our ears from Carolina's shore!
'Forever free!' and slavery is no more!
Ere time the hunter followed up the slave;
But now a Hunter, noble, true, and brave,
Proclaims the right, to each who draws a breath,
To lift himself from out a living death,
And plant his feet on Freedom's happy soil,
Content to take her wages for his toil,
And look to God, the author of his days,
For food and raiment, sounding forth His praise."

Deep indeed was the impression left upon the public mind by the orders of both Fremont and Hunter; and they hastened the policy which the President eventually adopted, to the great gratification of the friends of freedom everywhere.

CHAPTER XI.

HEROISM OF NEGROES ON THE HIGH SEAS.

Heroism of Negroes. — William Tillman re-captures " The S. G. Waring." — George Green. — Robert Small captures the Steamer " Planter." — Admiral Dupont's Opinion on Negro Patriotism.

In the month of June, 1861, the schooner " S. J. Waring," from New York, bound to South America, was captured on the passage by the rebel privateer "Jeff. Davis," a prize-crew put on board, consisting of a captain, mate, and four seamen ; and the vessel set sail for the port of Charleston, S.C. Three of the original crew were retained on board, a German as steersman, a Yankee who was put in irons, and a black man named William Tillman, the steward and cook of the schooner. The latter was put to work at his usual business, and told that he was henceforth the property of the Confederate States, and would be sold, on his arrival at Charleston, as a slave. Night comes on ; darkness covers the sea ; the vessel is gliding swiftly towards the South ; the rebels, one after another, retire to their berths ; the hour of midnight approaches ; all is silent in the cabin ; the captain is asleep ; the mate, who has charge of the watch, takes his brandy toddy, and reclines upon the quarter-deck. The negro thinks of home and all its endearments : he sees in the dim future chains and slavery.

He resolves, and determines to put the resolution into

practice upon the instant.   Armed with a heavy club,
he proceeds to the captain's room.   He strikes the fatal
blow : he feels the pulse, and all is still. He next goes to
the adjoining room : another blow is struck, and the black
man is master of the cabin.   Cautiously he ascends to
the deck, strikes the mate : the officer is wounded but
not killed. He draws his revolver, and calls for help. The
crew are aroused : they are hastening to aid their commander.   The negro repeats his blows with the heavy
club : the rebel falls dead at Tillman's feet. The African
seizes the revolver, drives the crew below deck, orders
the release of the Yankee, puts the enemy in irons, and
proclaims himself master of the vessel.

"The Waring's" head is turned towards New York,
with the stars and stripes flying, a fair wind, and she rapidly retraces her steps.   A storm comes up : more men
are needed to work the ship. Tillman orders the rebels
to be unchained, and brought on deck. The command is
obeyed ; and they are put to work, but informed, that, if
they show any disobedience, they will be shot down.
Five days more, and " The S. J. Waring " arrives in the
port of New York, under the command of William Tillman, the negro patriot.

"The New-York Tribune " said of this event, —
" To this colored man was the nation indebted for the
first vindication of its honor on the sea."   Another public journal spoke of that achievement alone as an offset
to the defeat of the Federal arms at Bull Run.   Un-
stinted praise from all parties, even those who are usually
awkward in any other vernacular than derision of the
colored man, has been awarded to this colored man.   At
Barnum's Museum he was the centre of attractive gaze
to daily increasing thousands.   Pictorials vied with each

other in portraying his features, and in graphic delinea-
tions of the scene on board the brig; while, in one of
them, Tillman has been sketched as an embodiment of
black action on the sea, in contrast with some delinquent
Federal officer as white inaction on land.

The Federal Government awarded to Tillman the sum
of six thousand dollars as prize-money for the capture
of the schooner. All loyal journals joined in praise of
the heroic act; and, even when the news reached England, the negro's bravery was applauded.[1] A few weeks
later, and the same rebel privateer captured the schooner
" Enchantress," bound from Boston to St. Jago, while off
Nantucket Shoals. A prize-crew was put on board, and,
as in the case of " The Waring," retaining the colored
steward; and the vessel set sail for a Southern port.
When off Cape Hatteras, she was overtaken by the Federal gunboat " Albatross," Capt. Prentice.

On speaking her, and demanding where from and
whence bound, she replied, " Boston, for St. Jago."   At
this moment the negro rushed from the galley, where the
pirates had secreted him, *and jumped into the sea,* exclaiming, " They are a privateer crew from The ' Jeff. Davis,'
and bound for Charleston !" The negro was picked up, and
taken on board " The Albatross." The prize was ordered
to heave to, which she did.   Lieut. Neville jumped
aboard of her, and ordered the pirates into the boats, and
to pull for " The Albatross," where they were secured in
irons. " The Enchantress " was then taken in tow by " The
Albatross," and arrived in Hampton Roads.[2] On the morning of the 13th of May, 1862, the rebel gunboat " Planter" was captured by her colored crew, while lying in the
port of Charleston, S.C., and brought out, and delivered
over to our squadron then blockading the place.   The

following is the dispatch from Com. Dupont to the Secretary of War, announcing the fact : —

"U. S. STEAMSHIP AUGUSTA,
off Charleston, May 13, 1862.

"Sir, — I have the honor to inform you that the rebel armed gunboat 'Planter' was brought out to us this morning from Charleston by eight contrabands, and delivered up to the squadron.   Five colored women and three children are also on board.   She was the armed despatch and transportation steamer attached to the engineer department at Charleston, under Brig.-Gen. Ripley.   At four in the morning, in the absence of the captain who was on shore, she left her wharf close to the government office and head-quarters, with the Palmetto and confederate flags flying, and passed the successive forts, saluting as usual, by blowing the steam-whistle.   After getting beyond the range of the last gun, they hauled down the rebel flags, and hoisted a white one.   "The Onward" was the inside ship of the blockading squadron in the main channel, and was preparing to fire when her commander made out the white flag.

"The armament of the steamer is a thirty-two pounder, on pivot, and a fine twenty-four-pound howitzer.   She has, besides, on her deck, four other guns, one seven-inch, rifled, which were to be taken on the following morning to a new fort on the middle ground.   One of the four belonged to Fort Sumter, and had been struck, in the rebel attack, on the muzzle.   Robert Small, the intelligent slave, and pilot of the boat, who performed this bold feat so skilfully, is a superior man to any who have come into our lines, intelligent as many of them have been.   His information has been most interesting, and

portions of it of the utmost importance. The steamer
is quite a valuable acquisition to the squadron by her
good machinery and very light draught. The bringing
out of this steamer would have done credit to any one.
I do not know whether, in the view of the Government,
the vessel will be considered a prize ; but, if so, I respectfully submit to the Department the claims of the
man Small and his associates. Very respectfully, your
obedient servant,

"S. F. DUPONT,

"Flag-Officer Commanding."

The New-York "Commercial Advertiser" said of the
capture, "We are forced to confess that this is a heroic
act, and that the negroes deserve great praise. Small is
a middle-aged negro, and his features betray nothing of
the firmness of character he displayed. He is said to be
one of the most skilful pilots of Charleston, and to have
a thorough knowledge of all the ports and inlets of South
Carolina."

A bill was introduced in Congress to give the prize to
Robert Small and his companions; and, while it was under
consideration, the "New-York Tribune" made the following timely remarks : "If we must still remember
with humiliation that the Confederate flag yet waves
where our national colors were struck, we should be all
the more prompt to recognize the merit that has put in
our possession the first trophy from Fort Sumter. And
the country should feel doubly humbled if there is not
magnanimity enough to acknowledge a gallant action,
because it was the head of a black man that conceived,
and the hand of a black man that executed it. It would
better, indeed, become us to remember that no small

share of the naval glory of the war belongs to the race which we have forbidden to fight for us; that one negro has captured a vessel from a Southern privateer, and another has brought away from under the very guns of the enemy, where no fleet of ours has yet dared to venture, a prize whose possession a commodore thinks worthy to be announced in a special despatch." The bill was taken up, passed both branches of Congress, and Robert Small, together with his associates, received justice at the hands of the American Government.

The "New-York Herald" gave the following account of the capture : —

"One of the most daring and heroic adventures since the war commenced was undertaken and successfully accomplished by a party of negroes in Charleston on Monday night last. Nine colored men, comprising the pilot, engineers, and crew of the rebel gunboat 'Planter,' took the vessel under their exclusive control, passed the batteries and forts in Charleston Harbor, hoisted the white flag, ran out to the blockading squadron, and thence to Port Royal, *via* St. Helena Sound and Broad River, reaching the flagship 'Wabash' shortly after ten o'clock last evening.

" 'The Planter' is just such a vessel as is needed to navigate the shallow waters between Hilton Head and the adjacent islands, and will prove almost invaluable to the Government. It is proposed, I hear, by the commodore, to recommend the appropriation of $20,000 as a reward to the plucky Africans who have distinguished themselves by this gallant service, $5,000 to be given to the pilot, and the remainder to be divided among his companions.

" 'The Planter' is a high-pressure, side-wheel steamer,

one hundred and forty feet in length, and about fifty feet beam, and draws about five feet of water. She was built in Charleston, was formerly used as a cotton boat, and is capable of carrying about 1,400 bales. On the organization of the Confederate navy, she was transformed into a gunboat, and was the most valuable war-vessel the Confederates had at Charleston. Her armament consisted of one thirty-two-pound rifle-gun forward, and a twenty-four-pound howitzer aft. Besides, she had on board, when she came into the harbor, one seven-inch rifle-gun, one eight-inch columbiad, one eight-inch howitzer, one long thirty-two pounder, and about two hundred rounds of ammunition, which had been consigned to Fort Ripley, and which would have been delivered at that fortification on Tuesday had not the designs of the rebel authorities been frustrated. She was commanded by Capt. Relay, of the Confederate Navy, all the other employees of the vessel, excepting the first and second mates, being persons of color.

"Robert Small, with whom I had a brief interview at Gen. Benham's headquarters this morning, is an intelligent negro, born in Charleston, and employed for many years as a pilot in and about that harbor. He entered upon his duties on board 'The Planter' some six weeks since, and, as he told me, adopted the idea of running the vessel to sea from a joke which one of his companions perpetrated. He immediately cautioned the crew against alluding to the matter in any way on board the boat; but asked them, if they wanted to talk it up in sober earnestness, to meet at his house, where they would devise and determine upon a plan to place themselves under the protection of the Stars and Stripes, instead of the stars and bars. Various plans were proposed; but finally the whole arrangement of the escape was left to the discretion and sagacity of Robert, his companions promising to obey him, and be ready at a moment's notice to accompany him. For three days he kept the provisions of the party secreted in the hold, awaiting an opportunity to slip away. At length, on Monday evening, the white officers of the vessel went on shore to spend the night, intending to start on the following morning for Fort Ripley, and to be absent from the city for some days. The families of the contrabands were notified, and came stealthily on board. At about three o'clock, the fires were lit under the boilers, and the vessel steamed quietly away down the harbor. The tide was against her, and Fort Sumter was not reached till broad daylight. However, the boat passed directly under its walls, giving the usual signal — two long pulls and a jerk at the whistle-cord — as she passed the sentinel.

"Once out of range of the rebel guns, the white flag was raised, and 'The Planter' steamed directly for the blockading steamer 'Augusta.' Capt. Parrott, of the latter vessel, as you may imagine, received them cordially, heard their report, placed Acting-Master Watson, of his ship, in charge of 'The Planter,' and sent the Confederate gunboat and crew forward to Commodore Dupont." [3]

CHAPTER XII.

GENERAL BUTLER AT NEW ORLEANS.

Recognition of Negro Soldiers with Officers of their own Color. — Society in New Orleans. — The Inhuman Master. — Justice. — Change of Opinion. — The Free Colored Population.

WHEN Major-Gen. Butler found himself in possession of New Orleans, he was soon satisfied of the fact that there were but few loyalists amongst the whites, while the Union feeling of the colored people was apparent from the hour of his landing; they having immediately called upon the commander, and, through a committee, offered their services in behalf of the Federal cause. Their offer was accepted, as the following will show : —

> "HEADQUARTERS DEPARTMENT OF THE GULF,
> NEW ORLEANS, Aug. 22, 1862.

"GENERAL ORDER, No. 63:

" Whereas, on the twenty-third day of April, in the year eighteen hundred and sixty-one, at a public meeting of the free colored population of the city of New Orleans, a military organization, known as the ' Native Guards ' (colored), had its existence, which military organization was duly and legally enrolled as a part of the military of the State, its officers being commissioned by Thomas O.

Moore, Governor, and Commander-in-Chief of the Militia, of the State of Louisiana, in the form following, that is to say : —

"'THE STATE OF LOUISIANA.

[Seal of the State.]

" ' By Thomas Overton Moore, Governor of the State of Louisiana, and Commander-in-Chief of the Militia thereof.

" ' In the name and by the authority of the State of Louisiana :

" ' Know ye that ———— ————, having been duly and legally elected Captain of the " Native Guards " (colored), First Division of the Militia of Louisiana, to serve for the term of the war,

"' I do hereby appoint and commission him Captain as aforesaid, to take rank as such, from the second day of May, 1861.

"' He is, therefore, carefully and diligently to discharge the duties of his office, by doing and performing all manner of things thereto belonging. And I do strictly charge and require all officers, non-commissioned officers, and privates under his command to be obedient to his orders as Captain; and he is to observe and follow such orders and directions, from time to time, as he shall receive from me, or the future Governor of the State of Louisiana, or other superior officers, according to the Rules and Articles of War, and in conformity to law.

" ' In testimony whereof, I have caused these letters to be made patent, and the seal of the State to be hereunto annexed.

" ' Given under my hand, at the city of Baton Rouge,

on the second day of May, in the year of our Lord one thousand eight hundred and sixty-two.

" ' (Signed)

" ' THOMAS O. MOORE.

" ' By the Governor.

" ' P. D. HARDY, *Secretary of State.*"

[INDORSED.]

" ' I, Maurice Grivot, Adjutant and Inspector-General of the State of Louisiana, do hereby certify that ————— ——, named in the within commission, did, on the twenty-second day of May, in the year 1861, deposit in my office his written acceptance of the office to which he is commissioned, and his oath of office taken according to law.

" ' M. GRIVOT,

" ' *Adjutant and Inspector-General La.*'

" And whereas such military organization elicited praise and respect, and was complimented in general orders for its patriotism and loyalty, and was ordered to continue during the war, in the words following: —

" ' HEADQUARTERS LOUISIANA MILITIA,

" ' Adjutant-General's Office, March 24, 1862.

" ' ORDER No. 426:

" ' I. The Governor and Commander-in-Chief, relying implicitly upon the loyalty of the free colored population of the city and State, for the protection of their homes, their property, and for Southern rights, from the pollution of a ruthless invader, and believing that the military organization which existed prior to the 15th February, 1862, and elicited praise and respect for the patriotic motives which prompted it, should exist for and during the war, calls upon them to maintain their organization, and hold themselves prepared for such orders as may be transmitted to them.

" 'II. The colonel commanding will report without delay to Major-Gen. Lewis, commanding State Militia.

" 'By order of

" 'THOS. O. MOORE, *Governor.*

" 'M. GRIVOT, *Adjutant-General.*'

" And whereas said military organization, by the same order, was directed to report to Major-Gen. Lewis for service, but did not leave the city of New Orleans when he did :

" Now, therefore, the commanding-general, believing that a large portion of this military force of the State of Louisiana are willing to take service in the volunteer forces of the United States, and be enrolled and organized to 'defend their homes from ruthless invaders;' to protect their wives and children and kindred from wrongs and outrages ; to shield their property from being seized by bad men ; and to defend the flag of their native country as their fathers did under Jackson at Chalmette against Packingham and his myrmidons, carrying the black flag of '.beauty and booty ' ;

" Appreciating their motives, relying upon their ' well-known loyalty and patriotism,' and with ' praise and respect ' for these brave men, it is ordered that all the members of the 'Native Guards' aforesaid, and all other free colored citizens recognized by the first and late governor and authorities of the State of Louisiana as a portion of the militia of the State, who shall enlist in the volunteer service of the United States, shall be duly organized by the appointment of proper officers, and accepted, paid, equipped, armed, and rationed as are other volunteer corps of the United States, subject to the ap-

proval of the President of the United States. All such
persons are required to report themselves at the Touro
Charity Building, Front Levee Street, New Orleans,
where proper officers will muster them into the service
of the United States.

" By command of

" Major-Gen. BUTLER.

"R. S. DAVIS, *Captain and A.A.A.G.*"

The commanding general soon discovered that he
was amongst a different people from those with whom he
had been accustomed to associate. New Orleans, however, though captured was not subdued. The city
had been for years the headquarters and focus of all
Southern rowdyism. An immense crowd of " loafers,"
many without regular occupation or means, infested
the streets, controlled the ballot-boxes, nominated the
judges, selected the police, and affected to rule every
one except a few immensely wealthy planters, who governed them by money. These rowdies had gradually
dissolved society, till New Orleans had become the most
blood-thirsty city in the world; a city where every man
went armed, where a sharp word was invariably answered by a stab, and where the average of murdered
men taken to one hospital was three a day. The mob
were bitter advocates of slavery, held all Yankees in
abhorrence, and guided by the astute brain of Pierre
Soulé, whilom ambassador to Spain, resolved to contest
with Gen. Butler the right to control the city. They
might as well have contested it with Bonaparte. The
first order issued by the general indicated a policy from
which he never swerved. The mob had surrounded the
St. Charles Hotel, threatening an attack on the building,
then the general's headquarters; and Gen. Williams,

commanding the troops round it, reported that he would be unable to control the mob. " Gen. Butler, in his serenest manner, replied, ' Give my compliments to Gen. Williams, and tell him, if he finds he cannot control the mob, to open upon them with artillery.' " The mob did that day endeavor to seize Judge Summers, the Recorder; and he was only saved by the determined courage of Lieut. Kinsman, in command of an armed party. From this moment the general assumed the attitude he never abandoned, that of master of New Orleans, making his own will the law. He at first retained the municipal organization; but, finding the officials incurably hostile, he sent them to Fort Lafayette, and thenceforward ruled alone, feeding the people, re-establishing trade, maintaining public order, and seeing that negroes obtained some reasonable measure of security. Their evidence was admitted, "Louisiana having, when she went out of the Union, taken her black code with her; " the whipping-house was abolished, and all forms of torture sternly prohibited.

The following interesting narrative, given by a correspondent of " The Atlantic Monthly," will show, to some extent, the scenes which Gen. Butler had to pass through in connection with slavery : —

" One Sunday morning, late last summer, as I came down to the breakfast-room, I was surprised to find a large number of persons assembled in the library.

" When I reached the door, a member of the staff took me by the arm, and drew me into a room toward a young and delicate mulatto girl, who was standing against the opposite wall, with the meek, patient bearing of her race, so expressive of the system of repression to which they have been so long subjected.

" Drawing down the border of her dress, my conduc-tor showed me a sight more revolting than I trust ever again to behold.

" The poor girl's back was flayed until the quivering flesh resembled a fresh beefsteak scorched on a gridiron. With a cold chill creeping through my veins, I turned away from the sickening spectacle, and, for an explana-tion of the affair, scanned the various persons about the room.

" In the centre of the group, at his writing-table, sat the general. His head rested on his hand, and he was evidently endeavoring to fix his attention upon the re-marks of a tall, swarthy-looking man who stood opposite, and who, I soon discovered, was the owner of the girl, and was attempting a defence of the foul outrage he had committed upon the unresisting and helpless person of his unfortunate victim, who stood smarting, but silent, under the dreadful pain inflicted by the brutal lash.

." By the side of the slave-holder stood our adjutant-gen eral, his face livid with almost irrepressible rage, and his fists tight clenched, as if to violently restrain him-self from visiting the guilty wretch with summary and retributive justice. Disposed about the room, in vari-ous attitudes, but all exhibiting in their countenances the same mingling of horror and indignation, were other members of the staff; while near the door stood three or four house-servants, who were witnesses in the case.

" To the charge of having administered the inhuman castigation, Landry (the owner of the girl) pleaded guilty, but urged, in extenuation, that the girl had dared to make an effort for that freedom which her in-stincts, drawn from the veins of her abuser, had taught her was the God-given right of all who possess the germ of immortality, no matter what the color of the casket in which it is hidden.

"I say 'drawn from the veins of her abuser,' because she declared she was his daughter; and every one in the room, looking upon the man and woman confronting each other, confessed that the resemblance justified the assertion.

"At the conclusion of all the evidence in the case, the general continued in the same position as before, and remained for some time apparently lost in abstraction. 1 shall never forget the singular expression on his face.

"I had been accustomed to see him in a storm of passion at any instance of oppression or flagrant injustice; but, on this occasion, he was too deeply affected to obtain relief in the usual way.

"His whole air was one of dejection, almost listlessness; his indignation too intense, and his anger too stern, to find expression, even in his countenance. After sitting in the mood which I have described at such length, the general again turned to the prisoner, and said, in a quiet, subdued tone of voice, —

"'Mr. Landry, I dare not trust myself to decide to-day what punishment would be meet for your offence; for I am in that state of mind that I fear I might exceed the strict demands of justice. I shall therefore place you under guard for the present, until I conclude upon your sentence.'

"A few days after, a number of influential citizens having represented to the general that Mr. Landry was not only a 'high-toned gentleman,' but a person of unusual 'AMIABILITY' of character, and was consequently entitled to no small degree of leniency, he answered, that, in consideration of the prisoner's 'high-toned' character, and

especially of his ' amiability,' of which he had seen so
remarkable a proof, he had determined to meet their
views ; and therefore ordered that Landry give a deed
of manumission to the girl, and pay a fine of five hundred dollars, to be placed in the hands of a trustee for
her benefit."

It was scenes like the above that changed Gen. Butler's views upon the question of slavery ; for it cannot
be denied, that, during the first few weeks of his command in New Orleans, he had a controversy with Gen.
Phelps, owing to the latter's real antislavery feelings.
Soon after his arrival, Gen. Butler gave orders that all
negroes not needed for service should be removed from
the camps. The city was sealed against their escape.
Even secession masters were assured that their property,
if not employed, should be returned. It is said that
pledges of reimbursement for loss of labor were made
to such. Gen. Phelps planted himself on the side of
the slave ; would not exile them from his camp ; branded
as cruel the policy that harbored, and then drove out the
slave to the inhuman revenge that awaited him.

Yet the latter part of Gen. Butler's reign compensated
for his earlier faults. It must be remembered, that, when
he landed in New Orleans, he was fresh from Washington, where the jails were filled with fugitive slaves,
awaiting the claim of their masters ; where the return
of the escaped bondman was considered a military duty.
Then how could he be expected to do better? The
stream cannot rise higher than the spring.

His removal from the Department of the Gulf, on account of the crushing blows which he gave the " peculiar institution," at once endeared him to the hearts of
the friends of impartial freedom throughout the land.

The following imitation of Leigh Hunt's celebrated poem is not out of place here : —

"ABOU BEN BUTLER.

"Abou Ben Butler (may his tribe increase!)
Awoke one night down by the old Balize,
And saw, outside the comfort of his room,
Making it warmer for the gathering gloom,
A black man, shivering in the Winter's cold.
Exceeding courage made Ben Butler bold ;
And to the presence in the dark he said,
"What wantest thou?" The figure raised its head,
And, with a look made of all sad accord,
Answered, "The men who'll serve the purpose of the Lord."
"And am I one?" said Butler. "Nay, not so,"
Replied the black man. Butler spoke more low,
But cheerly still, and said, "*As I am Ben*,
You'll not have cause to tell me that again!"

The figure bowed and vanished. The next night
It came once more, environed strong in light,
And showed the names whom love of Freedom blessed;
And, lo! Ben Butler's name led all the rest." — *Boston Transcript.*

It is probably well known that the free colored population of New Orleans, in intelligence, public spirit, and material wealth, surpass those of the same class in any other city of the Union. Many of these gentlemen have been highly educated, have travelled extensively in this and foreign countries, speak and read the French, Spanish, and English languages fluently, and in the Exchange Rooms, or at the Stock Boards, wield an influence at any time fully equal to the same number of white capitalists. Before the war, they represented in that city alone fifteen millions of property, and were heavily taxed to support the schools of the State, but were not allowed to claim the least benefit therefrom.

These gentlemen, representing so much intelligence,

culture, and wealth, and who would, notwithstanding the fact that they all have negro blood in their veins, adorn any circle of society in the North, who would be taken upon Broadway for educated and wealthy Cuban planters, rather than free negroes, although many of them have themselves held slaves, have always been loyal to the Union ; and, when New Orleans seemed in danger of being re-captured by the rebels under Gen. Magruder, these colored men rose *en masse*, closed their offices and stores, armed and organized themselves into six regiments, and for six weeks abandoned their business, and stood ready to fight for the defence of New Orleans, while, at the same time, not a single white regiment from the original white inhabitants was raised.

CHAPTER XIII.

THE DISTRICT OF COLUMBIA FREE.

Emancipation in the District. — Comments of the Press. — The Good Result. — Recognition of Hayti and Liberia. — The Slave-trader Gordon.

FOR many years previous to the Rebellion, efforts had been made to induce Congress to abolish slavery in the District of Columbia, without success. The "negro-pens" which adorned that portion of the national domain had long made Americans feel ashamed of the capital of their country; because it was well known that those pens were more or less connected with the American slave-trade, which, in its cruelty, was as bad as that of the African slave-trade, if not worse. It was expected, even by the democracy, that one of the first acts of the Republicans on coming into office would be the emancipation of the slaves of the District; and therefore no one was surprised at its being brought forward in the earliest part of Mr. Lincoln's administration. The bill was introduced into the Senate by Hon. Henry Wilson of Massachusetts. Its discussion caused considerable excitement among slave-holders, who used every means to prevent its passage. Nevertheless, after going through the Senate, it passed the House on the 11th of April, 1862, by a large majority, and soon received the sanction of the President. The Copperhead press howled over the doings of Congress, and appeared to

see the fate of the institution in this act. The " Louis-
ville Journal " said, —

" The President, contrary to our most earnest hopes,
has approved the bill for the abolition of slavery in the
District of Columbia.

" We need hardly say that the President's reasons for
approving the bill are not, in our opinion, such as should
have governed him at this extraordinary juncture of the
national history. They are not to us sufficient reasons.
On the contrary, we think they weigh as nothing compared with the grave reasons in the opposite scale.

" The enemies of the country will no doubt attempt so
to use the act by representing it as the first step towards
the abolition of slavery in the States ; but this represen-
tation, if made, will be a very gross misrepresentation.
The Republicans, as a body, our readers know full well,
always declared that Congress had the constitutional
power to abolish slavery in the District of Columbia, and
that Congress ought to exercise the power. They, however, have always declared, with the same unanimity,
that Congress does not possess the constitutional power
to interfere with slavery in the States. And they now
declare so with especial distinctness and solemnity.

" We, of course, except from the scope of the remarks
we have now made such abolitionists as Sumner and his
scattered followers in Congress. With the exception of
these few *raving zealots, of whom most Republicans are
heartily ashamed,* the men who voted to abolish slavery
in the District of Columbia avow themselves as resolutely
opposed to interfering with slavery in the States as the
men who voted against the measure are known to be.
Their avowals are distinct and emphatic.

" We hope that the majority in Congress are at length

through with such tricks, and will henceforth leave in peace the myrtle of party eye-sores, while they split the oak of the Rebellion."

However, the predictions and hopes of the "Journal" were not to avail any thing for the slavemongers. The Rebellion had sounded the death-knell of the crime of crimes. Too many brave men had already fallen by the hands of the upholders of the barbarous system to have it stop there. The God of liberty had proclaimed that —

> "In this, the District where my Temple stands,
> I burst indignant every captive's bands ;
> Here in my home my glorious work begin ;
> Then blush no more each day to see this sin.
> Thus finding room to freely breathe and stand,
> I'll stretch my sceptre over all the land,
> Until, unfettered, leaps the waiting slave,
> And echoes back the blessings of the brave."

The "Press," Forney's paper, spoke thus, a few days after slavery had died in the District : —

"The emancipation of slaves in the District of Columbia was one of the most suggestive events of the age. It was an example and an illustration. The great idea of the past century, the idea which had associated and identified itself with our institutions, was at last tried by a practical test. Good results came from it ; none of the evils dreaded and prophesied have been manifested. It was a simple measure of legislative policy, and was established amid great opposition and feeling. Yet it was succeeded by no agitation, no outbreaks of popular prejudice. The District of Columbia is now a free Territory by the easy operation of a statute law, — by what enemies of the measure called forcible emancipation ; and yet the District of Columbia is as pleasant and as prosperous as at any period of its history. There has been no negro saturnalia, no violent outbreak of social disorder, no attempt to invade those barriers of social distinction that must forever exist between the African and Anglo-Saxon [?]. It was said that property would depreciate ; that there would be excesses and violences ; that the negro would become insolent and unbearable; that the city of Washington would become a desolated metropolis ; that negro labor would become valueless ; that hundreds of the emancipated negroes would flock to the Northern States. We have seen no such results as yet ; we know that nothing of the kind is anticipated. We have yet to hear of the first emancipated negro coming to Philadelphia. Labor moves on in its accustomed way, with the usual supply and demand. We do not think a white woman has been insulted by an emancipated negro ; we are confident that no emancipated negro has sought the hand of any fair damsel of marriageable age and condition.

"Society is the same in Maryland and Kentucky. In accomplishing emancipation in the District of Columbia, we have shown the timid that their fears were but of the imagination, the mere prejudices of education. Slavery has been the cancer of the Southern social system. We employ an old metaphor, perhaps, but it is a forcible and appropriate illustration. It rooted itself into the body of Southern society, attacking the glands, terminating in an ill-conditioned and deep disease, and causing the republic excruciating pain. It became schirrous and indurated. It brought disaster and grief upon them, and the sorest of evils upon us. It brought us blood and civil war, ruined commerce and desolated fields, blockaded ports, and rivers that swarm with gunboats instead of mer-

chant vessels.   It was tolerated as a necessary evil, until
its extent and virulence made it incumbent upon us to ter-
minate it as such, or to be terminated by it.   The cham-
pions of this institution, not content with submitting to
the toleration and protection of our great Northern free
community, have made it the pretext for aggression and
insult, and by their own acts are accomplishing its downfall.   The emancipation of slavery in the District of Columbia was the necessary and natural result of the
Southern Rebellion.   It is but the beginning of the
results the Rebellion must surely bring.   The wedge has
only entered the log, and heavy blows are falling upon
it day by day."

Great was the rejoicing in Washington and throughout the Free States ; for every one saw " the end from the
beginning."   Our own Whittier strung his harp anew,
and sung, —

> " I knew that truth would crush the lie, —
>   Somehow, sometime the end would be ;
>   Yet scarcely dared I hope to see
> The triumph with my mortal eye.
>
> But now I see it.   In the sun
>   A free flag floats from yonder dome,
>   And at the nation's hearth and home
> The justice long delayed is done."

With the abolition of slavery in the District of Columbia, commenced a new era at our country's capital.
The representatives of the Governments of Hayti and
Liberia had both long knocked in vain to be admitted
with the representatives of other nations.   The slave
power had always succeeded in keeping them out.   But
a change had now come over the dreams of the people,

and Congress was but acting up to this new light in passing the following bill: —

"*Be it enacted by the Senate and House of Representatives of the United States of America in Congress assembled,* That the President of the United States be, and he hereby is, authorized, by and with the consent of the Senate, to appoint diplomatic representatives of the United States to the republics of Hayti and Liberia, respectively. Each of the said representatives so appointed shall be accredited as commissioner and consul general, and shall receive, out of any money in the treasury not otherwise appropriated, the compensation of commissioners provided for by the Act of Congress approved August 18, 1856: *Provided* that the compensation of the representative at Liberia shall not exceed $4,000."

The above bill was before the Senate some time, and elicited much discussion, and an able speech was made by Hon. Charles Sumner in favor of the recognition of the independence of Hayti and Liberia. To use his own expressive words, "Slavery in the national capital is now abolished: it remains that this other triumph shall be achieved. Nothing but the sway of a slave-holding despotism on the floor of Congress, hitherto, has prevented the adoption of this righteous measure; and now that that despotism has been exorcised, no time should be lost by Congress to see it carried into immediate execution. All other civilized nations have ceased to make complexion a badge of superiority or inferiority in the matter of nationality; and we should make haste, therefore, to repair the injury we have done, as a republic, in refusing to recognize Liberian and Haytian independence."

Even after all that had passed, the African slave-trade

was still being carried on between the Southern States and Africa. Ships were fitted out in Northern ports for the purpose of carrying on this infernal traffic. And, although it was prohibited by an act of Congress, none had ever been convicted for dealing in slaves. The new order of things was to give these traffickers a trial, and test the power by which they had so long dealt in the bodies and souls of men whom they had stolen from their native land. One Nathaniel Gordon was already in prison in New York, and his trial was fast approaching: it came, and he was convicted of piracy in the United States District Court in the city of New York; the piracy consisting in having fitted out a slaver, and shipped nine hundred Africans at Congo River, with a view to selling them as slaves. The same man had been tried for the same offence before; but the jury failed to agree, and he accordingly escaped punishment for the time. Every-effort was made which the ingenuity of able lawyers could invent, or the power of money could enforce, to save this miscreant from the gallows; but all in vain: for President Lincoln utterly refused to interfere in any way whatever, and Gordon was executed on the 7th of February.[1]

This blow appeared to give more offence to the commercial Copperheads than even the emancipation of the slaves in the District of Columbia; for it struck an effectual blow at a very lucrative branch of commerce, in which the New Yorkers were largely interested. Thus it will be seen that the nation was steadily moving on to the goal of freedom.

CHAPTER XIV.

THE BLACK BRIGADE OF CINCINNATI.

The Great Fright. — Cruel Treatment of the Colored People by the Police. — Bill Homer and his Roughs. — Military Training. — Col. Dickson. — The Work. — Mustering Out. — The Thanks.

HATRED to the negro is characteristic of the people of Cincinnati; more so, probably, than any other city in the West. Mobs in which the colored citizens have been the victims have more than once occurred in that place, to the utter disgrace of its white inhabitants, — mobs resulting often in the loss of life, and always in the destruction of property. The raid of John Morgan in the month of July, 1862, and, soon after, the defeat of the Union troops in Kentucky, had given warning of impending danger. This feeling of fear culminated on the first of September, in the mayor of Cincinnati calling on the people to organize and prepare for the defence of the city, in the following proclamation : —

"MAYOR'S OFFICE, *City of Cincinnati.*

"In accordance with a resolution passed by the City Council of Cincinnati on the first instant, I hereby request that all business of every kind or character be suspended at ten o'clock of this day, and that all persons, employers and employees, assemble in their respective wards, at the usual places of voting, and then and there organize themselves in such manner as may be thought best for the defence of the city. Every man, of every age, be he citizen or alien, who lives under the protection of our laws, is expected to take part in the organization.

" Witness my hand, and the corporate seal of the city of Cincinnati, this second day of September, A.D. 1862.

"GEORGE HATCH, *Mayor*."

At two o'clock on the morning of the same day, the mayor issued another proclamation, notifying the citizens that the police force would perform the duty of a provost-guard, under the direction of Gen. Wallace.

The mayor's proclamation, under ordinary circumstances, would be explicit enough. " Every man, of every age, be he citizen or alien," surely meant the colored people. A number thought themselves included in the call ; but, remembering the ill-will excited by former offers for home defence, they feared to come forward for enrolment. The proclamation ordered the people to assemble " in the respective wards, at the usual places of voting." The colored people had no places of voting. Added to this, George Hatch was the same mayor who had broken up the movement for home defence, before mentioned. Seeking to test the matter, a policeman was approached, as he strutted in his new dignity of provost-guard. To the question, humbly, almost tremblingly, put, "Does the mayor desire colored men to report for service in the city's defence ? " he replied, " You know d——d well he does'nt mean you. Niggers ain't citizens." — " But he calls on all, citizens and aliens. If he does not mean all, he should not say so." — " The mayor knows as well as you do what to write, and all he wants is for you niggers to keep quiet." This was at nine o'clock on the morning of the second. The military authorities had determined, however, to impress the colored men for work upon the fortifications. The privilege of volunteering, extended to others, was to be denied to them. Permission to volunteer would imply some freedom, some dignity, some independent manhood. For this the commanding officer is alone chargeable.

If the guard appointed to the duty of collecting the colored people had gone to their houses, and notified them to report for duty on the fortifications, the order would have been cheerfully obeyed. But the brutal ruffians who composed the regular and special police took every opportunity to inflict abuse and insult upon the men whom they arrested. The special police was entirely composed of that class of the population, which, only a month before, had combined to massacre the colored population, and were only prevented from committing great excesses by the fact that John Morgan, with his rough riders, had galloped to within forty miles of the river, when the respectable citizens, fearing that the disloyal element within might combine with the raiders without, and give the city over to pillage, called a meeting on 'Change, and demanded that the riot be stopped. The special police was, in fact, composed of a class too cowardly or too traitorous to aid, honestly and manfully, in the defence of the city. They went from house to house, followed by a gang of rude, foul-mouthed boys. Closets, cellars, and garrets were searched; bayonets were thrust into beds and bedding; old and young, sick and well, were dragged out, and, amidst shouts and jeers, marched like felons to the pen on Plum Street, opposite the Cathedral. No time was given to prepare for camp-life; in most cases no information was given of the pur-

pose for which the men were impressed.   The only
answers to questions were curses, and a brutal " Come
along now; you will find out time enough."   Had the
city been captured by the Confederates, the colored people would have suffered no more than they did at the
hands of these defenders.   Tuesday night, Sept. 2, was
a sad night to the colored people of Cincinnati.   The
greater part of the male population had been dragged
from home, across the river, but where, and for what,
none could tell.

The captain of these conscripting squads was one William Homer, and in him organized ruffianism had its
fitting head.   He exhibited the brutal malignity of his
nature in a continued series of petty tyrannies.   Among
the first squads marched into the yard was one which
had to wait several hours before being ordered across
the river.   Seeking to make themselves as comfortable
as possible, they had collected blocks of wood, and piled
up bricks, upon which they seated themselves on the
shaded side of the yard.   Coming into the yard, he ordered all to rise, marched them to another part, then
issued the order, " D—n you, squat."   Turning to the
guard, he added, " Shoot the first one who rises."
Reaching the opposite side of the river, the same squad
were marched from the sidewalk into the middle of the
dusty road, and again the order, " D—n you, squat,"
and the command to shoot the first one who should rise.

The drill of this guard of white ruffians was unique,
and not set down in either Scott or Hardee.   Calling up
his men, he would address them thus : " Now, you fellows, hold up your heads.   Pat, hold your musket
straight; don't put your tongue out so far; keep your eyes
open : I believe you are drunk.   Now, then, I want you

fellows to go out of this pen, and bring all the niggers
you can catch. Don't come back here without niggers:
if you do, you shall not have a bit of grog. Now be off,
you shabby cusses, and come back in forty minutes, and
bring me niggers; that's what I want." This barbarous
and inhuman treatment of the colored citizens of Cincinnati continued for four days, without a single word of
remonstrance, except from the "Gazette."

Finally, Col. Dickson, a humane man and gentlemanly
officer, was appointed to the command of the "Black
Brigade," and brutality gave way to kind treatment.
The men were permitted to return to their homes, to
allay the fears of their families, and to prepare themselves the better for camp-life. The police were relieved
of provost-guard duty, and on Friday morning more men
reported for duty than had been dragged together by
the police. Many had hidden too securely to be found;
others had escaped to the country. These now
came forward to aid in the city's defence. With aug-
mented numbers, and glowing with enthusiasm, the
Black Brigade marched to their duty. Receiving the
treatment of men, they were ready for any thing. Being
in line of march, they were presented with a national
flag by Capt. Lupton, who accompanied it with the following address: —

"I have the kind permission of your commandant,
Col. Dickson, to hand you, without formal speech or presentation, this national flag, — my sole object to encourage and cheer you on to duty. On its broad folds is
inscribed, 'THE BLACK BRIGADE OF CINCINNATI.' I am
confident, that, in your hands, it will not be dishonored.

"The duty of the hour is *work*, — hard, severe labor
on the fortifications of the city. In the emergency upon

us, the highest and the lowest alike owe this duty. Let it be cheerfully undertaken. He is no *man* who now, in defence of home and fireside, shirks duty.

" A flag is the emblem of sovereignty, a symbol and guaranty of *protection*. Every nation and people are proud of the flag of their country. England, for a thousand years, boasts her Red Flag and Cross of St. George; France glories in her Tri-color and Imperial Eagle ; ours, the ' Star-spangled Banner,' far more beautiful than they, — *this dear old flag!* — the sun in heaven never looked down on so proud a banner of beauty and glory. Men of the Black Brigade, rally around it ! Assert your *manhood;* be loyal to duty; be obedient, hopeful, patient. Slavery will soon die ; the slave-holders' rebellion, accursed of God and man, will shortly and miserably perish. There will then be, through all the coming ages, in very truth, a land of the free, — one country, one flag, one destiny.

" I charge you, *men of the Black Brigade of Cincinnati,* remember that for you, and for me, and for your children, and your children's children, there is but *one flag,* as there is but one Bible, and one GOD, the Father of us all."

For nearly three weeks the Black Brigade labored upon the fortifications, their services beginning, as we have seen, Sept. 2, and terminating Sept. 20.

When the brigade was mustered out, the commander thanked them in the following eloquent terms : —

" SOLDIERS OF THE BLACK BRIGADE ! You have finished the work assigned to you upon the fortifications for the defence of the city. You are now to be discharged. You have labored faithfully ; you have made miles of military roads, miles of rifle-pits, felled hundreds

of acres of the largest and loftiest forest trees, built
magazines and forts.   The hills across yonder river will
be a perpetual monument of your labors.   You have, in
no spirit of bravado, in no defiance of established prejudice, but in submission to it, intimated to me your willingness to defend with your lives the fortifications your
hands have built.   *Organized companies of men of your
race have tendered their services to aid in the defence of the city.*   In obedience to the policy of the Government, the authorities have denied you this privilege.
In the department of labor permitted, you have, however,
rendered a willing and cheerful service.   Nor has your
zeal been dampened by the cruel treatment received.
The citizens, of both sexes, have encouraged you with
their smiles and words of approbation ; the soldiers have
welcomed you as co-laborers in the same great cause.
But a portion of the police, ruffians in character, early
learning that your services were accepted, and seeking
to deprive you of the honor of voluntary labor, before
opportunity was given you to proceed to the field, rudely
seized you in the streets, in your places of business, in
your homes, everywhere, hurried you into filthy pens,
thence across the river to the fortifications, not permit-
ting you to make any preparation for camp-life.   You
have borne this with the accustomed patience of your
race; and when, under more favorable auspices, you have
received only the protection due to a common humanity,
you have labored cheerfully and effectively.

" Go to your homes with the consciousness of having
performed your duty, — of deserving, if you do not receive, the protection of the law, and bearing with you
the gratitude and respect of all honorable men.   You
have learned to suffer and to wait ; but, in your hours of

adversity, remember that the same God who has numbered the hairs of our heads, who watches over even the fate of a sparrow, is the God of your race as well as mine. The sweat-blood which the nation is now shedding at every pore is an awful warning of how fearful a thing it is to oppress the humblest being."

A letter in " The Tribune," dated Cincinnati, Sept. 7, giving an account of the enthusiasm of the people in rallying for the city's defence, says, " While all have done well, the negroes, as a class, must bear away the palm. When martial law was declared, a few prominent colored men tendered their services in any capacity desired. As soon as it became known that they would be accepted, Mayor Hatch's police commenced arresting them everywhere, dragging them away from their houses and places of business without a moment's notice, shutting them up in negro-pens, and subjecting them to the grossest abuse and indignity. Mr. Hatch is charged with secession proclivities. During the recent riots against the negroes, the *animus* of his police was entirely hostile to them, and many outrages were committed upon that helpless and unoffending class. On this occasion, the same course was pursued. No opportunity was afforded the negro to volunteer ; but they were treated as public enemies. They were taken over the river, ostensibly to work upon the fortification ; but were scattered, detailed as cooks for white regiments, some of them half-starved, and all so much abused that it finally caused a great outcry. When Gen. Wallace's attention was called to the matter, he requested Judge William M. Dickson, a prominent citizen, who is related by marriage to President Lincoln, to take the whole matter in charge. Judge Dickson undertook the thankless task : organized the negroes into two regiments of three hundred each, made the proper provision for their comfort, and set them at work upon the trenches. They have accomplished more than any other six hundred of the whole eight thousand men upon the fortifications. Their work has been entirely voluntary. Judge Dickson informed them at the outset that all could go home who chose; that it must be entirely a labor of love with them. *Only one man* of the whole number has availed himself of the privilege ; the rest have all worked cheer. fully and efficiently. One of the regiments is officered by white captains, the other by negroes. The latter proved so decidedly superior that both regiments will hereafter be commanded by officers of their own race. They are not only working, but drilling ; and they already go through some of the simpler military movements very creditably. Wherever they appear, they are cheered by our troops. Last night, one of the colored regiments, coming off duty for twenty-four hours, was halted in front of headquarters, at the Burnet House, front faced, and gave three rousing cheers for Gen. Wallace, and three more for Judge Dickson."

CHAPTER XV.

PROCLAMATION OF FREEDOM.

Emancipation Proclamation. — Copperhead View of It. — "Abraham Spare the South." — The Contrabands Rejoicing. — The Songs. — Enthusiasm. — Faith in God. — Negro Wit. — "Forever Free."

ON the 22d of September, 1862, President Lincoln sent forth his proclamation, warning the rebel States that he would proclaim emancipation to their slaves if such States did not return to the Union before the first day of the following January. Loud were the denunciations of the copperheads of the country; and all the stale arguments against negro emancipation which had been used in the West Indies thirty years before, and since then in our country, were newly vamped, and put forward to frighten the President and his Cabinet.

The toleration of a great social wrong in any country is ever accompanied by blindness of vision, hardness of heart, and cowardice of mind, as well as moral deterioration and industrial impoverishment. Hence, whenever an earnest attempt is made for the removal of the wrong, those without eyes noisily declare that they see clearly that nothing but disastrous consequences will follow; those who are dead to all sensibility profess to be shocked beyond measure in contemplating the terrible scenes that must result from the change; and those who have no faith in justice are thrown into spasms at the mention of its impartial administration. For a whole generation, covering the period of the antislavery struggle in this

country, have they not incessantly raised their senseless
clamors and indignant outcries against the simplest claim
of bleeding humanity to be released from its tortures, as
though it were a proposition to destroy all order, inaugurate universal ruin, and " let chaos come again ? "

" The proclamation won't reach the slaves," said one.
" They wont heed it," said another.

" This proclamation is an invitation to the blacks to
murder their masters," remarked a Boston copperhead
newspaper. " The slaves will fight for their masters,"
said the same journal, the following day.

" " It will destroy the Union." — " It is harmless and im-
potent." — " It will excite slave insurrection." — " The
slaves will never hear of it." — " It will excite the South
to desperation." — " The rebels will laugh it to scorn."

Delegation after delegation waited on the President,
and urged a postponement of emancipation. The Kentucky Congressional delegation did all in their power to
put back the glorious event. Conservative old-line
Whigs and backsliding antislavery men were afraid to
witness the coming day.

> " Abraham, spare the South,
>   Touch not a single slave,
> Nor e'en by word of mouth
>   Disturb the thing, we crave.
> 'Twas our forefathers' hand
>   That slavery begot :
> There, Abraham, let it stand ;
>   Thine acts shall harm it not," —

cried thousands who called at the White House.
Washington, Alexandria, and Georgetown were crowded
with " contrabands ; " and hundreds were forwarded to
the Sea Islands, to be occupied in cultivating the deserted
plantations. As the day drew near, reports were circu-

lated that the President would re-call the pledge. The friends of the negro were frightened; the negro himself trembled for fear that the cause would be lost. The blacks in all the Southern departments were behaving well, as if to deepen the already good impression made by them on the Government officials. Rejoicing meetings were advertised at the Tremont Temple, Boston; Cooper Institute, New York, and the largest hall in Philadelphia, and in nearly every city and large town in the north. Great preparation was made at the " Contraband Camp," in the District of Columbia. At the latter place, they met on the last night in December, 1862, in the camp, and waited patiently for the coming day, when they should become free. The fore part of the night was spent in singing and prayer, the following being sung several times : —

> " Oh, go down, Moses, [1]
>   Way down into Egypt's land ;
>   Tell king Pharaoh
>   To let my people go.
>
> Oh, Pharaoh said he would go cross,
>   Let my people go.
> But Pharaoh and his host was lost,
>   Let my people go.
>   *Chorus* — Oh, go down, Moses, &c.
>
> O Moses, stretch your hands across,
>   Let my people go.
> And don't get lost in the wilderness,
>   Let my people go.
>   *Chorus* — Oh, go down, Moses, &c.
>
> You may hinder me here, but you can't up there,
>   Let my people go.
> He sits in heaven, and answers prayer,
>   Let my people go.
>   *Chorus* — Oh, go down, Moses, &c."

After this an old man struck up, in a clear and powerful voice, " I am a free man now : Jesus Christ has made
me free ! " the company gradually joining in ; and, before
the close, the whole assemblage was singing in chorus.

It was quite evident, through the exercises of the day
and night, that the negroes regard the condition of the
Israelites in Egypt as typical of their own condition in
slavery ; and the allusions to Moses, Pharaoh, the Egyp-
tian task-masters, and the unhappy condition of the captive Israelites, were continuous ; and any reference to
the triumphant escape of the Israelites across the Red
Sea, and the destruction of their pursuing masters, was
certain to bring out a strong " Amen ! "

An old colored preacher, who displays many of the
most marked peculiarities of his race, calling himself
" John de Baptis," and known as such by his companions,
from his habit of always taking his text, as he expresses
it, from the " regulations ob de 2d chapter of Matthew,
'And in those days came John de Baptis,' " came forward,
and, taking his usual text, went on to show the necessity
of following good advice, and rebuked his hearers for
being more lawless than they were in Dixie.

Then came another contraband brother, who said, —

" Onst, the time was dat I cried all night. What's de
matter ? What's de matter ? Matter enough. De nex
mornin' my child was to be sold, an' she was sold ; an' I
neber spec to see her no more till de day ob judgment.
Now, no more dat ! no more dat ! no more dat ! Wid
my hands agin my breast I was gwine to my work, when
de overseer used to whip me along. Now, no more dat !
no more dat ! no more dat ! When I tink what de Lord's
done for us, an' brot us thro' de trubbles, I feel dat I
ought go inter his service. We'se free now, bress de

Lord ! (Amens ! were vociferated all over the building.)
Dey can't sell my wife an' child any more, bress de Lord !
(Glory, glory ! from the audience.)   No more dat ! no
more dat ! no more dat, now ! (Glory !)   Presurdund
Lincum hav shot de gate !   Dat's what de matter ! " and
there was a prolonged response of Amens !

A woman on her knees exclaimed at the top of her
voice, —

> " If de Debble do not ketch
> Jeff. Davis, dat infernal retch,
> An roast and frigazee dat rebble,
> Wat is de use ob any Debble ? "

" Amen ! amen ! amen ! " cried many voices.

At this juncture of the meeting, an intelligent contraband broke out in the following strain : —

> " The first of January next, eighteen sixty-three, —
> So says the Proclamation, — the slaves will all be free !
> To every kindly heart 'twill be the day of jubilee ;
>   For the bond shall all go free !
>
> John Brown, ̤he dauntless hero, with joy is looking on ;
> From his home among the angels he sees the coming dawn ;
> Then up with Freedom's banners, and hail the glorious morn
>   When the slaves shall all go free !
>
> We've made a strike for liberty ; the Lord is on our side ;
> And Christ, the friend of bondmen, shall ever be our guide ;
> And soon the cry will ring, throughout this glorious land so wide,
>   ' Let the bondmen all go free ! '
>
> No more from crushed and bleeding hearts we hear the broken sigh ;
> No more from brothers bound in chains we'll hear the pleading cry ;
> For the happy day, the glorious day, is coming by and by,
>   When the slaves shall all go free !
>
> We're bound to make our glorious flag the banner of the free,
> The first of January next, eighteen sixty-three ;
> Of every loyal Northern heart the glad cry then shall be,
>   ' Let the bondmen all go free ! '

'No Compromise with Slavery!' we hear the cheering sound,
The road to peace and happiness 'Old Abe' at last has found:
With earnest hearts and willing hands to stand by him we're bound,
    While he sets the bondmen free!

The morning light is breaking: we see its cheering ray, —
The light of Truth and Justice, that can never fade away;
And soon the light will brighten to a great and glorious day,
    When the slaves shall all go free!

And when we on the 'other side' do all together stand,
As children of one family we'll clasp the friendly hand:
We'll be a band of brothers in that brighter, better land,
    Where the bond shall all be free!"

After several others had spoken, George Payne, another contraband, made a few sensible remarks, somewhat in these words: "Friends, don't you see de han' of God in dis? Haven't we a right to rejoice? You all know you couldn't have such a meetin' as dis down in Dixie! Dat you all knows. I have a right to rejoice; an' so have you; for we shall be free in jus' about five minutes. Dat's a fact. I shall rejoice that God has placed Mr. Lincum in de president's chair, and dat he wouldn't let de rebels make peace until after dis new year. De Lord has heard de groans of de people, and has come down to deliver! You all knows dat in Dixie you worked de day long, an' never got no satisfacshun. But here, what you make is yourn. I've worked six months; and what I've made is mine! Let me tell you, though, don't be too free! De lazy man can't go to heaven. You must be honest, an' work, an' show dat you is fit to be free; an' de Lord will bless you an' Abrum Lincum. Amen!"

A small black man, with a rather cracking voice, appearing by his jestures to be inwardly on fire, began jumping, and singing the following: —

" Massa gone, missy too;
    Cry ! niggers, cry !
Tink I'll see de bressed Norf,
    'Fore de day I die.
        Hi ! hi ! Yankee shot 'im ;
        Now I tink de debbil's got 'im."

The whole company then joined in singing the annexed song, which made the welkin ring, and was heard
far beyond the camp.

I.

" Oh ! we all longed for freedom,
Oh ! we all longed for freedom,
Oh ! we all longed for freedom,
    Ah ! we prayed to be free ;
    Yes, we prayed to be free,
    Oh ! we prayed to be free,
Though the day was long in coming,
Though the day was long in coming,
Though the day was long in coming,
    That we so longed to see,
    That we so longed to see,
    That we so longed to see,
Though the day was long in **coming**
    That we so longed to see.

II.

But bless the great Jehovah,
But bless the great Jehovah,
But bless the great Jehovah,
    At last the glad day's come,
    At last the glad day's come,
    At last the glad day's come.
By fire and sword he brought **us**,
By fire and sword he brought **us**,
By fire and sword he brought **us**,
    From slavery into freedom,
    From slavery into freedom,
    From slavery into Freedom ;
By fire and sword he brought **us**
    From slavery into freedom.

III.

We'll bless the great Redeemer,
We'll bless the great Redeemer,
We'll bless the great Redeemer,
   And glorify his name,
   And glorify his name,
   And glorify his name,
And all who helped to bring us,
And all who helped to bring us,
And all who helped to bring us
   From sorrow, grief, and shame,
   From sorrow, grief, and shame,
   From sorrow, grief, and shame,
And all who helped to bring us
   From sorrow, grief, and shame.

IV.

And blessed be Abraham Lincoln,
And blessed be Abraham Lincoln,
And blessed be Abraham Lincoln,
   And the Union army too,
   And the Union army too.
May the choicest of earth's blessings,
May the choicest of earth's blessings,
May the choicest of earth's blessings,
   Their pathways ever strew,
   Their pathways ever strew,
   Their pathways ever strew !
May the choicest of earth's blessings
   Their pathways ever strew !

V.

We'll strive to learn our duty,
We'll strive to learn our duty,
We'll strive to learn our duty,
   That all our friends may see,
   That all our friends may see,
   That all our friends may see,
Though so long oppressed in bondage,
Though so long oppressed in bondage,
Though so long oppressed in bondage,

We were worthy to be free,
We were worthy to be free,
We were worthy to be free :
Though so long oppressed in bondage,
We were worthy to be free."

Just before midnight, Dr. Nichols requested all present to kneel, and to silently invoke the blessing of the Almighty. The silence was almost deadly when the clock announced the new year; and Dr. Nichols said, " Men and women (for you are this day to be declared free, and I can address you as men and women), I wish you a happy new year!" An eloquent prayer was then offered by an aged negro; after which, all rose, and joined in singing their version of " Glory! glory! hallelujah!" shaking each other by the hand, and indulging in joyous demonstrations. They then promenaded the grounds, singing hymns, and finally serenaded the superintendent, in whose honor a sable improvisatore carolled forth an original ode, the chorus of which was, " Free forever! Forever free!"

" Ring, ring! O Bell of Freedom, ring!
And to the ears of bondmen bring
Thy sweet and freeman-thrilling tone.
On Autumn's blast, from zone to zone,
The joyful tidings go proclaim,
In Liberty's hallowed name :
Emancipation to the slave,
The rights which his Creator gave,
To live with chains asunder riven,
To live free as the birds of heaven,
To live free as the air he breathes,
Entirely free from galling greaves ;
The right to act, to know, to feel,
That bands of iron and links of steel
Were never wrought to chain the mind,
Nor human flesh in bondage bind ;

That Heaven, in its generous plan,
Gave like and equal rights to man.
Go send thy notes from shore to shore,
Above the deep-voiced cannon's roar;
Go send Emancipation's peal
Where clashes North with Southern steel,
And nerve the Southern bondmen now
To rise and strike the final blow,
To lay Oppression's minions low.
Oh! rouse the mind and nerve the arm
To brave the blast and face the storm;
And, ere the war-cloud passes by,
We'll have a land of liberty.

Our God has said, "Let there be light
Where Error palls the land with night."
Then send forth now, O Freedom's bell,
Foul Slavery's last and fatal knell!
Oh! speed the tidings o'er the land,
That tells that stern Oppression's hand
Has yielded to the power of Right:
That Wrong is weak, that Truth is might!
. . . .
Then Union shall again return,
And Freedom's fires shall brightly burn;
And PEACE and JOY, sweet guests, shall come,
And dwell in every heart and home."

" Free forever!   Forever free! "

No pen can fitly portray the scene that followed this
announcement.   Every heart seemed to leap for joy:
some were singing, some praying, some weeping, some
dancing, husbands embracing wives, friends shaking
hands, and appearing to feel that the Day of Jubilee
had come.   A sister broke out in the following strain,
which was heartily joined in by the vast assembly : —

" Go down, Abraham, away down in Dixie's land,
Tell Jeff. Davis to let my people go.

Our bitter tasks are ended, all our unpaid labor done;
Our galling chains are broken, and our onward march begun :
    Go down, Abraham, away down in Dixie's land,
    Tell Jeff. Davis to let my people go.

Down in the house of bondage we have watched and waited long ;
The oppressor's heel was heavy, the oppressor's arm was strong :
    Go down, Abraham, away down in Dixie's land,
    Tell Jeff. Davis to let my people go.

Not vainly have we waited through the long and darkened years ;
Not vain the patient watching, 'mid our sweat and blood and tears :
    Go down, Abraham, away down in Dixie's land,
    Tell Jeff. Davis to let my people go.

Now God is with Grant, and he'll surely whip Lee;
For the Proclamation says that the niggers must be free :
    Go down, Abraham, away down in Dixie's land,
    Tell Jeff. Davis to let my people go."

Thus ended the last night of slavery in the contraband camp at Washington.

The morning of Jan. 1, 1863, was anxiously looked for by the friends of freedom throughout the United States; and, during the entire day, the telegraph offices in the various places were beset by crowds, waiting to hear the news from the Nation's capital. Late in the day the following proclamation made its appearance : —

WASHINGTON, Jan. 1, 1863. — I Abraham Lincoln, President of the United States of America, do issue this my Proclamation : —

Whereas, On the 22d day of September, in the year of our Lord one thousand eight hundred and sixty-three, a proclamation was issued by the President of the United States, containing, among other things, the following, to wit : —

" That, on the first day of January, in the year of our

Lord one thousand eight hundred and sixty-three, all persons held as slaves within any State or any designated part of a State, the people whereof shall then be in rebellion against the United States, shall be then, henceforward, and forever, free ; and the Executive Government of the United States, including the military and naval force thereof, will recognize and maintain the freedom of such persons, and will do no act or acts to repress such persons, or any of them, in any effort they may make for their actual freedom ; that the Executive will, on the first day of January aforesaid, by proclamation, designate the States and parts of States, if any, in which the people therein respectively shall then be in rebellion against the United States ; and the fact that any State or people thereof shall on that day be in good faith represented in the Congress of the United States by members chosen thereto, at elections wherein a majority of the qualified voters of such States shall have participated, shall, in the absence of strong countervailing testimony, be deemed conclusive evidence that such State and the people thereof are not then in rebellion against the United States.

" Now, therefore, I, Abraham Lincoln, President of the United States, by virtue of the power in me vested, as Commander-in-Chief of the Army and Navy of the United States in times of actual rebellion against the authorities and Government of the United States, and as a fit and necessary war measure for suppressing this rebellion, do on this, the first day of January, in the year of our Lord one thousand eight hundred and sixty-three, and in accordance with my purpose so to do, publicly proclaimed for the full period of one hundred days from the date of the first above-mentioned order, do designate as

the States and parts of States wherein the people thereof, respectively, are this day in rebellion against the
United States. The following, to wit : —

"Arkansas, Texas, Louisiana, Mississippi, Alabama,
Florida, Georgia, South Carolina, North Carolina, and
Virginia.

"Louisiana (except the parishes of St. Bernard, Plac-
quemines, Jefferson, St. John, St. Charles, St. James,
Ascension, Assumption, Terre Bonne, Lafourche, St.
Mary, St. Martin, and Orleans, including the city of New
Orleans), Mississippi, Alabama, Florida, Georgia, South
Carolina, North Carolina, and Virginia, except the forty-
eight counties designated as West Virginia, and also the
counties of Berkley, Accomac, Northampton, Elizabeth
City, York, Princess Anne, and Norfolk, including the
cities of Norfolk and Portsmouth, which excepted parts
are for the present left precisely as if this proclamation
were not made.

"And by virtue of the power, for the purpose aforesaid,
I do order and declare that all persons held as slaves
within said designated States and parts of States are, and
henceforward shall be, FREE; and the Executive Government of the United States, including the military and
naval authorities thereof, will recognize and maintain
the freedom of such persons.

"And I hereby enjoin upon the people so declared to
be free to abstain from all violence, unless in necessary
self-defence ; and I recommend to them, that, in all cases
where allowed, they labor faithfully for reasonable wages.

"And I further declare and make known, that such persons, if in suitable condition, will be received into the
armed service of the United States, to garrison forts, positions, stations, and other places, and to man vessels of

all sorts in said service. And upon this, sincerely believed to be an act of justice warranted by the Constitution, and upon military necessity, I invoke the consid-
erate judgment of mankind and the gracious favor of
Almighty God.

"In witness whereof, I have hereunto set my hand, and
caused the seal of the United States to be affixed.

"Done at the city of Washington, this first day of January, in the year of our Lord one thousand eight hundred
and sixty-three, and of the independence of the United
States of America the eighty-seventh.

[L. s.]   (Signed)   "ABRAHAM LINCOLN.

" By the President.

" WM. H. SEWARD, *Secretary of State.*"

This was the beginning of a new era : the word had
gone forth, and a policy was adopted.

> " The deed is done. Millions have yearned
>   To see the spear of Freedom cast :
> The dragon writhed and roared and burned ;
>   You've smote him full and square at last."

The proclamation gave new life and vigor to our men
on the battle-field. The bondmen everywhere caught up
the magic word, and went with it from farm to farm, and
from town to town. Black men flocked to recruiting stations, and offered themselves for the war. Everybody saw
light in the distance. What newspapers and orators had
failed to do in months was done by the proclamation in
a single week. Frances Ellen Harper,[2] herself colored,
cheered in the following strain : —

"It shall flash through coming ages;
   It shall light the distant years;
And eyes now dim with sorrow
   Shall be brighter through their **tears.**

It shall flush the mountain ranges,
   And the valleys shall grow **bright**;
It shall bathe the hills in radiance,
   And crown their brows with light.

It shall flood with golden splendor
   All the huts of Caroline;
And the sun-kissed brow of labor
   With lustre new shall shine.

It shall gild the gloomy prison,
   Darkened with the age's crime,
Where the dumb and patient millions
   Wait the better coming time.

By the light that gilds their prison,
   They shall seize its mouldering key;
And the bolts and bars shall vibrate
   With the triumphs of the free.

Like the dim and ancient Chaos,
   Shuddering at Creation's light,
Oppression grim and hoary
   Shall cower at the sight.

And her spawn of lies and malice
   Shall grovel in the dust;
While joy shall thrill the bosoms
   Of the merciful and just.

Though the morning seems to linger
   O'er the hill-tops far away,
The shadows bear the promise
   Of the quickly coming day.

Soon the mists and murky shadows
   Shall be fringed with crimson light,
And the glorious dawn of freedom
   Break resplendent on the sight."

CHAPTER XVI.

THE NEW POLICY.

A New Policy announced. — Adjutant-Gen. Thomas. — Major-Gen. Prentiss. — Negro Wit and Humor. — Proslavery Correspondents. — Feeling in the Army. — Let the Blacks fight.

ATTORNEY-GEN. BATES had already given his opinion with regard to the citizenship of the negro, and that opinion was in the black man's favor. The Emancipation Proclamation was only a prelude to calling on the colored men to take up arms, and the one soon followed the other; for the word "Emancipation" had scarcely gone over the wires, ere Adjutant-Gen. Thomas made his appearance in the valley of the Mississippi. At Lake Providence, La., he met a large wing of the army, composed of volunteers from all parts of the country, and proclaimed to them the new policy of the administration; and he did it in very plain words, as will be seen: —

" FELLOW-SOLDIERS, — Your commanding general has so fully stated the object of my mission, that it is almost unnecessary for me to say any thing to you in reference to it. Still, as I come here with full authority from the President of the United States to announce the policy, which, after mature deliberation, has been determined upon by the wisdom of the nation, it is my duty to make known to you clearly and fully the features of that policy. It is a source of extreme gratification to me to come

124

before you this day, knowing, as I do full well, how glorious have been your achievements on the field of battle. No soldier can come before soldiers of tried valor, without having the deepest emotions of his soul stirred within him. These emotions I feel on the present occasion; and I beg you will listen to what I have to say, as soldiers receiving from a soldier the commands of the President of the United States.

"I came from Washington clothed with the fullest power in this matter. With this power, I can act as if the President of the United States were himself present. I am directed to refer nothing to Washington, but to act promptly, — what I have to do to do at once; to strike down the unworthy and to elevate the deserving.

"Look along the river, and see the multitude of deserted plantations upon its banks. These are the places for these freedmen, where they can be self-sustaining and self-supporting. All of you will some day be on picket-duty; and I charge you all, if any of this unfortunate race come within your lines, that you do not turn them away, but receive them kindly and cordially. They are to be encouraged to come to us; they are to be received with open arms; they are to be fed and clothed; *they are to be armed.*

"This is the policy that has been fully determined upon. I am here to say that I am authorized to raise as many regiments of blacks as I can. I am authorized to give commissions, from the highest to the lowest; and I desire those persons who are earnest in this work to take hold of it. I desire only those whose hearts are in it, and to them alone will I give commissions. I don't care who they are, or what their present rank may be. I do not hesitate to say, that all proper persons will receive commissions.

" While I am authorized thus in the name of the Secretary of War, I have the fullest authority to dismiss from the army any man, be his rank what it may, whom I find maltreating the freedmen. This part of my duty I will most assuredly perform if any case comes before me. I would rather do that than give commissions, because such men are unworthy the name of soldiers.

" This, fellow-soldiers, is the determined policy of the Administration. You all know, full well, when the President of the United States, though said to be slow in coming to a determination, once puts his foot down, it is there; and he is not going to take it up. He has put his foot down. I am here to assure you that my official influence shall be given that he shall not raise it."

Major-Gen. B. M. Prentiss, after the cheering had subsided which greeted his appearance, indorsed, in a forcible and eloquent speech, the policy announced by Adjutant-Gen. Thomas, and said, that, "from the time he was a prisoner, and a negro sentinel, with firm step, *beat* in front of his cell, and with firmer voice commanded silence within, he prayed God for the day of revenge; and he now thanked God that it had come."

Turning to Gen. Thomas, the speaker continued, " Yes: tell the President for me, I will receive them into the lines; I will beg them to come in; *I will make them come in!* and if any officer in my command, high or low, *neglects to receive them friendly, and treat them kindly, I will put them outside the lines.* (Tremendous applause.) Soldiers, when you go to your quarters, if you hear any one condemning the policy announced here to-day, put him down as a contemptible copperhead traitor. Call them what you please, copperheads, secesh, or traitors, they are all the same to me : *enemies of our country*, against whom I have taken a solemn oath, and called God as my witness, to whip them wherever I find them."

Congress had already passed a bill empowering the President " to enroll, arm, equip, and receive into the land and naval service of the United States, such a number of volunteers of African descent as he may deem equal to suppress the present rebellion, for such term of service as he may prescribe, not exceeding five years; the said volunteers to be organized according to the regulations of the branch of the service into which they may be enlisted, to receive the same rations, clothing, and equipments as other volunteers, and a monthly pay not to exceed that of the volunteers."

Proslavery newspaper correspondents from the North, in the Western and Southern departments, still continued to report to their journals that the slaves would not fight if an opportunity was offered to them. Many of these were ridiculously amusing. The following is a sample: —

" I noticed upon the hurricane-deck, to-day, an elderly negro, with a very philosophical and retrospective cast of countenance, squatted upon his bundle, toasting his shins against the chimney, and apparently plunged into a state of profound meditation. Finding by inquiry that he belonged to the Ninth Illinois, one of the most gallantly-behaved and heavily-losing regiments at the Fort-Donelson battle, and part of which was aboard, I began to interrogate him upon the subject. His philosophy was so much in the Falstaffian vein that I will give his views in his own words, as near as my memory serves me: —

" ' Were you in the fight ? '

" ' Had a little taste of it, sa.'

" ' Stood your ground, did you?'

" ' No, sa; I runs.'

" ' Run at the first fire, did you?'

" ' Yes, sa; and would ha' run soona had I know'd it war comin'.'

" ' Why, that wasn't very creditable to your courage.'

" ' Dat isn't in my line, sa; cookin's my perfeshun.'

" ' Well, but have you no regard for your reputation?'

" ' Refutation's nuffin by the side ob life.'

" ' Do you consider your life worth more than other people's?'

" ' It's worth more to me, sa.'

" ' Then you must value it very highly.'

" ' Yes, sa, I does; more dan all dis wuld; more dan a million of dollars, sa: for what would dat be wuf to a man wid de bref out of him. Self-perserbashum am de fust law wid me.'

" ' But why should you act upon a different rule from other men?'

" ' Because different men set different values upon dar lives: mine is not in de market.'

" ' But if you lost it, you would have the satisfaction of knowing that you died for your country.'

" ' What satisfaction would dat be to me when de power ob feelin' was gone?'

" ' Then patriotism and honor are nothing to you?'

" ' Nuffin whatever, sa: I regard dem as among de vanities; and den de gobernment don't know me; I hab no rights; may be sold like old hoss any day, and dat's all.'

" ' If our old soldiers were like you, traitors might have broken up the Government without resistance.'

"'Yes, sa; dar would hab been no help for it. I wouldn't put my life in de scale 'ginst any gobernment dat ever existed; for no gobernment could replace de loss to me.'

"'Do you think any of your company would have missed you if you had been killed ?'

"'May be not, sa; a dead white man ain't much to dese sogers, let alone a dead nigga; but I'd a missed myself, and dat was de pint wid me.'

"It is safe to say that the dusky corpse of that African will never darken the field of carnage."

CHAPTER XVII.

ARMING THE BLACKS.

Department of the South. — Gen. Hunter Enlisting Colored Men. — Letter to Gov. Andrew. — Success. — The Earnest Prayer. — The Negro's Confidence in God.

THE Northern regiments stationed at the South, or doing duty in that section, had met with so many reverses on the field of battle, and had been so inhumanly treated by the rebels, both men and women, that the new policy announced by Adjutant-Gen. Thomas, at Lake Providence and other places, was received with great favor, especially when the white soldiers heard from their immediate commanders, that the freedmen, when enlisted, would be employed in doing fatigue-duty, when not otherwise needed. The slave, regarding the use of the musket as the only means of securing his freedom permanently, sought the nearest place of enlistment with the greatest speed.

The appointment of men from the ranks of the white regiments over the blacks caused the former to feel still more interest in the new levies. The position taken by Major-Gen. Hunter, in South Carolina, and his favorable reports of the capability of the freedmen for military service, and the promptness with which that distinguished scholar and Christian gentleman, Thomas Wentworth Higginson, accepted the colonelcy of the First South Carolina, made the commanding of negro regiments respectable, and caused a wish on the part of white volunteers to seek commissions over the blacks.

The new regiments filled up rapidly; the recruits adapted themselves to their new condition with a zeal that astonished even their friends; and their proficiency in the handling of arms, with only a few days' training, set the minds of their officers at rest with regard to their future action. The following testimonial from Gen. Hunter is not without interest: —

"HEADQUARTERS DEPARTMENT OF THE SOUTH,
Hilton Head, Port Royal, S.C., May 4, 1863.

" *To His Excellency the Governor of Massachusetts, Boston, Mass.*

.   .   .   .

"I am happy to be able to announce to you my complete and eminent satisfaction with the results of the organization of negro regiments in this department. In the field, so far as tried, they have proved brave, active, enduring, and energetic, frequently outrunning, by their zeal, and familiarity with the Southern country, the restrictions deemed prudent by certain of their officers. They have never disgraced their uniform by pillage or cruelty, but have so conducted themselves, upon the whole, that even our enemies, though more anxious to find fault with these than with any other portion of our troops, have not yet been able to allege against them a single violation of any of the rules of civilized warfare.

"These regiments are hardy, generous, temperate, patient, strictly obedient, possessing great natural aptitude for arms. and deeply imbued with that religious sentiment — call it fanaticism, such as like — which

made the soldiers of Cromwell invincible. They believe
that now is the time appointed by God for their deliverance; and, under the heroic incitement of this faith, I
believe them capable of showing a courage, and persist-
ency of purpose, which must, in the end, extort both
victory and admiration.

" In this connection, I am also happy to announce to
you that the prejudices of certain of our white soldiers
and officers against these indispensable allies are rapidly softening, or fading out; and that we have now
opening before us in this department, which was the
first in the present war to inaugurate the experiment of
employing colored troops, large opportunities of putting
them to distinguished and profitable use.

" With a brigade of liberated slaves already in the
field, a few more regiments of intelligent colored men
from the North would soon place this force in a condition to make extensive incursions upon the main land,
through the most densely populated slave regions; and,
from expeditions of this character, I make no doubt the
most beneficial results would arise.

"I have the honor to be, Governor,
" Very respectfully,
" Your most obedient servant,
" D. HUNTER,
" *Major-Gen. Commanding.*"

Reports from all parts of the South gave corroborative
evidence of the deep religious zeal with which the
blacks entered the army. Every thing was done for
" God and liberty."

Col. T. W. Higginson, in " The Atlantic Monthly,"
gives the following prayer, which he heard from one
of his contraband soldiers: —

"'Let me so lib dat when I die I shall *hab manners;* dat I shall know what to say when I see my heabenly Lord.

"'Let me lib wid de musket in one hand, an' de Bible in de oder — dat if I die at de muzzle of de musket, die in de water, die on de land, I may know I hab de bressed Jesus in my hand, an' hab no fear.

"'I hab lef my wife in de land o' bondage; my little ones dey say eb'ry night, "Whar is my fader?" But when I die, when de bressed mornin' rises, when I shall stan' in de glory, wid one foot on de water an' one foot on de land, den, O Lord! I shall see my wife an' my little chil'en once more.'"

"These sentences I noted down, as best I could, beside the glimmering camp-fire last night. The same person was the hero of a singular little *contre-temps* at a funeral in the afternoon. It was our first funeral. The man had died in hospital, and we had chosen a picturesque burial place above the river, near the old church, and beside a little nameless cemetery, used by generations of slaves. It was a regular military funeral, the coffin being draped with the American flag, the escort marching behind, and three volleys fired over the grave. During the services, there was singing, the chaplain deaconing out the hymn in their favorite way. This ended, he announced his text: 'This poor man cried, and the Lord heard him, and delivered him out of all his trouble.' Instantly, to my great amazement, the cracked voice of the chorister was uplifted, intoning the text, as if it were the first verse of another hymn. So calmly was it done, so imperturbable were all the black countenances that I half began to conjecture that the chaplain himself intended it for a hymn, though I could imagine no prospective rhyme for *trouble,* unless it were approximated by *debbil;* which is, indeed, a favorite reference, both with the men and with his reverence. But the chaplain, peacefully awaiting, gently repeated his text after the chant, and to my great relief the old chorister waived all further recitative, and let the funeral discourse proceed.

" Their memories are a vast bewildered chaos of Jewish history and biography ; and most of the great events of the past, down to the period of the American Revolution, they instinctively attribute to Moses. There is a fine bold confidence in all their citations, however, and the record never loses piquancy in their hands, though strict accuracy may suffer. Thus one of my captains, last Sunday, heard a colored exhorter at Beaufort proclaim, ' Paul may plant, *and may polish wid water,* but it won't do,' in which the sainted Apollos would hardly have recognized himself.

A correspondent of the Burlington " Free Press " gives an account of a Freedmen's meeting at Belle Plain, Va. " Some of the negro prayers and exhortations were very simple and touching. One said in his prayer,' O Lord ! we's glad for de hour when our sins nailed us to de foot of de cross, and de bressed Lord Jesus put his soft arm around us, and tole us dat we's his chillen: we's glad we's sinners, so dat we can be saved by his grace.' Another thus earnestly prayed for the army of freedom: ' O Lord ! bress de Union army ; be thou their bulwarks and ditches. O Lord ! as thou didst hear our prayer when we's down in de Souf country, as we held de plow and de hoe in the hot sun, so hear our prayer at dis time for de Union army. Guard 'em on de right, and on de lef,' and in de rear : don't lef' 'em 'lone, though they's

mighty wicked.' Another (a young man) thus energeti-
cally desired the overthrow of Satan's empire : ' O Lord !
if you please, sir, won't you come forth out of de heaven,
and take ride 'round about hell, and give it a mighty
shake till de walls fall down.'

"A venerable exhorter got the story of the Prodigal
Son slightly mixed, but not so as to damage the effect at
all. He said, ' He rose up and went to his fader's house.
And I propose he was ragged. And I propose de road
dirty. But when his fader saw him coming over de hill,
ragged and dirty, he didn't say, " Dat ain't my son." He
go and meet him. He throw his arms round his neck
and kiss ; and, while he was hugging and kissing him, he
thought of dat robe in de wardroom, and he said, " Bring
dat robe, and put it on him." And when dey was a putting
on de robe, he thought of de ring, dat splendid ring ! and
he said, " My son, dat was dead and is alive again, he like
dat ring, cos it shine so." And he made dem bring de ring
and put it on his hand ; and he put shoes on his feet, and
killed de fatted calf. And here, my friends, see de 'fection
of de prodigal for his son. But, my bredren, you are a
great deal better off dan de prodigal's son. For he
hadn't no gemmen of a different color to come and tell
him dat his fader was glad to hab him come home again.
But dese handmaid bredren has kindly come dis evening
to tell us dat our heabenly Father wants us to come
back now. He's ready to gib us de robe and de ring.
De bressed Lord Jesus stands leaning over de bannis-
ters of heaven, and reaching down his arms to take us
up. O my friends ! I ask you dis night to repent. If
you lose your soul, you'll never get anoder. I tell you
all, if you don't repent you're goin' straight to hell ; and
in de last day, when de Lord say to you, " Depart from

me, ye cursed, into everlastin' fire," if you're 'onorable, you'll own up, and say it's right. O my friends! I tell you de truth : it's de best way to come to de Lord Jesus dis night.' "

Regiment after regiment of blacks were mustered into the United-States service, in all the rebel States, and were put on duty at once, and were sooner or later called to take part in battle.

CHAPTER XVIII.

BATTLE OF MILLIKEN'S BEND.

Contraband Regiments; their Bravery; the Surprise. — Hand to hand Fight. — "No Quarters." — Negroes rather die than surrender. — The Gunboat and her dreadful Havoc with the Enemy.

ON the 7th of June, 1863, the first regular battle was fought between the blacks and whites in the valley of the Mississippi. The planters had boasted, that, should they meet their former slaves, a single look from them would cause the negroes to throw down their weapons, and run. Many Northern men, especially copperheads, professed to believe that such would be the case. Therefore, all eyes were turned to the far off South, the cotton, sugar, and rice-growing States, to see how the blacks would behave on the field of battle; for it is well known that the most ignorant of the slave population belonged in that section.

The following account of the fight is from an eye witness: —

" My informant states that a force of about five hundred negroes, and two hundred men of the Twenty-third Iowa, belonging to the second brigade, Carr's division (the Twenty-third Iowa had been up the river with prisoners, and was on its way back to this place), was surprised in camp by a rebel force of about two thousand men. The first intimation that the commanding officer received was from one of the black men, who went into the colonel's tent, and said, 'Massa, the secesh are in camp." The colonel ordered him to have the men load their guns at once. He instantly replied, "We have done did dat now, massa." Before the colonel was ready, the men were in line, ready for action. As before stated, the rebels drove our force towards the gunboats, taking colored men prisoners and murdering them. This so enraged them that they rallied, and charged the enemy more heroically and desperately than has been recorded during the war. It was a genuine bayonet-charge, a hand-to-hand fight, that has never occurred to any extent during this prolonged conflict. Upon both sides men were killed with the butts of muskets. White and black men were lying side by side, pierced by bayonets, and in some instances transfixed to the earth. In one instance, two men — one white and the other black — were found dead, side by side, each having the other's bayonet through his body. If facts prove to be what they are now represented, this engagement of Sunday morning will be recorded as the most desperate of this war. Broken limbs, broken heads, the mangling of bodies, all prove that it was a contest between enraged men: on the one side, from hatred to a race; and, on the other, desire for self-preservation, revenge for past grievances, and the inhuman murder of their comrades. One brave man took his former master prisoner, and brought him into camp with great gusto. A rebel prisoner made a particular request, that *his own* negroes should not be placed over him as a guard."

Capt. M. M. Miller, of Galena, Ill., who commanded a company in the Ninth Louisiana (colored) Regiment, in a letter, gives the following account of the battle: —

"We were attacked here on June 7, about three o'clock

in the morning, by a brigade of Texas troops, about two thousand five hundred in number. We had about six hundred men to withstand them, five hundred of them negroes. I commanded Company I, Ninth Louisiana. We went into the fight with thirty-three men. I had sixteen killed, eleven badly wounded, and four slightly. I was wounded slightly on the head, near the right eye, with a bayonet, and had a bayonet run through my right hand, near the forefinger; that will account for this miserable style of penmanship.

" Our regiment had about three hundred men in the fight. We had one colonel wounded, four captains wounded, two first and two second lieutenants killed, five lieutenants wounded, and three white orderlies killed, and one wounded in the hand, and two fingers taken off. The list of killed and wounded officers comprised nearly all the officers present with the regiment, a majority of the rest being absent recruiting.

" We had about fifty men killed in the regiment and eighty wounded; so you can judge of what part of the fight my company sustained. I never felt more grieved and sick at heart, than when I saw how my brave soldiers had been slaughtered, — one with six wounds, all the rest with two or three, none less than two wounds. Two of my colored sergeants were killed; both brave, noble men, always prompt, vigilant, and ready for the fray. I never more wish to hear the expression, ' The niggers won't fight.' Come with me, a hundred yards from where I sit, and I can show you the wounds that cover the bodies of sixteen as brave, loyal, and patriotic soldiers as ever drew bead on a rebel.

" The enemy charged us so close that we fought with our bayonets, hand to hand. I have six broken bayo-

nets to show how bravely my men fought. The Twenty-
third Iowa joined my company on the right; and I
declare truthfully that they had all fled before our regiment fell back, as we were all compelled to do.

" Under command of Col. Page, I led the Ninth and
Eleventh Louisiana when the rifle-pits were retaken and
held by our troops, our two regiments doing the work.

" I narrowly escaped death once. A rebel took deliberate aim at me with both barrels of his gun; and the
bullets passed so close to me that the powder that remained on them burnt my cheek. Three of my men,
who saw him aim and fire, thought that he wounded me
each fire. One of them was killed by my side, and he
fell on me, covering my clothes with his blood; and,
before the rebel could fire again, I blew his brains out
with my gun.

"It was a horrible fight, the worst I was ever engaged
in, — not even excepting Shiloh. The enemy cried,
'No quarter!' but some of them were very glad to
take it when made prisoners.

"Col. Allen, of the Sixteenth Texas, was killed in front
of our regiment, and Brig.-Gen. Walker was wounded.
We killed about one hundred and eighty of the enemy.
The gunboat "Choctaw" did good service shelling them.
I stood on the breastworks after we took them, and
gave the elevations and direction for the gunboat by
pointing my sword; and they sent a shell right into
their midst, which sent them in all directions. Three
shells fell there, and sixty-two rebels lay there when the
fight was over.

" My wound is not serious but troublesome. What
few men I have left seem to think much of me, because
I stood up with them in the fight. I can say for them

that I never saw a braver company of men in my life.

"Not one of them offered to leave his place until ordered to fall back. I went down to the hospital, three miles, to-day to see the wounded. Nine of them were there, two having died of their wounds. A boy I had cooking for me came and begged a gun when the rebels were advancing, and took his place with the company; and, when we retook the breastworks, I found him badly wounded, with one gun-shot and two bayonet wounds. A new recruit I had issued a gun to the day before the fight was found dead, with a firm grasp on his gun, the bayonet of which was broken in three pieces. So they fought and died, defending the cause that we revere. They met death coolly, bravely : not rashly did they expose themselves, but all were steady and obedient to orders."

This battle satisfied the slave-masters of the South that their charm was gone; and that the negro, as a slave, was lost forever. Yet there was one fact connected with the battle of Milliken's Bend which will descend to posterity, as testimony against the humanity of slave-holders; and that is, that no negro was ever found alive that was taken a prisoner by the rebels in this fight.

CHAPTER XIX.

RAISING BLACK REGIMENTS AT THE NORTH.

Prejudices at the North. — Black Laws of Illinois and Indiana. — Ill-treatment of Negroes. — The Blacks forget their Wrongs, and come to the Rescue.

In the struggle between the Federal Government and the rebels, the colored men asked the question, " Why should we fight ? " The question was a legitimate one, at least for those residing in the Northern States, and especially in those States where there were any considerable number of colored people. In every State north of Mason and Dixon's Line, except Massachusetts and Rhode Island, which attempted to raise a regiment of colored men, the blacks are disfranchised, excluded from the jury-box, and in most of them from the public schools. The iron hand of prejudice in the Northern States is as circumscribing and unyielding upon him as the manacles that fettered the slave of the South.

Now, these are facts, deny it who will. The negro has little to hope from Northern sympathy or legislation. Any attempt to engraft upon the organic law of the States provisions extending to the colored man political privileges is overwhelmingly defeated by the people. It makes no difference that here is a pen, and there a voice, raised in his behalf: the general verdict is against him; and its repetition in any case where it is demanded shows that it is inexorable. We talk a great deal about

142

the vice of slavery, and the cruelty of denying to our
fellowmen their personal freedom and a due reward of
labor ; but we are very careful not to concede the co-
rollary, that the sin of withholding that freedom is not
vastly greater than withholding the rights to which he
who enjoys it is entitled.

When the war broke out, it was the boast of the
Administration that the status of the negro was not to
be changed in the rebel States.   President Lincoln, in
his inaugural address, took particular pains to commit
himself against any interference with the condition of
the blacks.

When the Rebellion commenced, and the call was made
upon the country, the colored men were excluded.   In
some of the Western States into which slaves went
when escaping from their rebel masters, in the first and
second years of the war, the black-laws were enforced
to drive them out.   Read what " The Daily Alton Democrat " said for Illinois, in the year 1862 : —

" NOTICE TO THE ' FREE NEGROES.' — I hereby give
public notice to all free negroes who have arrived here
from a foreign State within the past two months, or may
hereafter come into the city of Alton with the intention
of being residents thereof, that they are allowed the
space of thirty days to remove ; and, upon failure to
leave the city, will, after that period, be proceeded
against by the undersigned, as by law directed.   The
penalty is a heavy fine, to liquidate which the law-
officer is compelled to offer all free negroes arrested at
public auction, unless the fine and all costs of suit are
promptly paid.   I hope the city authorities will be
spared the *necessity* of putting the above law *in execu-*

tion. All railroad companies and steamboats are also forbidden to land free negroes within the city under the penalty of the law. No *additional* notice will be given. Suits will POSITIVELY be instituted against all offenders.

"JAMES W. DAVIS,

"May 27, 1862."   " *Prosecuting Attorney Alton-City Court.*

The authorities of the State of Indiana also got on the track of the contrabands from the rebel States; and the old black-laws were put forth as follows : —

" Any person who shall employ a negro or mulatto who shall have come into the State of Indiana subsequent to the thirty-first day of October, in the year one thousand eight hundred and fifty-one, or shall hereafter come into said State, or who shall encourage such negro or mulatto to remain in the State, shall be fined in any sum not less than ten dollars, nor more than five hundred dollars."

The following will show how Illinois treated the colored people, even after the proclamation of freedom was put forth by President Lincoln.

" The Whiteside (Ill.) Sentinel " says the following official notice is posted in the post-office and other public places in the city of Carthage, Hancock County, Ill. It is a practical exemplication of the Illinois " black-laws." The notice reads as follows : —

" PUBLIC SALE. — Whereas, The following negroes and one mulatto man were, on the fifth and sixth days of February, 1863, tried before the undersigned, a Justice of the Peace within and for Hancock County, Ill., on a charge of high misdemeanor, having come into this State and county, and remaining therein for ten days and more, with the evident intention of residing in this State, and were found guilty by a jury, and were each severally fined in the sum of fifty dollars, and the judgment was rendered against said negroes and mulatto man for fifty dollars' fine each, and costs of suit, which fines and costs are annexed opposite to each name, to wit : —

	Age.	Fine.	Costs.
John, a negro man, tall and slim, about .	35	$50	$33.17
Sambo, a negro man, about	21	50	32.17
Austin, a negro man, heavy set, about . .	20	50	30.10
Andrew, a negro man, about	—	50	30.33
Amos, a negro man, about	40	50	29.67
Nelson, a mulatto man, about	55	50	30.07

" And whereas. Said fines and costs have not been paid, notice is therefore given that the undersigned will, on Thursday, the nineteenth day of February, A.D. 1863, between the hours of one and five o'clock, P.M., of said day, at the west end of the Court House, in Carthage, Hancock County, Ill., sell each of said negro men, John, Austin, Sambo, Andrew, Amos, and said mulatto man, Nelson, at public auction, to the person or persons who will pay the said fine and costs appended against each respectively for the shortest time of service of said negroes and mulatto.

" The purchaser or purchasers will be entitled to the control and services of the negroes and mulatto purchased for the period named in the sale, and no longer, and will be required to furnish said negroes and mulatto with comfortable food, clothing, and lodging during said servitude. The fees for selling will be added on completion of the sale.

" C. M♪ CHILD, J.P.

" CARTHAGE, Feb. 9, 1863."

It will be seen that these odious laws were rigidly enforced. With what grace could the authorities in those States ask the negro to fight? Yet they called upon him; and he, forgetting the wrongs of the past, and demanding no pledge for better treatment, left family, home, and every thing dear, enlisted, and went forth to battle. And even Connecticut, with her proscription of the negro, called on him to fight. How humiliating·it must have been! And yet Connecticut, after appealing to black men, and receiving their aid in fighting her battles, retains her negro "black-laws" upon her statute-book by a vote of more than six thousand.

CHAPTER XX.

THE Fifty-fourth Regiment of Massachusetts Volunteer Infantry was called into the service of the United States by the President, under an act of Congress, passed July 21, 1861, entitled " An Act to authorize the Employment of Volunteers to aid in enforcing the Laws and protecting Public Property." Recruiting began Feb. 9, 1863, in Boston. A camp of rendezvous was opened at "Camp Meigs," Readville, Mass., on the 21st of February, with a squad of twenty-seven men ; and, by the end of March, five companies were recruited, comprising four hundred and fourteen men. This number was doubled during April; and, on the 12th of May, the regiment was full.

Orders being received for it to proceed to the Department of the South, the regiment broke camp on the 28th of May, and took cars for Boston. After passing through the principal streets, and reaching the Common, they prepared to receive the colors which were to be presented by the Governor.

The regiment was formed in a hollow square, the distinguished persons present occupying the centre. The flags were four in number, comprising a national flag,

147

presented by young colored ladies of Boston; a national ensign, presented by the " Colored Ladies' Relief Society; " an emblematic banner, presented by ladies and gentlemen of Boston, friends of the regiment; and a flag presented by relatives and friends of the late Lieut. Putnam. The emblematic banner was of white silk, handsomely embroidered, having on one side a figure of the Goddess of Justice, with the words, " Liberty, Loyalty, and Unity," around it. The fourth flag bore a cross with a blue field, surmounted with the motto, "*In hoc signo vinces.*" All were of the finest texture and workmanship.

Prayer having been offered by the Rev. Mr. Grimes,[1] Gov. Andrew presented the various flags, with the following speech : —

PRESENTATION SPEECH OF GOV. ANDREW.

" Col. Shaw, — As the official representative of the Commonwealth, and by favor of various ladies and gentlemen, citizens of the Commonwealth, and friends of the Fifty-fourth Regiment of Massachusetts Volunteers, I have the honor and the satisfaction of being permitted to join you this morning for the purpose of presenting to your regiment the national flag, the State colors of Massachusetts, and the emblematic banner which the cordial, generous, and patriotic friendship of its patrons has seen fit to present to you.

" Two years of experience in all the trials and vicissitudes of war, attended with the repeated exhibition of Massachusetts regiments marching from home to the scenes of strife, have left little to be said or suggested which could give the interest of novelty to an occasion like this.   But, Mr. Commander, one circumstance pertaining to the composition of the Fifty-fourth Regiment, exceptional in its character when compared with any thing we have seen before, gives to this hour an interest and importance, solemn and yet grand, because the occasion marks an era in the history of the war, of the Commonwealth, of the country, and of humanity.   I need not dwell upon the fact that the enlisted men constituting the rank and file of the Fifty-fourth Regiment of Massachusetts Volunteers are drawn from a race not hitherto connected with the fortunes of the war.   And yet I cannot forbear to allude to the circumstance, because I can but contemplate it for a brief moment, since it is uppermost in your thoughts, and since this regiment, which for many months has been the desire of my own heart, is present now before this vast assembly of friendly citizens of Massachusetts, prepared to vindicate by its future, as it has already begun to do by its brief history of camp-life here, to vindicate in its own person and in the presence, I trust, of all who belong to it, the character, the manly character, the zeal, the manly zeal, of the colored citizens of Massachusetts and of those other States which have cast their lot with ours.   (Applause.)

"I owe to you, Mr. Commander, and to the officers who, associated with you, have assisted in the formation of this noble corps, composed of men selected from among their fellows for fine qualities of manhood, — I owe to you, sir, and to those of your associates who united with me in the original organization of this body, the heartiest and most emphatic expression of my cordial thanks.   I shall follow you, Mr. Commander, your officers, and your men, with a friendly and personal solicitude, to say nothing of official care, which can hardly be said of any other corps which has marched from Massachusetts. My own personal honor, if I have any, is identified with yours. I stand or fall, as a man and a magistrate, with the rise or fall in the history of the Fifty-fourth Massachusetts Regiment. (Applause.) I pledge not only in behalf of myself, but of all those whom I have the honor to represent to-day, the utmost generosity, the utmost kindness, the utmost devotion of hearty love, not only for the cause, but for you that represent it. We will follow your fortunes in the camp and in the field with the anxious eyes of brethren and the proud hearts of citizens.

"To those men of Massachusetts, and of surrounding States who have now made themselves citizens of Massachusetts, I have no word to utter fit to express the emotions of my heart. These men, sir, have now, in the Providence of God, given to them an opportunity which, while it is personal to themselves, is still an opportunity for a whole race of men. (Applause.) With arms possessed of might to strike a blow, they have found breathed into their hearts an inspiration of devoted patriotism, and regard for their brethren of their own color, which has inspired them with a purpose to nerve that arm, that it may strike a blow which, while it shall help to raise aloft their country's flag — *their* country's flag now as well as ours — by striking down the foes which oppose it, strikes also the last blow, I trust, needful to rend the last shackle which binds the limb of the bondman in the rebel States. (Applause.)

"I know not, Mr. Commander, when, in all human history, to any given thousand men in arms there has been given a work so proud, so precious, so full of hope and glory, as the work committed to you. (Applause.) And

may the infinite mercy of Almighty God attend you
every hour of every day, through all the experiences
and vicissitudes of that dangerous life in which you have
embarked ! may the God of our fathers cover your heads
in the day of battle ! may he shield you with the arms
of everlasting power ! may he hold you always most of
all, first of all, and last of all, up to the highest and holi-
est conception of duty ; so that if, on the field of stricken
fight, your souls shall be delivered from the thraldom of
the flesh, your spirits shall go home to God, bearing aloft
the exulting thought of duty well performed, of glory
and reward won even at the hands of the angels who
shall watch over you from above!

" Mr. Commander, you, sir, and most of your officers,
have been carefully selected from among the most intelligent and experienced officers who have already performed illustrious service upon the field during the last
two years of our national conflict.   I need not say, sir,
with how much confidence and with how much pride we
contemplate the leadership which we know this regiment
will receive at your hands.   In yourself, sir, your staff
and line officers, we are enabled to declare a confidence
which knows no hesitation and no doubt.   Whatever
fortune may betide you, we know from the past that all
will be done for the honor of the cause, for the protection
of the flag, for the defence of the right, for the glory of
your country, and for the safety and the honor of these
men whom we commit to you, that shall lie either in the
human heart or brain or arm.   (Applause.)

" And now, Mr. Commander, it is my most agreeable
duty and high honor to hand to you, as the representa
tive of the Fifty-fourth Regiment of Massachusetts Volunteers, the American flag, the star-spangled banner

of the Republic. Wherever its folds shall be unfurled, it will mark the path of glory. Let its stars be the inspiration of yourselves, your officers, and your men. As the gift of the young ladies of the city of Boston to their brethren in arms, they will cherish it as the lover cherishes the recollection and fondness of his mistress; and the white stripes of its field will be red with their blood before it shall be surrendered to the foe. (Applause.)

"I have also the honor, Mr. Commander, to present to you the State colors of Massachusetts, — the State colors of the old Bay State, borne already by fifty-three regiments of Massachusetts soldiers, white men thus far, now to be borne by the Fifty-fourth Regiment of soldiers, not less of Massachusetts than the others. Whatever may be said, Mr. Commander, of any other flag which has ever kissed the sunlight, or been borne on any field, I have the pride and honor to be able to declare before you, your regiment, and these witnesses, that, from the beginning up till now, the State colors of Massachusetts have never been surrendered to any foe. (Cheers.) The Fifty-fourth now holds in possession this sacred charge in the performance of their duties as citizen-soldiers. You will never part with that flag so long as a splinter of the staff, or a thread of its web, remains within your grasp. (Applause.) The State colors are presented to the Fifty-fourth by the Relief Society, composed of colored ladies of Boston.

"And now let me commit to you this splendid emblematic banner. It is prepared for your acceptance by a large and patriotic committee, representing many others beside ladies and gentlemen of Boston, to whose hearty sympathy, and powerful co-operation and aid, much of the success which has hitherto attended the organization of this regiment is due.   The Goddess of Liberty, erect in beautiful guise and form (liberty, loyalty, and unity are the emblems it bears), — the Goddess of Liberty shall be the lady-love whose fair presence shall inspire your hearts; liberty, loyalty, unity, the watchwords in the fight.

"And now, Mr. Commander, the sacred, holy cross, representing passion, the highest heroism, I scarcely dare to trust myself to present to you.   It is the emblem of Christianity.   I have parted with the emblems of the State, of the nation, — heroic, patriotic emblems they are, dear, inexpressibly dear, to all our hearts; but now, *In hoc signo vinces*, the cross which represents the passion of our Lord, I dare to pass into your soldier hands; for we are fighting now a battle not merely for country, not merely for humanity, not only for civilization, but for the religion of our Lord itself.   When this cause shall ultimately fall, if ever failure at the last shall be possible, it will only fail when the last patriot, the last philanthropist, and the last Christian shall have tasted death, and left no descendants behind them upon the soil of Massachusetts.   (Applause.)

"This flag, Mr. Commander, has connected with its history the most touching and sacred memory.   It comes to your regiment from the mother, sister, friends, family relatives, of one of the dearest and noblest soldier-boys of Massachusetts.   I need not utter the name of Lieut. Putnam in order to excite in every heart the tenderest emotions of fond regard, or the strongest feeling of patriotic fire.   May you, sir, and these, follow not only on the field of battle, but in all the walks and ways of life, in camp, and hereafter, when, on returning peace, you shall resume the more quiet and peaceful duties of citi-

zens, — may you but follow the splendid example, the
sweet devotion mingled with manly, heroic character, of
which the life, character, and death of Lieut. Putnam
was one example! How many more there are we know
not : the record is not yet complete ; but, oh ! how many
there are of these Massachusetts sons, who, like him,
have tasted death for this immortal cause ! Inspired by
such examples, fired by the heat and light of love and
faith which illumined and warmed these heroic and noble
hearts, may you, sir, and these, march on to glory, to
victory, and to every honor! This flag I present to you,
Mr. Commander, and your regiment. *In hoc signo vinces.*

RESPONSE OF COL. SHAW.

"*Your Excellency*, — We accept these flags with feelings of deep gratitude. They will remind us not only of
the cause we are fighting for, and of our country, but of
the friends we have left behind us, who have thus far
taken so much interest in this regiment, and who, we
know, will follow us in our career. Though the greater
number of men in this regiment are not Massachusetts
men, I know there is not one who will not be proud to
fight and serve under our flag.[2] May we have an opportunity to show that you have not made a mistake in in-
trusting the honor of the State to a colored regiment !
— the first State that has sent one to the war.

"I am very glad to have this opportunity to thank the
officers and men of the regiment for their untiring fidelity and devotion to their work from the very beginning.
They have shown that sense of the importance of our
undertaking, without which we should hardly have attained our end. (Applause.)

At the conclusion of Col. Shaw's remarks, the colors were borne to their place in the line by the guard, and the regiment was reviewed by the Governor. Thence they marched out of the Common, down Tremont Street, down Court Street, by the Court House, chained hardly a decade ago to save slavery and the Union. Thence down State Street, trampling on the very pavement over which Sims and Burns marched to their fate, encompassed by soldiers of the United States.

" Their sisters, sweethearts, and wives " — a familiar quotation in the notices of previous departing regiments, but looking a little odd in this new place — ran along beside " the boys," giving their parting benediction of smiles and tears, telling them to be brave, and to show their blood.

They marched in good time, and wheeled with a readiness which showed that they had a clear idea of what was required, and only needed a little more practice to equal the best regiments that left the State.

The regiment marched down State Street at a quarter past twelve o'clock to the tune of " John Brown," and was vociferously cheered by the vast crowds that covered the sidewalks and filled the windows. Nowhere was the reception of the regiment more hearty.

All attempts to express the feeling of the crowd or the soldiers seem to read stale and flat. Yet, as Goldsmith said that the weakest jokes were received as wit by the circle of the happy vicar, so these attempts were treated as successes by-the happy crowd. One man said it was a verification of Shakspeare : —

> " Know you not *Pompey ?*
> You have climbed up to the walls and battlements
> To see *Great Pompey* pass the streets of Rome."

One fact should be chronicled. Their regimental banner, of superb white silk, had on one side the coat-of-arms of Massachusetts, and on the other a golden cross on a golden star, with IN HOC SIGNO VINCES beneath. *This is the first Christian banner that has gone into our war.* By a strange, and yet not strange, providence, God has made this despised race the bearers of his standard. They are thus the real leaders of the nation.

On reaching the wharf at a quarter before one, every thing had been placed on board through the efforts of Capt. McKim; the guns were placed in boxes, the horses put aboard, and the men began to embark. At four o'clock, the vessel steamed down the harbor, bound for Port Royal, S.C.

THE COMPLETE ROSTER OF THE REGIMENT.

Colonel. — Robert G. Shaw.

Lieut.-Colonel. — Norwood P. Hallowell.

Major. — Edward N. Hallowell.

Surgeon. — Lincoln R. Stone.

Assistant Surgeon. — C. B. Brigham.

Captains. — Alfred S. Hartwell, David A. Partridge, Samuel Willard, John W. M. Appleton, Watson W. Bridge, George Pope, William H. Simpkins, Cabot J. Russell, Edward L. Jones, and Louis F. Emilo.

1st. Lieutenants. — John Ritchie, Garth W. James, William H. Hemans, Orin E. Smith, Erik Wulff, Walter H. Wild, Francis L. Higginson, James M. Walton, James M. Grace, R. K. L. Jewett.

2d Lieutenants. — Thomas L. Appleton, Benjamin F. Dexter, J. Albert Pratt, Charles F. Smith, Henry W. Littlefield, William Nutt, David Reid, Charles E. Tucker, and William Howard.

Many of the men in the Fifty-Fourth had once been slaves at the South; some had enjoyed freedom for years; others had escaped after the breaking out of the Rebellion. Most of them had relatives still there, and had a double object in joining the regiment. They were willing to risk their lives for the freedom of those left behind; and, if they failed in that, they might, at least, have an opportunity of settling with the " ole boss " for a long score of cruelty.

> " From many a Southern field they trembling came,
> Fled from the lash, the fetter, and the chain ;
> Return they now, not at base Slavery's claim,
> To meet the oppressor on the battle-plain."

" The following song was written by a private in Company A, Fifty-Fourth (colored) Regiment, Massachusetts Volunteers, and has been sent to us for publication by a friend of the regiment." — *Boston Transcript.*

> " *Air.* — ' *Hoist up the Flag.*'

> "Fremont told them, when the war it first begun,
> How to save the Union, and the way it should be done ;
> But Kentucky swore so hard, and old Abe he had his fears,
> Till every hope was lost but the colored volunteers.

> *Chorus.* — Oh ! give us a flag all free without a slave,
> We'll fight to defend it as our fathers did so brave :
> The gallant Comp'ny A will make the rebels dance ;
> And we'll stand by the Union, if we only have a chance.

> McClellan went to Richmond with two hundred thousand brave :
> He said, ' keep back the niggers,' and the Union he would save.
> Little Mac he had his way, still the Union is in tears :
> *Now* they call for the help of the colored volunteers.
> *Chor.* — Oh ! give us a flag, &c.

Old Jeff says he'll hang us if we dare to meet him armed :
A very big thing, but we are not at all alarmed ;
For he first has got to catch us before the way is clear,
And ' that's what's the matter ' with the colored volunteer.
   Chor. — Oh ! give us a flag, &c.

So rally, boys, rally, let us never mind the past :
We had a hard road to travel, but our day is coming fast;
For God is for the right, and we have no need to fear :
The Union must be saved by the colored volunteer.
   Chor. — Oh ! give us a flag, &c."

CHAPTER XXI.

BLACKS UNDER FIRE IN SOUTH CAROLINA.

Expedition up the St. Mary's River. — The Negroes Long for a Fight. —
Their Gallantry in Battle.

THE Department of the South, under Major-Gen.
Hunter, was the first in which the negro held the musket. By consent of the commanding-general, I give the
following interesting report from Col. T. W. Higginson : —

"ON BOARD STEAMER 'BEN DEFORD,'
Sunday, Feb. 1, 1863.

"*Brig.-Gen. Saxton, Military Governor, &c.*

"GENERAL, — I have the honor to report the safe re-
turn of the expedition under my command, consisting
of four hundred and sixty-two officers and men of the
First Regiment of South-Carolina Volunteers, who left
Beaufort on Jan. 23, on board the steamers 'John
Adams,' 'Planter,' and 'Ben Deford.'

"The expedition has carried the regimental flag and
the President's proclamation far into the interior of
Georgia and Florida. The men have been repeatedly
under fire ; have had infantry, cavalry, and even artillery, arrayed against them ; and have, in every instance,
come off, not only with unblemished honor, but with undisputed triumph. At Township, Fla., a detachment of
the expedition fought a cavalry company which met

159

us unexpectedly, on a midnight march through pine woods, and which completely surrounded us. They were beaten off with a loss on our part of one man killed and seven wounded; while the opposing party admits twelve men killed (including Lieut. Jones, in command of the company), besides many wounded. So complete was our victory, that the enemy scattered, hid in the woods all night, not returning to his camp, which was five miles distant, until noon next day; a fact which was unfortunately unknown until too late to follow up our advantage. Had I listened to the urgent appeals of my men, and pressed the flying enemy, we could have destroyed his camp; but, in view of the darkness, his uncertain numbers and swifter motions, with your injunctions of caution, I judged it better to rest satisfied with the victory already gained.

"On another occasion, a detachment of about two hundred and fifty men, on board the 'John Adams,' fought its way forty miles up and down a river, the most dangerous in the department, — the St. Mary's; a river left untraversed by our gunboats for many months, as it required a boat built like the 'John Adams' to ascend it successfully. The stream is narrow, swift, winding, and bordered at many places with high bluffs, which blazed with rifle-shots. With our glasses, as we approached these points, we could see mounted men by the hundreds galloping through the woods, from point to point, to await us; and, though fearful of our shot and shell, they were so daring against musketry, that one rebel actually sprang from the shore upon the large boat which was towed at our stern, where he was shot down by one of my sergeants. We could see our shell scatter the rebels as they fell among them, and some terrible execution must have been done; but not a man of this regiment was killed or wounded, though the steamer is covered with bullet-marks, one of which shows where our brave Capt. Clifton, commander of the vessel, fell dead beside his own pilot-house, shot through the brain by a Minie-ball.   Major Strong, who stood beside him, escaped as if by magic, both of them being unnecessarily exposed without my knowledge.   The secret of our safety was in keeping the regiment below, except the gunners; but this required the utmost energy of the officers, as the men were wild to come on deck, and even implored to be landed on shore, and charge on the enemy.   Nobody knows any thing about these men who has not seen them in battle.   I find that I myself knew nothing.   There is a fiery energy about them beyond any thing of which I have ever read, unless it be the French Zouaves.   It requires the strictest discipline to hold them in hand.   During our first attack on the river, before I got them all penned below, they crowded at the open ends of the steamer, loading and firing with inconceivable rapidity, and shouting to each other, 'Never give it up!'   When collected into the hold, they actually fought each other for places at the few port-holes from which they could fire on the enemy.

"Meanwhile, the black gunners, admirably trained by Lieuts. Stockdale and O'Neil (both being accomplished artillerists), and Mr. Heron, of the gunboat, did their duty without the slightest protection, and with great coolness, amid a storm of shot.

"No officer in this regiment now doubts that the key to the successful prosecution of this war lies in the unlimited employment of black troops.   Their superiority lies simply in the fact that they know the country, which white troops do not; and, moreover, that they have peculiarities of temperament, position, and motive, which belong to them alone. Instead of leaving their homes and families to fight, they are fighting for their homes and families; and they show the resolution and sagacity which a personal purpose gives. It would have been madness to attempt with the bravest white troops what I have successfully accomplished with black ones.

"Every thing, even to the piloting of the vessel, and the selection of the proper points for cannonading, was done by my own soldiers; indeed, the real conductor of the whole expedition at the St. Mary's was Corporal Robert Sutton, of Company G, formerly a slave upon the St. Mary's River; a man of extraordinary qualities, who needs nothing but a knowledge of the alphabet to entitle him to the most signal promotion. In every instance where I followed his advice, the predicted result followed; and I never departed from it, however slightly, without having reason for subsequent regret.

"I have the honor to be, &c.,

"T. W. HIGGINSON,
"*Col. Com. First Regiment South-Carolina Vols.*"

CHAPTER XXII.

FREEDMEN UNDER FIRE IN MISSISSIPPI.

Bravery of the Freedmen. — Desperation of the Rebels. — Severe Battle. Negroes Triumphant.

WHILE the people along the banks of the Mississippi, above New Orleans, were discussing the question as to whether the negro would fight, if attacked by white men, or not, Col. Daniels, of the Second Regiment Louisiana Volunteers, gave one side of the subject considerable of a "hist," on the 9th of April, 1863. His official report will speak for itself.

> " HEADQUARTERS, SHIP ISLAND (Miss.),
> April 11, 1863.

" Brig.-Gen. Sherman, commanding Defences of New Orleans.

"SIR, — In compliance with instructions from your headquarters, to keep you promptly informed of any movements that the enemy might be known to be making up the Mississippi Sound, upon learning that repeated demonstrations had been made in the direction of Pascagoula, by Confederate troops ashore, and in armed boats along the coast; and, furthermore, having reliable information that the greater part of the forces at Mobile were being sent to re-enforce Charleston, I determined to make a reconnoissance within the enemy's lines, at or near Pascagoula, for the purpose of not only breaking up their demonstrations, but of creating a di-

163

version of the Mobile forces from Charleston, and pre-
cipitating them along the Sound; and accordingly embarked with a detachment of a hundred and eighty
men of my command on United-States Transport ' General Banks,' on the morning of the 9th of April, 1863, and
made for Pascagoula, Miss., where we arrived about
nine o'clock, A.M., landed, and took possession of wharf
and hotel, hoisted the stars and stripes upon the building, threw out pickets, and sent small detachments in
various directions to take possession of the place, and
hold the roads leading from the same. Immediately
thereafter, a force of over three hundred Confederate
cavalry came down the Mobile Road, drove in the pickets, and attacked the squad on the left, from whom they
received a warm reception. They then fell back in
some confusion, re-formed, and made a dash upon the
detachment stationed at the hotel, at which point they
were again repulsed ; Confederate infantry, meanwhile,
attacking my forces on the extreme left, and forcing a
small detachment to occupy a wharf, from which they
poured volley after volley into the enemy's ranks, killing and wounding many, with a loss of one man only.
The fight had now extended along the road from the
river to the wharf, the enemy being under cover of the
houses and forest; whilst my troops were, from the nature of the ground, unavoidably exposed. The Confederates had placed their women and children in front of
their houses, for a cover, and even armed their citizens, and forced them to fight against us. After an
hour's continuous skirmishing, the enemy retreated to
the woods, and my forces fell back to the hotel and
wharf. Then the enemy sallied forth again, with apparently increased numbers, attempting to surround the

hotel, and obtain possession of the wharf; but they were again repulsed, and driven back to their cover, — the forest. It was here that Lieut. Jones, with a detachment of only seven men, having been placed on the extreme right, cut his way through a large force of the enemy's cavalry, and arrived at the hotel without losing a man, but killing and wounding a considerable number of the enemy.

" After continuous fighting, from ten o'clock, A.M., to two o'clock, P.M., and on learning that heavy re-enforcements of infantry and artillery had arrived from the camps up the Pascagoula River, I withdrew my forces from the hotel, and returned to Ship Island. The enemy's loss was over twenty killed, and a large number wounded. From my own knowledge, and from information derived from prisoners taken in the fight, and from refugees since arrived, the enemy had over four hundred cavalry and infantry at Pascagoula, and heavy re-enforcements within six miles of the place. Refugees who have arrived since the engagement report the enemy's loss as greater than mentioned in my first report.

" The expedition was a perfect success, accomplishing all that was intended; resulting in the repulse of the enemy in every engagement with great loss; whilst our casualty was only two killed and eight wounded. Great credit is due to the troops engaged, for their unflinching bravery and steadiness under this their first fire, exchanging volley after volley with the coolness of veterans; and for their determined tenacity in maintaining their position, and taking advantage of every success that their courage and valor gave them; and also to their officers, who were cool and determined through-

out the action, fighting their commands against five
times their numbers, and confident throughout of success, — all demonstrating to its fullest extent that the
oppression which they have heretofore undergone from
the hands of their foes, and the obloquy that had been
showered upon them by those who should have been
friends, had not extinguished their manhood, or suppressed their bravery, and that they had still a hand to
wield the sword, and a heart to vitalize its blow.

"I would particularly call the attention of the Department to Major F. E. Dumas, Capt. Villeverd, and Lieuts.
Jones and Martin, who were constantly in the thickest
of the fight, and by their unflinching bravery, and admirable handling of their commands, contributed to the
success of the attack, and reflected great honor upon
the flag under and for which they so nobly struggled.
Repeated instances of individual bravery among the
troops might be mentioned; but it would be invidious
where all fought so manfully and so well.

"I have the honor to be, most respectfully,

"Your obedient servant,

"N. U. DANIELS,
"*Col. Second Regiment La. N. O. Vols., Commanding Post.*"

CHAPTER XXIII.[1]

BATTLE OF PORT HUDSON.

The Louisiana Native Guard. — Capt. Callioux. — The Weather. — Spirit of the Troops. — The Battle begins. — " Charge." — Great Bravery. — The Gallant Color-bearer. — Grape, Canister, and Shell sweep down the Heroic Men. — Death of Callioux. — Comments.

ON the 26th of May, 1863, the wing of the army under Major-Gen. Banks was brought before the rifle-pits and heavy guns of Port Hudson. Night fell — the lovely Southern night — with its silvery moonshine on the gleaming waters of the Mississippi, that passed directly by the intrenched town. The glistening stars appeared suspended in the upper air as globes of liquid light, while the fresh soft breeze was bearing such sweet scents from the odoriferous trees and plants, that a poet might have fancied angelic spirits were abroad, making the atmosphere luminous with their pure presence, and every breeze fragrant with their luscious breath. The deep-red sun that rose on the next morning indicated that the day would be warm; and, as it advanced, the heat became intense. The earth had been long parched, and the hitherto green verdure had begun to turn yellow. Clouds of dust followed every step and movement of the troops. The air was filled with dust : clouds gathered, frowned upon the earth, and hastened away.

The weatherwise watched the red masses of the morning, and still hoped for a shower to cool the air, and lay the dust, before the work of death commenced ; but none came, and the very atmosphere seemed as if it were from an overheated oven.   The laying-aside of all unnecessary articles or accoutrements, and the preparation that showed itself on every side, told all present that the conflict was near at hand.   Gen. Dwight, whose antecedents with regard to the rights of the negro, and his ability to fight, were not of the most favorable character, was the officer in command over the colored brigade ; and busy Rumor, that knows every thing, had whispered it about that the valor of the black man was to be put to the severest test that day.

The black forces consisted of the First Louisiana, under Lieut.-Col. Bassett, and the Third Louisiana, under Col. Nelson.   The line-officers of the Third were white ; and the regiment was composed mostly of freedmen, many of whose backs still bore the marks of the lash, and whose brave, stout hearts beat high at the thought that the hour had come when they were to meet their proud and unfeeling oppressors.   The First was the noted regiment called " The Native Guard," which Gen. Butler found when he entered New Orleans, and which so promptly offered its services to aid in crushing the Rebellion.   The line-officers of this regiment were all colored, taken from amongst the most wealthy and influential of the free colored people of New Orleans.   It was said that not one of them was worth less than twenty-five thousand dollars.   The brave, the enthusiastic, and the patriotic, found full scope for the development of their powers in this regiment, of which all were well educated ; some were fine scholars.   One of the most efficient officers was Capt. André Callioux, a man whose identity with his race could not be mista-

ken ; for he prided himself on being the blackest man in
the Crescent City.   Whether in the drawing-room or on
the parade, he was ever the centre of attraction.   Finely
educated, polished in his manners, a splendid horseman,
a good boxer, bold, athletic, and daring, he never lacked
admirers.   His men were ready at any time to follow
him to the cannon's mouth ; and he was as ready to lead
them.   This regiment petitioned their commander to
allow them to occupy the post of danger in the battle,
and it was granted.

As the moment of attack drew near, the greatest suppressed excitement existed ; but all were eager for the
fight.   Capt. Callioux walked proudly up and down the
line, and smilingly greeted the familiar faces of his company.   Officers and privates of the white regiments
looked on as they saw these men at the front, and asked
each other what they thought would be the result.
Would these blacks stand fire ?   Was not the test by
which they were to be tried too severe ?   Col. Nelson
being called to act as brigadier-general, Lieut-Col. Finnegas took his place.   The enemy in his stronghold felt
his power, and bade defiance to the expected attack.
At last the welcome word was given, and our men
started.   The enemy opened a blistering fire of shell,
canister, grape, and musketry.   The first shell thrown
by the enemy killed and wounded a number of the
blacks ; but on they went.   " Charge " was the word.

> " Charge ! "   Trump and drum awoke :
> Onward the bondmen broke ;
> Bayonet and sabre-stroke
> Vainly opposed their rush."

At every pace, the column was thinned by the falling

dead and wounded. The blacks closed up steadily as
their comrades fell, and advanced within fifty paces of
where the rebels were working a masked battery, situated on a bluff where the guns could sweep the whole
field over which the troops must charge. This battery
was on the left of the charging line. Another battery
of three or four guns commanded the front, and six
heavy pieces raked the right of the line as it formed,
and enfiladed its flank and rear as it charged on the
bluff. It was ascertained that a bayou ran under the
bluff where the guns lay, — a bayou deeper than a man
could ford. This charge was repulsed with severe loss.
Lieut-Col. Finnegas was then ordered to charge, and in
a well-dressed steady line his men went on the double-
quick down over the field of death. No matter how
gallantly the men behaved, no matter how bravely
they were led, it was not in the course of things that
this gallant brigade should take these works by charge.
Yet charge after charge was ordered and carried out
under all these disasters with Spartan firmness. Six
charges in all were made. Col. Nelson reported to Gen.
Dwight the fearful odds he had to contend with. Says
Gen. Dwight, in reply, "Tell Col. Nelson I shall consider
that he has accomplished nothing unless he take those
guns." Humanity will never forgive Gen. Dwight for
this last order; for he certainly saw that he was only
throwing away the lives of his men. But what were
his men? "Only niggers." Thus the last charge was
made under the spur of desperation.

The ground was already strewn with the dead and
wounded, and many of the brave officers had fallen
early in the engagement. Among them was the gallant
and highly cultivated Anselmo. He was a standard-

bearer, and hugged the stars and stripes to his heart as he fell forward upon them pierced by five balls. Two corporals near by struggled between themselves as to who should have the honor of again raising those blood-stained emblems to the breeze. Each was eager for the honor ; and during the struggle a missile from the enemy wounded one of them, and the other corporal shouldered the dear old flag in triumph, and bore it through the charge in the front of the advancing lines.

> "Now," the flag-sergeant cried,
> " Though death and hell betide,
> Let the whole nation see
> If we are fit to be
> Free 'in this land, or bound
> Down, like the whining hound, —
> Bound with red stripes and pain
> In our old chains again."
> Oh ! what a shout there went
> From the black regiment !

Shells from the rebel guns cut down trees three feet in diameter, and they fell, at one time burying a whole company beneath their branches. Thus they charged bravely on certain destruction, till the ground was slippery with the gore of the slaughtered, and cumbered with the bodies of the maimed. The last charge was made about one o'clock. At this juncture, Capt. Callioux was seen with his left arm dangling by his side, — for a ball had broken it above the elbow, — while his right hand held his unsheathed sword gleaming in the rays of the sun ; and his hoarse, faint voice was heard cheering on his men. A moment more, and the brave and generous Callioux was struck by a shell, and fell far in advance of his company. The fall of this officer so exasperated his men, that they appeared to be filled with new enthusiasm; and they rushed forward with a reck-lessness that probably has never been surpassed. Seeing it to be a hopeless effort, the taking of these batteries, order was given to change the programme; and the troops were called off. But had they accomplished any thing more than the loss of many of their brave men? Yes: they had. The self-forgetfulness, the undaunted heroism, and the great endurance of the negro, as ex-hibited that day, created a new chapter in American history for the colored man.

Many Persians were slain at the battle of Thermopylæ; but history records only the fall of Leonidas and his four hundred companions. So in the future, when we shall have passed away from the stage, and rising generations shall speak of the conflict at Port Hudson, and the cele-brated charge of the negro brigade, they will forget all others in their admiration for André Callioux and his colored associates. Gen. Banks, in his report of the bat-tle of Port Hudson, says, " Whatever doubt may have existed heretofore as to the efficiency of organizations of this character, the history of this day proves conclu-sively to those who were in a condition to observe the conduct of these regiments, that the Government will find in this class of troops effective supporters and de-fenders. The severe test to which they were subjected, and the determined manner in which they encountered the enemy, leaves upon my mind no doubt of their ulti-mate success."

Hon. B. F. Flanders paid them the following tri-bute: —

" The unanimous report of all those who were in the recent battle at Port Hudson, in regard to the negroes,

is, that they fought like devils. They have completely
conquered the prejudice of the army against them.
Never before was there such an extraordinary revolution of sentiment as that of this army in respect to the
negroes as soldiers."

This change was indeed needed ; for only a few days
previous to the battle, while the regiments were at Baton
Rouge, the line-officers of the New-England troops,
either through jealousy or hatred to the colored men on
account of their complexion, demanded that the latter,
as officers, should be dismissed. And, to the disgrace of
these white officers, the colored men, through the mean
treatment of their superiors in office, the taunts and
jeers of their white assailants, were compelled to throw
up their commissions. The colored soldiers were deeply
pained at seeing the officers of their own color and
choice taken from them ; for they were much attached to
their commanders, some of whom were special favorites
with the whole regiment. Among these were First Lieut.
Joseph Howard of Company I, and Second Lieut. Joseph
G. Parker, of Company C. These gentlemen were both
possessed of ample wealth, and had entered the army, not
as a matter of speculation, as too many have done, but
from a love of military life. Lieut. Howard was a man
of more than ordinary ability in military tactics ; and a
braver or more daring officer could not be found in the
Valley of the Mississippi. He was well educated, speaking the English, French, and Spanish languages fluently,
and was considered a scholar of rare literary attainments. He, with his friend Parker, felt sorely the humiliation attending their dismissal from the army, and
seldom showed themselves on the streets of their native
city, to which they had returned. When the news

reached New Orleans of the heroic charge made by the
First Louisiana Regiment, at Port Hudson, on the 27th of
May, Howard at once called on Parker; and they were
so fired with the intelligence, that they determined to
proceed to Port Hudson, and to join their old regiment as
privates. That night they took passage, and the following
day found them with their former friends in arms. The
regiment was still in position close to the enemy's works,
and the appearance of the two lieutenants was hailed with
demonstrations of joy. Instead of being placed as privates in the ranks, they were both immediately assigned
the command of a company each, not from any compliment to them, but from sheer necessity, because the
white officers of these companies, feeling that the colored
soldiers were put in the front of the battle owing to their
complexion, were not willing to risk their lives, and had
thrown up their commissions.

On the 5th of June, these two officers were put to
the test, and nobly did they maintain their former reputation for bravery. Capt. Howard leading the way,
they charged upon the rebel's rifle-pits, drove them
out, and took possession, and held them for three hours,
in the face of a raking fire of artillery. Several times
the blacks were so completely hidden from view by the
smoke of their own guns and the enemy's heavy cannon,
that they could not be seen. It was at this time, that
Capt. Howard exhibited his splendid powers as a commander. The negroes never hesitated. Amid the roar
of artillery, and the rattling of musketry, the groans of
the wounded, and the ghastly appearance of the dead,
the heroic and intrepid Howard was the same. He never
said to his men, " Go," but always, " Follow me." At
last, when many of their men were killed, and the

severe fire of the enemy's artillery seemed to mow down
every thing before it, these brave men were compelled
to fall back from the pits which they had so triumphantly
taken.   At nightfall, Gen. Banks paid the negro officers
a high compliment, shaking the hand of Capt. Howard,
and congratulating him on his return, and telling his aides
that this man was worthy of a more elevated position.

Although the First Louisiana had done well, its great
triumph was reserved for the 14th of June, when Capt.
Howard and his associates in arms won for themselves
immortal renown. Never, in the palmy days of Napoleon,
Wellington, or any other general, was more true hero·
ism shown.   The effect of the battle of the 27th of
May, is thus described in "The New-York Herald,"
June 6 : —

"The First Regiment Louisiana Native Guard, Col.
Nelson, were in this charge. *They went on the advance,
and, when they came out, six hundred out of nine hundred
men could not be accounted for. It is said on every side
that they fought with the desperation of tigers.* One negro
was observed with a rebel soldier in his grasp, tearing
the flesh from his face with his teeth, other weapons
having failed him.   There are other incidents connected
with the conduct of this regiment *that have raised them
very much in my opinion as soldiers. After firing one
volley, they did not deign to load again, but went in with
bayonets; and, wherever they had a chance, it was all up
with the rebels.*"

From " The New-York Tribune," June 8 : —

" Nobly done, First Regiment of Louisiana Native
Guard ! though you failed to carry the rebel works
against overwhelming numbers, you did not charge and
fight and fall in vain.   That heap of six hundred corpses,

lying there dark and grim and silent before and within the rebel works, is a better proclamation of freedom than even President Lincoln's.   A race ready to die thus was never yet retained in bondage, and never can be. Even the Wood copperheads, who will not fight themselves, and try to keep others out of the Union ranks, will not dare to mob negro regiments if this is their style of fighting.

" Thus passes one regiment of blacks to death and everlasting fame."

Humanity should not forget, that, at the surrender of Port Hudson, not a single colored man could be found alive, although thirty-five were known to have been taken prisoners during the siege.   All had been murdered.

CHAPTER XXIV.

GENERAL BANKS IN LOUISIANA.

Gen. Banks at New Orleans. — Old Slave-laws revived. — Treatment of Free
Colored Persons. — Col. Jonas H. French. — Ill Treatment at Port Hudson.

GEN. BANKS'S antecedents were unfavorable to him
when he landed in New Orleans. True, he was from
Massachusetts, and was a Republican; but he belonged
to the conservative portion of the party. The word
"white" in the militia law, which had so long offended
the good taste and better judgment of the majority of
the people, was stricken out during the last term
of Gov. Banks's administration, but failed to receive his sanction. In his message vetoing the bill,
he resorted to a laborious effort of special pleading to
prove that the negro was not a citizen. The fact is, he
was a Democrat dressed up in Republican garments.
Gen. Butler had brought the whites and blacks nearly
to a level with each other as citizens of New Orleans,
when he was succeeded by Gen. Banks. The latter at
once began a system of treatment to the colored people,
which showed that his feelings were with the whites,
and against the blacks. The old slave-law, requiring
colored persons to be provided with passes to enable
them to be out from their homes after half-past eight
o'clock at night was revived by Gen. Banks's under-
strappers, as the following will show : —

"ST. CHARLES HOTEL, NEW ORLEANS, Jan. 25.

"On Tuesday evening last, at half-past eight o'clock, while passing up St. Charles Street in company with F. S. Schell, Esq., the artist of 'Frank Leslie's Pictorial,' who is attached to the Banks Expedition, I was suddenly accosted by two colored women, one of whom, a beautiful mulatto very tastily attired, besought me to protect her from the watchmen, who, she said, were following close behind her on the opposite side of the street, and were about to arrest her and her mother for being out without passes.

"I offered her and her mother all the protection in my power until they should reach their home, which was but a few blocks distant; and I had but scarcely made the proffer, when two powerful and muscular watchmen came running across the street, club in hand, and at once proceeded to arrest the women. I inquired of the officers by what authority they arrested slaves or free colored people. They informed me that they were acting under orders received from the chief of police, Col. Jonas H. French.

"The women begged, with tears in their eyes, for their liberty, that they might return to their homes, where a sister was lying dangerously ill, and towards whom they were hastening when seized by the watchmen. Being enough of a 'Yankee abolitionist' to feel a glow of indignation at this flagrant violation of human rights, and, as I supposed, illegal assumption of power, I proceeded to the prison or watch-house, adjoining the city hall, from the roof of which flies the flag of freedom.

"What a sight was revealed to me on my visit to that prison! Such a scene may I never be permitted to visit again! Securing permission, I went into the corridor, from which lead the cells. There I saw, in one cell, fifteen feet by twenty feet, fifty colored women and girls packed like so many cattle : there were six or eight wooden berths, with *pine mattresses* and *oak pillows,* for these poor creatures to rest their limbs upon. Of course, the most of them were obliged to stand uprightly, or lie upon the wet flooring of the cell.

" I never shall forget the emotions that arose within my bosom as I stood intently gazing upon the sorrowing faces of these unfortunates as they cast wistful glances through the heavy iron bars of their cell, and in supplicating tones implored me to secure them their release. One pretty young girl of fifteen, with a beautiful face, whose complexion was that of a pretty Boston brunette, and with long flowing hair, slightly crimpled, was sobbing as though her heart would break for her mother. She was terrified at the surroundings of her new position, and the hideous yells of drunken soldiers and sailors in the next cell.

" There were confined in this cell several women, who, in New York or Boston, would pass for white women without the slightest difficulty or suspicion.   And there were many darker countenances in that cell, that were intelligent, and indicated the existence and beating of hearts beneath those tinged and sable hues.   In the opposite cells were over one hundred colored men and boys of all colors, from the ebony, thick-lipped African, to the mulatto, and delicately-tinged colored man. They were there from all ages, from the little child of nine years, to the aged and decrepit negro of seventy-five. There were the dandy darkey, slave and free; the laborer, slave and free; the mechanic and waiter, slave and free.

"Some of these men were the fathers, husbands, and brothers of the women in the opposite cells. It was but a little while after, when, the jailer having barred the door which leads into the stone corridor, I heard distinctly the swelling notes of 'John Brown's body lies mouldering,' &c., and shortly after the grand chorus of an ancient Methodist hymn, 'For Jesus' sake, we'll serve the Lord.' The next evening, I visited the cells, and found that nearly all who had been imprisoned the previous evening had been released on paying a fine of one dollar and a quarter for free people, and one dollar and a half for slaves.

"There were several likely-looking negro-girls still in the cell, and three mothers. All of these mothers had sons in the Union army, enlisted in the colored Native-Guard Regiment. One of them had *three* sons in one regiment; the other had two sons, her only children; and the only child of the third, a boy of nineteen years, was a sergeant in a colored company. These mothers were all the *property* of rebels; for they told me their masters and mistresses swore they would 'never take the oath of allegiance to the abolition Yankee Government.' I asked them how they happened to be imprisoned, and was informed that their masters and mistresses had them 'sent to prison for safe-keeping.'

"One mother told me she was always treated well until her sons joined the negro regiment, since which time she had been whipped and otherwise sadly abused. She was not allowed so much liberty at home, and her mistress had put her off on a short allowance of food, because she did not prevent her sons from enlisting.

"Here is a verbatim copy of the official order requiring the arrest by the police of all colored people found in the streets. Beyond the simple written notice, nothing more has been made public in regard to this important matter : —

        " ' OFFICE CHIEF OF POLICE.

" ' *Lieut. J. Duan*, — You are hereby ordered to arrest all negroes out without passes after half past eight, P.M.

       " ' By order of

              " ' COL. J. H. FRENCH,

        " ' *Provost-marshal General and Chief of Police.*' "

" Notices of this kind were sent to all the station-houses, and were posted in the offices. It is a most despotic law to put in force at such an hour as this, to protect the property, in the shape of human flesh and blood, in God's creatures, belonging or *owned*, as they say, by the very fiends who have no compulsion at shedding the precious life's blood of our sons and brothers, husbands and fathers.

" We, who profess to be Christian people, contributing blood and treasure for the suppression of this cursed Rebellion, are now called upon to provide cells for the safe-keeping of their slaves."—*Correspondence of The Boston Traveller.*

The following private letter (says " The New-York Tribune ") from a colored man in New Orleans, cancelling an order he had previously sent to New York for a banner, may throw some light on the state of things in the Southern metropolis : —

" SIR, — If you have not had the banner commenced, it is useless to have it made at all, as, since the issuing of the President's proclamation, Jonas H. French has stopped all of our night-meetings, and has caused us to get permits to hold meetings on Sunday, and sends his police around to all of the colored churches every Sunday to examine all of the permits. He had all the slaves that were turned out of their former owners' yards re-arrested and sent back; those who belonged to rebels as well as those who belong to loyal persons. The slaves were mustered into the rebel army. He has them confined in jail to starve and die, and refuses their friends to see them. He is much worse than our rebel masters, he being the chief of police. Last night, after Gen. Banks left the city, Col. French issued a secret order to all the police-stations to arrest all the negroes who may be found in the streets, and at the places of amusement, and placed in jail. There were about five hundred, both free and slave, confined, without the least notice or cause, — persons who thought themselves free by the President's proclamation, from the parishes of Natchitoches, Ouachita, Rapides, Catahoula, Concordia, Aragules, Jaques, Iberville, West Baton Rouge, Point Coupee, Filiciana, East Baton Rouge, St. Helena, Washington, St. Samany. Free persons of color from any of these parishes, who are found within the limits of the city, are immediately arrested and placed in jail by order of Col. French. Therefore it is useless to have the banner made, as there is no use for it since Gen. Butler has left.   R. K. T."

All colored persons, even those who had been born free, and had resided in the city from infancy, were included in the order of the provost-marshal. It is a fact beyond dispute, that both officers and soldiers under Gen. Banks's rule in Louisiana manifested a degree of negro hate that was almost unknown before their advent.

At the siege of Port Hudson, this prejudice against the blacks was exhibited by all, from Gen. Banks down to the most ignorant private. A correspondent in "The Boston Commonwealth," dated at Port Hudson, July 17, 1864, says, —

" Thus, in the siege of Port Hudson, no one knew an instance of such terrible assaults, without possibility of success, but only repeated in obedience to Gen. Dwight's order to 'continue charging till further orders.' The white troops were unanimous in praising the valor of this devoted regiment. How was it when the provisions of Paragraph 11, Appendix B, Revised Army Regulations, 1863, were carried out? A General Order from Gen. Banks authorizes 'Port Hudson' to be inscribed on every banner but those of the colored regiments, which are *overlooked*. Do those people who speak so loudly in praise of these regiments at Port Hudson know they are the only ones not authorized to inscribe 'Port Hudson' on their flags? Does *Adjutant-Gen. Thomas* know it? The only inscription on the banner of the glorious Seventy-third is the blood-stain of the noble sergeant who bore it in this fierce assault, and the rents made in the struggle of the corporals to obtain the dear rag from the dying man who had rolled himself up in its fold. Regiments which were ridiculed as cowards and vagabonds have Port Hudson on their flags. Let us be cautious how we praise the First Native Guards: they have it not on their flag. Thank God there were thousands of honest privates in the ranks of the white regiments who will tell the story of the First Native Guards! The changes of its designation and consolidation with other regiments will not entirely obliterate its fame. The blood of the heroic Callioux and his fellow-victims at Port Hudson will cry to Heaven, and will be heard.

"And how has it run in the campaign of 1864? This same devoted regiment followed the army of Gen. Banks to Pleasant Hill; but Fort Pillow rushed red on the general's sight, and he dare not let them fight. They were therefore made to 'boost' along the wagon-trains of the white troops; to build the greater part of the famous bridge which saved the fleet, and got Lieut.-Col. Bailey a star; to endure the kicks and insults of white soldiers; the officers to be put in arrest by inferior officers of white regiments, and returned to Morganzia. Every available man is detailed daily, rain or shine, to work on the fortifications under the jeers of loafing white soldiers and officers."

The labor-system adopted by Gen. Banks for the freedmen was nothing less than slavery under another name. Having no confidence in the negro's ability to take care of himself, he felt that, even in freedom, he needed a master, and therefore put him in leading-strings. The general evidently considered that the wishes of the white planters, whether rebel or not, were to be gratified, although it were done at the expense of the black man. In reconstructing the civil authorities of the city of New Orleans, he carried out the same policy of ignoring the rights of the colored people, as will be seen by the following extract from a petition of the colored citizens to President Lincoln : —

"Your petitioners aver that they have applied in respectful terms to Brig.-Gen. George F. Shepley, Military Governor of Louisiana, and to Major-Gen. N. P. Banks, commanding the Department of the Gulf, praying to be placed upon the registers as voters, to the end that they might participate in the re-organization of civil government in Louisiana; and that their petition has met with no response from those officers."

This petition was signed by the men, who, when the city was threatened by the rebels during the siege of Port Hudson, took up arms for its defence; all of whom were loyal to the American Union.

CHAPTER XXV.

HONORS TO THE NOBLE DEAD.

Capt. André Callioux. — His Body lies in State. — Personal Appearance. — His Enthusiasm. — His Popularity. — His Funeral. — The great Respect paid the Deceased. — General Lamentation.

THE death of Capt. André Callioux created a profound sensation throughout Louisiana, and especially in New Orleans, where the deceased had lived from childhood. This feeling of sorrow found vent at the funeral, which took place on the 11th of July, 1863. We give the following, written at the time by a correspondent of a New-York Journal : —

"NEW ORLEANS, Saturday, Aug. 1, 1863.

" The most extraordinary local event that has ever been seen within our borders, and, I think, one of the most extraordinary exhibitions brought forth by this Rebellion, was the funeral of Capt. André Callioux, Company E, First Louisiana National Guards. Here, in this Southern emporium, was performed a funeral ceremony that for numbers and impressiveness never had its superior in this city ; and it was originated and carried through in honor of a gallant soldier of the despised race, to enslave which, it is said, will soothe this State back into the Union.

" Capt. Callioux was fine-looking, and, in his military dress, had an imposing appearance. I remember seeing him at Gen. Banks's headquarters, in company with at least fifteen of our prominent military officers; and he was a marked personage among them all. In the celebrated assault and repulse on Port Hudson by Gen. Banks, Capt. Callioux fell, at the head of his company, on the 27th of May last, while gallantly leading it on to the enemy's works. His body, along with others of the national regiments, after the battle, lay within deadly reach of the rebel sharpshooters; and all attempts to recover the body were met with a shower of Minie-bullets. Thus guarded by the enemy, or, I might say, thus honored by their attention, the body lay exposed until the surrender of the place, the 8th of July, when it was recovered, and brought to this city to receive the astonishing ovation connected with the last rights of humanity.

" The arrival of the body developed to the white population here that the colored people had powerful organizations in the form of civic societies; as the Friends of the Order, of which Capt. Callioux was a prominent member, received the body, and had the coffin containing it, draped with the American flàg, exposed in state in the commodious hall. Around the coffin, flowers were strewn in the greatest profusion, and candles were kept continually burning. All the rights of the Catholic Church were strictly complied with. The guard paced silently to and fro, and altogether it presented as solemn a scene as was ever witnessed.

" In due time, the band of the Forty-second Massachusetts Regiment made their appearance, and discoursed the customary solemn airs. The officiating priest, Father Le Maistre, of the Church of St. Rose of Lima, who has paid not the least attention to the excommunication and denunciations issued against him by the archbishop of this diocese, then performed the Catholic service for the dead.   After the regular services, he ascended to the president's chair, and delivered a glowing and eloquent eulogy on the virtues of the deceased.   He called upon all present to offer themselves, as Callioux had done, martyrs to the cause of justice, freedom, and good government.   It was a death the proudest might envy.

" Immense crowds of colored people had by this time gathered around the building, and the streets leading thereto were rendered almost impassable.   Two companies of the Sixth Louisiana (colored) Regiment, from their camp on the Company Canal, were there to act as an escort; and Esplanade Street, for more than a mile, was lined with colored societies, both male and female, in open order, waiting for the hearse to pass through.

" After a short pause, a sudden silence fell upon the crowd, the band commenced playing a dirge; and the body was brought from the hall on the shoulders of eight soldiers, escorted by six members of the society, and six colored captains, who acted as pall-bearers.   The corpse was conveyed to the hearse through a crowd composed of both white and black people, and in silence profound as death itself.   Not a sound was heard save the mournful music of the band, and not a head in all that vast multitude but was uncovered.

" The procession then moved off in the following order: The hearse containing the body, with Capts. J. W. Ringgold, W. B. Barrett, S. J. Wilkinson, Eugene Mailleur, J. A. Gléa, and A. St. Leger (all of whom, we believe, belong to the Second Louisiana Native Guards), and six members of The Friends of the Order, as pall-bearers; about a hundred convalescent sick and wounded colored soldiers; the two companies of the Sixth Regiment; a large number of colored officers of all native guard regiments ; the carriages containing Capt. Cal-

lioux's family, and a number of army officers; winding
up with a large number of private individuals, and the
following-named societies: —

Friends of the Order.
Society of Economy and Mutual Assistance.
United Brethren.
Arts' and Mechanics' Association.
Free Friends.
Good Shepherd Conclave, No. 2.
Artisans' Brotherhood.
Good Shepherd Conclave, No. 1.
Union Sons' Relief.
Perseverance Society.
Ladies of Bon Secours.
La Fleur de Marie.
Saint Rose of Lima.
The Children of Mary Society.
Saint Angela Society.
The Immaculate Conception Society.
The Sacred Union Society.
The Children of Jesus.
Saint Veronica Society.
Saint Alphonsus Society.
Saint Joachim Society.
Star of the Cross.
Saint Theresa Society.
Saint Eulalia Society.
Saint Magdalen Society.
God Protect Us Society.
United Sisterhood.
Angel Gabriel Society.
Saint Louis Roi Society.
Saint Bénoit Society.
Benevolence Society.
Well Beloved Sisters' Society.
Saint Peter Society.
Saint Michael Archangel Society
Saint Louis de Gonzague Society.
Saint Ann Society.
The Children of Moses

" After moving through the principal down-town streets, the body was taken to the Bienville-street cemetery, and there interred with military honors due his rank.

" Capt. Callioux was a native of this city, aged forty-three years, and was one of the first to raise a company under the call of Gen. Butler for colored volunteers. 'The Union,' of this city, a paper of stanch loyalty, which is devoted to the interests of the colored people, speaking of Capt. Callioux, says ' By his gallant bearing, his gentlemanly deportment, his amiable disposition, and his capacities as a soldier, — having received a very good education, — he became the idol of his men, and won the respect and confidence of his superior officers. He was a true type of the Louisianian. In this city, where he passed his life, he was loved and respected by all who knew him.

" ' In Capt. Callioux, the cause of the Union and freedom has lost a valuable friend. Capt. Callioux, defending the integrity of the sacred cause of liberty, vindicated his race from the opprobrium with which it was charged. He leaves a wife and several children, who will have the consolation that he died the death of the patriot and the righteous.'

" The long pageant has passed away ; but there is left deeply impressed on the minds of those who witnessed this extraordinary sight the fact that thousands of people born in slavery had, by the events of the Rebellion, been disinthralled enough to appear in the streets of New Orleans, bearing to the tomb a man of their own color, who had fallen gallantly fighting for the flag and his country, — a man who had sealed with his blood the inspiration he received from Mr. Lincoln's Emanci-

pation Proclamation. The thousands of the unfortunates who followed his remains had the flag of the
Union in miniature form waving in their hands, or
pinned tastefully on their persons.

" We would ask, Can these people ever again be subjected to slavery? Are these men who have been
regenerated by wearing the United-States uniform,
these men who have given their race to our armies to
fight our would-be oppressors, — are these people
to be, can they ever again be, handed over to the task-
master? Would a Government that would do such a
thing be respected by the world, be honored of God?
Could the Christianized people of the globe have witnessed the funeral of Capt. Callioux, there would have
been but one sentiment called forth, and that is this, —
that the National Government can make no compromise
on this slave question. It is too late to retreat: the responsibility has been taken, and the struggle must go on
until there is not legally a slave under the folds of the
American flag."

CHAPTER XXVI.

THE NORTHERN WING OF THE REBELLION.

The New-York Mob. — Murder, Fire, and Robbery. — The City given
up to the Rioters. — Whites and Blacks robbed in Open Day in the
Great Thoroughfares. — Negroes murdered, burned, and their Bodies
hung on Lamp-posts. — Southern Rebels at the Head of the Riot.

THE partial successes which the rebels had achieved
at Bull Run, Ball's Bluff, and Big Bethel, together with
the defiant position of Gen. Lee on the one hand, and
the bad management of Gen. McClellan on the other,
had emboldened the rebels, and made them feel their
strength.

Those who had served out their terms of service in the
Union army were not very anxious to re-enlist. The Con-
script Act had been passed by Congress, and the copperhead press throughout the land was urging the people
to resist the draft, when the welcome news of the surrender of Vicksburg and Port Hudson came over the wires.
The agents of the Confederacy were at once despatched
to New York to " let loose the dogs of war."

As the blacks of the South had assisted in the capture
of Vicksburg and Port Hudson, the colored people of
the North must be made to suffer for it.

The mob was composed of the lowest and most degraded of the foreign population (mainly Irish), raked
from the filthy cellars and dens of the city, steeped in
crimes of the deepest dye, and ready for any act, no

matter how dark and damnable; together with the worst type of our native criminals, whose long service in the prisons of the country, and whose training in the Democratic party, had so demoralized their natures, that they were ever on the hunt for some deed of robbery or murder.

This conglomerated mass of human beings were under the leadership of men standing higher than themselves in the estimation of the public, but, if possible, really lower in moral degradation. Cheered on by men holding high political positions, and finding little or no opposition, they went on at a fearful rate.

Never, in the history of mob-violence, was crime carried to such an extent. Murder, arson, robbery, and cruelty reigned triumphant throughout the city, day and night, for more than a week.

Breaking into stores, hotels, and saloons, and helping themselves to strong drink, *ad libitum*, they became inebriated, and marched through every part of the city. Calling at places where large bodies of men were at work, and pressing them in, their numbers rapidly increased to thousands, and their fiendish depredations had no bounds. Having been taught by the leaders of the Democratic party to hate the negro, and having but a few weeks previous seen regiments of colored volunteers pass through New York on their way South, this infuriated band of drunken men, women, and children paid special visits to all localities inhabited by the blacks, and murdered all they could lay their hands on, without regard to age or sex. Every place known to employ negroes was searched: steamboats leaving the city, and railroad depots, were watched, lest some should escape their vengeance.

Hundreds of the blacks, driven from their homes, and hunted and chased through the streets, presented themselves at the doors of jails, prisons, and police-stations, and begged admission.   Thus did they prowl about the city, committing crime after crime; indeed, in point of cruelty, the Rebellion was transferred from the South to the North.

These depredations were to offset the glorious triumphs of our arms in the rebel States.

Peaceful o'er the placid waters rose the radiant summer sun,
Loyal voices shouted anthems o'er the conquest bravely won;
For the walls of Vicksburg yielded to the Union shot and shell,
While Port Hudson, trembling, waited but a clearer tale to tell.

But, alas! day's golden image scarce had left its impress there,
When above a Northern city rose the sounds of wild despair:
Fiends and demons yet unnumbered rallied forth in bold array;
Deeds of darkness, scenes of carnage, marked the traitors' onward way.

Blind to feeling, deaf to mercy, who may judge the depth of crime?
None but God may know the misery traced upon the Book of Time.

The following account of the mob is from "The New-York Times" July 14, 1863: —

"The Orphan Asylum for Colored Children was visited by the mob about four o'clock.   This institution is situated on Fifth Avenue; and the building, with the grounds and gardens adjoining, extends from Forty-third to Forty-fourth Street.   Hundreds and perhaps thousands of the rioters, the majority of whom were women and children, entered the premises, and, in the most excited and violent manner, ransacked and plundered the building from cellar to garret.   The building was located in the most healthy portion of the city.   It was purely

a charitable institution.   In it there was an average of
six or eight hundred homeless colored orphans.   The
building was a large four-story one, with two wings of
three stories each.

" When it became evident that the crowd designed to
destroy it, a flag of truce appeared on the walk opposite, and the principals of the establishment made an
appeal to the excited populace ; but in vain.

"Here it was, that Chief-Engineer Decker showed himself one of the bravest of the brave.   After the entire
building had been ransacked, and every article deemed
worth carrying had been taken, — *and this included even
the little garments for the orphans, which were contributed
by the benevolent ladies of the city, — the premises were
fired on the first floor.*   Mr. Decker did all he could to
prevent the flames from being kindled ; but, when he was
overpowered by superior numbers, with his own hands
he scattered the brands, and effectually extinguished the
flames.   A second attempt was made, and this time in
three different parts of the house.   Again he succeeded,
with the aid of half a dozen of his men, in defeating the
incendiaries.   The mob became highly exasperated at
his conduct, and threatened to take his life if he repeated the act.   On the front steps of the building, he
stood up amid an infuriated and half-drunken mob of
two thousand, and begged of them to do nothing so disgraceful to humanity as to burn a benevolent institution,
which had for its object nothing but good.   He said it
would be a lasting disgrace to them and to the city of
New York.

" These remarks seemed to have no good effect upon
them, and meantime the premises were again fired, —
this time in all parts of the house.   Mr. Decker, with

his few brave men, again extinguished the flames. This last act brought down upon him the vengeance of all who were bent on the destruction of the asylum;· and but for the fact that some firemen surrounded him, and boldly said that Mr. Decker could not be taken except over their bodies, he would have been despatched on the spot. The institution was destined to be burned; and, after an hour and a half of labor on the part of the mob, it was in flames in all parts. Three or four persons were horribly bruised by the falling walls; but the names we could not ascertain. There is now scarcely one brick left on another of the Orphan Asylum.

"At one o'clock yesterday, the garrison of the Seventh-avenue arsenal witnessed a sad and novel sight. Winding slowly along Thirty-fourth Street into Seventh Avenue, headed by a strong police force, came the little colored orphans, whose asylum had been burned down on Monday night. The boys, from two and three to fifteen years of age, followed by little girls of the same ages, to the number of about two hundred each, trotted along, and were halted in front of the arsenal.

"Then came a large number of men and women, several having babes in their arms, who had been forced to seek refuge in adjacent station-houses from the fury of the mob. Most of them carried small bundles of clothing and light articles of furniture, all they had been able to save from the wreck of their property. The negroes who had sought safety under the guns of the arsenal were then taken out, and ordered to join their friends outside. The procession was then re-formed, and, headed by the police, marched back again down Thirty-fifth Street to the North River.

"A strong detachment of Hawkins's Zouaves guarded

the flanks of the procession; while a company of the Tenth New-York Volunteers, and a squad of police, closed up the rear.   Col. William Meyer had command of the escort; and on arriving at the pier, where a numerous crowd had followed them, he placed his men, with fixed bayonets, facing the people to keep them in check; and the negroes were all safely embarked, and conveyed to Ricker's Island.

.   .   .   .

"The poor negroes have had a hard time.   Finding they were to be slaughtered indiscriminately, they have hid themselves in cellars and garrets, and have endeavored, under cover of darkness, to flee to neighboring places. The Elysian Fields, over in Hoboken, has been a pretty safe refuge for them, as there are but few Irish living in that city.   They have a sort of improvised camp there, composed mainly of women and children."

Blacks were chased to the docks, thrown into the river, and drowned; while some, after being murdered, were hung to lamp-posts.   Between forty and fifty colored persons were killed, and nearly as many maimed for life.   But space will not allow us to give any thing like a detailed account of this most barbarous outrage.

CHAPTER XXVII.

ASSAULT ON FORT WAGNER.

The Fifty-fourth Massachusetts Regiment. — Col. Shaw. — March to the Island. — Preparation. — Speeches. — The Attack. — Storm of Shot, Shell, and Canister. — Heroism of Officers and Men. — Death of Col. Shaw. — The Color-sergeant. — The Retreat. — "Buried with his Niggers." — Comments.

On the 16th of July, the Fifty-fourth Regiment (colored), Col. R. G. Shaw, was attacked by the enemy, on James Island, in which a fight of two hours' duration took place, the Rebels largely outnumbering the Union forces. The Fifty-fourth, however, drove the enemy before them in confusion. The loss to our men was fourteen killed and eighteen wounded. During the same day, Col. Shaw received orders from Gen. Gillmore to evacuate the island. Preparations began at dusk. The night was dark and stormy, and made the movement both difficult and dangerous. The march was from James Island to Cole Island, across marshes, streams, and dikes, and part of the way upon narrow foot-bridges, along which it was necessary to proceed in single-file. The whole force reached Cole Island the next morning, July 17, and rested during the day on the beach opposite the south end of Folly Island. About ten o'clock in the evening, the colonel of the Fifty-fourth received orders directing him to report, with his command, to Gen. George C. Strong, at Morris Island, to whose brigade the regiment was transferred.

From eleven o'clock of Friday evening until four
o'clock of Saturday, they were being put on the transport, "The Gen. Hunter," in a boat which took about fifty
at a time. There they breakfasted on the same fare, and
had no other food before entering into the assault on
Fort Wagner in the evening.

"The Gen. Hunter" left Cole Island for Folly Island
at six, A.M.; and the troops landed at Pawnee Landing
about nine and a half, A.M., and thence marched to the point
opposite Morris Island, reaching there about two o'clock
in the afternoon. They were transported in a steamer
across the inlet, and at four, P.M., began their march for
Fort Wagner. They reached Brigadier-Gen. Strong's
quarters, about midway on the island, about six or six
and a half o'clock, where they halted for five minutes.

Gen. Strong expressed a great desire to give them
food and stimulants; but it was too late, as they had to
lead the charge. They had been without tents during
the pelting rains of Thursday and Friday nights. Gen.
Strong had been impressed with the high character of
the regiment and its officers; and he wished to assign
them the post where the most severe work was to be
done and the highest honor was to be won.

The march across Folly and Morris Islands was over a
sandy road, and was very wearisome. The regiment
went through the centre of the island, and not along the
beach, where the marching was easier.

When they had come within six hundred yards of
Fort Wagner, they formed in line of battle, the colonel
heading the first, and the major the second battalion.
This was within musket-shot of the enemy. There was
little firing from the enemy; a solid shot falling between
the battalions, and another falling to the right, but no

musketry. At this point, the regiment, together with the next supporting regiment, the Sixth Connecticut, Ninth Maine, and others, remained half an hour. The regiment was addressed by Gen. Strong and by Col. Shaw. Then, at seven and a half or seven and three-quarters o'clock, the order for the charge was given. The regiment advanced at quick time, changed to double-quick when at some distance on.

The intervening distance between the place where the line was formed and the fort was run over in a few minutes.

When about one hundred yards from the fort, the rebel musketry opened with such terrible effect, that, for an instant, the first battalion hesitated, — but only for an instant ; for Col. Shaw, springing to the front and waving his sword, shouted, " Forward, my brave boys ! " and with another cheer and a shout they rushed through the ditch, gained the parapet on the right, and were soon engaged in a hand-to-hand conflict with the enemy. Col. Shaw was one of the first to scale the walls. He stood erect to urge forward his men, and, while shouting for them to press on, was shot dead, and fell into the fort. His body was found, with twenty of his men lying dead around him ; two lying on his own body.

The Fifty-fourth did well and nobly ; only the fall of Col. Shaw prevented them from entering the fort. They moved up as gallantly as any troops could, and, with their enthusiasm, they deserved a better fate.

Sergeant-major Lewis H. Douglass, son of Frederick Douglass, the celebrated orator, sprang upon the parapet close behind Col. Shaw, and cried out, " Come, boys, come, let's fight for God and Governor Andrew." This brave young man was the last to leave the parapet. Be-

fore the regiment reached the parapet, the color-sergeant
was wounded ; and, while in the act of falling, the colors
were seized by Sergt. William H. Carney, who bore them
up, and mounted the parapet, where he, too, received
three severe wounds.   But, on orders being given to retire, the color-bearer, though almost disabled, still held
the emblem of liberty in the air, and followed his regiment by the aid of his comrades, and succeeded in reaching the hospital, where he fell exhausted and almost lifeless on the floor, saying, "The old flag never touched the
ground, boys." Capt. Lewis F. Emilio, the junior captain,—all of his superiors having been killed or wounded,
— took command, and brought the regiment into camp.
In this battle, the total loss in officers and men, killed
and wounded, was two hundred and sixty-one.

When John Brown was led out of the Charlestown
jail, on his way to execution, he paused a moment, it will
be remembered, in the passage-way, and, taking a little
colored child in his arms, kissed and blessed it.[1] The
dying blessing of the martyr will descend from generation to generation; and a whole race will cherish for
ages the memory of that simple caress, which, degrading
as it seemed to the slaveholders around him, was as sub-
lime and as touching a lesson, and as sure to do its work
in the world's history, as that of Him who said, " Suffer
little children to come unto me."

When inquiry was made at Fort Wagner, under flag
of truce, for the body of Col. Shaw of the Massachusetts
Fifty-fourth, the answer was, " We have buried him with
his niggers ! "   It is the custom of savages to outrage
the dead, and it was only natural that the natives of
South Carolina should attempt to heap insult upon the
remains of the brave young soldier ; but that wide **grave**

on Morris Island will be to a whole race a holy sepul-
chre. No more fitting burial-place, no grander obsequies,
could have been given to him who cried, as he led that
splendid charge, " On, my brave boys ! " than to give
to him and to them one common grave. As they clus-
tered around him in the fight ; as they rallied always to
the clear ring of his loved voice ; as they would have
laid down their lives, each and all of them, to save his ;
as they honored and reverenced him, and lavished on
him all the strong affections of a warm-hearted and im-
pulsive people : so when the fight was over, and he was
found with the faithful dead piled up like a bulwark
around him, the poor savages did the only one fitting
thing to be done when they buried them together.
Neither death nor the grave has divided the young
martyr and hero from the race for which he died ; and a
whole people will remember in the coming centuries,
when its new part is to be played in the world's history,
that " he was buried with his niggers ! "

> " They buried him with his niggers ! "
>   Together they fought and died.
>   There was room for them all where they laid him
>   (The grave was deep and wide),
>   For his beauty and youth and valor,
>   Their patience and love and pain ;
>   And at the last day together
>   They shall all be found again.
>
> " They buried him with his niggers ! "
>   Earth holds no prouder grave :
>   There is not a mausoleum
>   In the world beyond the wave,
>   That a nobler tale has hallowed,
>   Or a purer glory crowned,
>   Than the nameless trench where they buried
>   The brave so faithful found.

> " They buried him with his niggers ! "
>   A wide grave should it be.
>   They buried more in that shallow trench
>   Than human eye could see.
>   Ay : all the shames and sorrows
>   Of more than a hundred years
>   Lie under the weight of that Southern soil
>   Despite those cruel sneers.
>
> " They buried him with his niggers ! "
>   But the glorious souls set free
>   Are leading the van of the army
>   That fights for liberty.
>   Brothers in death, in glory
>   The same palm-branches bear ;
>   And the crown is as bright o'er the sable brows
>   As over the golden hair. [2]

Only those who knew Col. Shaw can understand how
fitting it seems, when the purpose of outrage is put aside
and forgotten, that he should have been laid in a common grave with his black soldiers. The relations between colored troops and their officers — if these are
good for any thing, and fit for their places — must need
be, from the circumstances of the case, very close and
peculiar. They were especially so with Col. Shaw and
his regiment. His was one of those natures which attract first through the affections. Most gentle tempered,
genial as a warm winter's sun, sympathetic, full of kind-
liness, unselfish, unobtrusive, and gifted with a manly
beauty and a noble bearing, he was sure to win the love,
in a very marked degree, of men of a race peculiarly
susceptible to influence from such traits of character as
these. First, they loved him with a devotion which
could hardly exist anywhere else than in the peculiar relation he held to them as commander of the first regiment of free colored men permitted to fling out a military

banner in this country, — a banner that, so raised, meant to them so much! But, then, came closer ties; they found that this young man, with education and habits that would naturally lead him to choose a life of ease, with wealth at his command, with peculiarly happy social relations (one most tender one just formed), accepted the position offered him in consideration of his soldierly as well as moral fitness, because he recognized a solemn duty to the black man ; because he was ready to throw down all that he had, all that he was, all that this world could give him, for the negro race ! Beneath that gentle and courtly bearing which so won upon the colored people of Boston when the Fifty-fourth was in camp, beneath that kindly but unswerving discipline of the commanding officer, beneath that stern but always cool and cheerful courage of the leader in the fight, was a clear and deep conviction of a duty to the blacks. He hoped to lead them, as one of the roads to social equality, to fight their way to true freedom ; and herein he saw his path of duty. Of the battle two days before that in which he fell, and in which his regiment, by their bravery, won the right to lead the attack on Fort Wagner, he said, " I wanted my men to fight by the side of whites, and they have done it; " thinking of others, not of himself; thinking of that great struggle for equality in which the race had now a chance to gain a step forward, and to which he was ready to devote his life. Could it have been for him to choose his last resting-place, he would, no doubt, have said, " Bury me with my men if I earn that distinction."

> Buried with a band of brothers
>   Who for him would fain have died;
> Buried with the gallant fellows
>   Who fell fighting by his side ;

Buried with the men God gave him,
  Those whom he was sent to save;
Buried with the martyred heroes,
  He has found an honored grave.

Buried where his dust so precious
  Makes the soil a hallowed spot;
Buried where, by Christian patriot,
  He shall never be forgot;

Buried in the ground accursed,
  Which man's fettered feet have trod;
Buried where his voice still speaketh,
  Appealing for the slave to God;

Fare thee well, thou noble warrior,
  Who·in youthful beauty went
On a high and holy mission,
  By the God of battles sent.

Chosen of Him, " elect and precious,"
  Well didst thou fulfil thy part:
When thy country " counts her jewels,"
  She shall wear thee on her heart. [3]

One who was present, speaking of the incidents before the battle, says of Col. Shaw, —

" The last day with us, or, I may say, the ending of it, as we lay flat on the ground before the assault, his manner was more unbending than I had ever noticed before in the presence of his men. He sat on the ground, and was talking to the men very familiarly and kindly. He told them how the eyes of thousands would look upon the night's work they were about to enter on; and he said, 'Now, boys, I want you to be men!' He would walk along the line, and speak words of cheer to his men.

" We could see that he was a man who had counted the cost of the undertaking before him; for his words were spoken ominously, his lips were compressed, and now and then there was visible a slight twitching of the corners of the mouth, like one bent on accomplishing or dying.   One poor fellow, struck no doubt by the colonel's determined bearing, exclaimed, as he was passing him, ' Colonel, I will stay by you till I die ; ' and he kept his word : he has never been seen since.   For one so young, Col. Shaw showed a well-trained mind, and an ability of governing men not possessed by many older or more experienced men.   In him the regiment has lost one of its best and most devoted friends.   Col. Shaw was only about twenty-seven years of age, and was married a few weeks before he joined the army of the South."

The following correspondence between the father of Col. Shaw and Gen. Gillmore needs no comment, but is characteristic of the family : —

" *Brig.- Gen. Gillmore, commanding Department of the South.*

" SIR, — I take the liberty to address you, because I am informed that efforts are to be made to recover the body of my son, Col. Shaw, of the Fifty-fourth Massachusetts Regiment, which was buried at Fort Wagner.   My object in writing is to say that such efforts are not authorized by me, or any of my family, and that they are not approved by us.   We hold that a soldier's most appropriate burial-place is on the field where he has fallen. I shall, therefore, be much obliged, general, if, in case the matter is brought to your cognizance, you will forbid the desecration of my son's grave, and prevent the disturbance of his remains or of those buried with him. With most earnest wishes for your success, I am, sir, with respect and esteem,

" Your most obedient servant,
                                                  " FRANCIS GEORGE SHAW.
" NEW YORK, Aug. 24, 1863."

" HEADQUARTERS DEPARTMENT OF THE SOUTH,
Morris Island, S.C., Sept. 5, 1863.

" *F. G. Shaw, Esq., Clifton, Staten Island, N. Y.*

" SIR, — I have just received your letter, expressing the disapprobation of yourself and family of any effort to recover the body of your son, the late Col. Shaw, of the Fifty-fourth Massachusetts Volunteers, buried in Fort Wagner; and requesting me to forbid the desecration of his grave or disturbance of his remains.

" Had it been possible to obtain the body of Col. Shaw immediately after the battle in which he lost his life, I should have sent it to his friends, in deference to a sentiment which I know to be widely prevalent among the friends of those who fall in battle, although the practice is one to which my own judgment has never yielded assent.

" The views expressed in your letter are so congenial to the feelings of an officer, as to command not only my cordial sympathy, but my respect and admiration. Surely no resting-place for your son could be found more fitting than the scene where his courage and devotion were so conspicuously displayed.

" I beg to avail myself of this opportunity to express my deep sympathy for yourself and family in their great bereavement, and to assure you that on no authority less than your own shall your son's remains be disturbed.

" Very respectfully, your obedient servant,

" Q. A. GILLMORE,
" *Brigadier-General commanding.*"

The following address of the Military Governor of South Carolina to the people of color in the Department of the South pays a fit tribute to the memory of the lamented Col. Shaw : —

" *To the Colored Soldiers and Freedmen in this Department.*

"It is fitting that you should pay a last tribute of respect to the memory of the late Col. Robert Gould Shaw, Colonel of the Fifty-fourth Regiment of Massachusetts Volunteers.   He commanded the first regiment of colored soldiers from a free State ever mustered into the United-States service.

"He fell at the head of his regiment, while leading a storming-party against a rebel stronghold.   You should cherish in your inmost hearts the memory of one who did not hesitate to sacrifice all the attractions of a high social position, wealth and home, and his own noble life, for the sake of humanity ; another martyr to your cause that death has added; still another hope for your race. The truths and principles for which he fought and died still live, and will be vindicated.   On the spot where he fell, by the ditch into which his mangled and bleeding body was thrown, on the soil of South Carolina, I trust that you will honor yourselves and his glorious memory by appropriating the first proceeds of your labor as free men toward erecting an enduring monument to the hero, soldier, martyr, Robert Gould Shaw.

"R. SAXTON,
" *Brigadier-General and Military Governor.*"

We are glad to be able to say, that the noble proposition of Gen. Saxton met with success.

Col. Shaw was singularly fortunate in being surrounded by officers, like himself, young, brave, and enthusiastic.   Major Hallowell, the next in command, was wounded while urging forward his men.   Adjutant G. W. James, Capts. S. Willard, J. W. M. Appleton, E. L.

Jones, G. Pope, W. H. Simpkins, C. J. Russell, and C.
E. Tucker, and Lieuts. O. E. Smith, W. H. Homan, R. H.
Jewett, and J. A. Pratt, — were severely wounded. A
large proportion of the non-commissioned officers fell in
the engagement or were badly wounded. Among these
was Sergt. R. J. Simmons, a young man of more than
ordinary ability, who had learned the science of war in
the British army. The writer enlisted him in the city of
New York, and introduced him to Francis George Shaw,
Esq., who remarked at the time that Simmons would
make "a valuable soldier." Col. Shaw, also, had a high
opinion of him. He died of his wounds in the enemy's
hospital at Charleston, from bad treatment. The heroic
act of Sergt. Carney, to which we have already alluded,
called forth the following correspondence, which needs
no comments, from the Adjutant-General's Report of
the State of Massachusetts for the year 1865 : —

> " NEW YORK, 596 Broadway, Room 10,
> Dec. 13, 1865.

" *To Adjutant-General of Massachusetts, Boston.*

" SIR, — Will you be pleased to give me the name of
some officer of the Fifty-fourth Massachusetts colored
regiment, so that I can obtain information concerning
the famous assault that regiment made on Fort Wagner?
I wish to learn the facts relating to the wounded color-
bearer, who, though wounded severely, bore the flag
heroically while crawling from the parapet to his retreating or repulsed regiment. It would make a splendid
subject for a statuette.

" Respectfully,

" T. H. BARTLETT,
" *Sculptor.*"

I immediately forwarded the letter to Col. Hallowell, with a request that he would furnish me with all the facts relating to the incident which he possessed. The following is Col. Hallowell's reply: —

" Boston, Dec. 18, 1865.

" *William Schouler, Adjutant-General.*

" Dear Sir, — Your letter of the 15th to my brother, enclosing one from Mr. Bartlett, and requesting me to furnish a statement of facts relating to Sergt. Carney, of the Fifty-fourth Regiment Massachusetts Volunteers, is received. The following statement is, to the best of my knowledge and belief, correct; but you must remember it is made up principally from hearsay, no one person having seen every incident, except the sergeant. During the assault upon Fort Wagner, July 18, 1863, the sergeant carrying the national colors of the Fifty-fourth Massachusetts Volunteers fell; but, before the colors reached the ground, Sergt. Carney, of Company C, grasped them, and bore them to the parapet of the fort ; where he received wounds in both legs, in the breast, and in the right arm : he, however, refused to give up his trust. When the regiment retired from the fort, Sergt. Carney, by the aid of his comrades, succeeded in reaching the hospital, still holding on to the flag, where he fell, exhausted and almost lifeless, on the floor, saying, ' The old flag never touched the ground, boys.' At the time the above happened, I was not in a condition to verify the truth of the statements made to me ; but they come to me from very reliable parties, and from very different people ; so, after a close cross-examination of the sergeant (who was known as a truthful man), I have concluded that the statement I have made is substantially correct.

" Sergt. Carney was an African, of, I should think, full blood; of very limited education, but very intelligent; bright face, lips and nose (comparatively) finely cut, head rather round, skin very dark, height about five feet eight inches, not very athletic or muscular; had lived in New Bedford, Mass., for many years. Hoping this will be of service to Mr. Bartlett, I have the honor to be, very respectfully,

" Your obedient servant,

" E. N. HALLOWELL,
" Late Colonel, &c."

CHAPTER XXVIII.

THE SLAVE-MARTYR.

The Siege of Washington, N.C. — Big Bob, the Negro Scout. — The Perilous Adventure. — The Fight. — Return. — Night Expedition. — The Fatal Sandbar. — The Enemy's Shells. — "Somebody's got to die to get us out of this, and it may as well be me." — Death of Bob. — Safety of the Boat.

THE siege of Washington, N.C., had carried consternation among the planters of the surrounding country, and contrabands were flocking in by hundreds, when, just at day-break one morning, a band of seventeen came to the shore, and hailed the nearest gunboat. The blacks were soon taken on board, when it was ascertained that they had travelled fifty miles the previous night, guided by their leader, a negro whom they called "Big Bob." This man was without a drop of Anglo-Saxon blood in his veins, if color was a true index. It was also soon known that he was a preacher, or had been, among his fellow-slaves. These men all expressed a desire to be put to work, and, if allowed, to fight for "de ole flag." "Big Bob" sported a suit of rebel gray, which his fellow-slaves could not; and the way in which he obtained it was rather amusing. In the region from which they escaped, the blacks were being enrolled in the rebel army; and Bob and his companions were taken, and put under guard, preparatory to their being removed to the nearest military post. Bob, however,

212

resolved that he would not fight for the rebel cause, and induced his comrades to join in the plan of seizing the guard, and bringing him away with them; which they did, Bob claiming the rebel soldier's clothes, when that individual was dismissed, after a march of thirty miles from their home. Bob made an amusing appearance, being above six feet in height, and dressed in a suit, the legs of the pants of which were five or six inches too short, and the arms of the coat proportionally short.

A few days after the arrival of the contrabands, their services were needed in an important expedition in the interior. These negroes, upon being told what was wanted of them, although knowing that the enterprise would be attended with the greatest danger, and would require the utmost skill, volunteered their services, and, upon being furnished with arms and implements, immediately started upon the expedition. Being landed upon a point some little distance from Washington, they succeeded in penetrating the enemy's country, arresting three very important rebels, and conveying them to the fleet. In the return march, the rebels complained at their being made to walk so far and so fast; but Bob, the captain of the company, would occasionally be heard urging them along after this style: "March along dar, massa; no straggling to de rear: come, close up dar, close up dar! we're boss dis time." On the arrival of the party, the blacks were highly complimented by the commander.

A week had scarcely passed, and the slaves rested, before they were sent upon a more difficult and dangerous expedition; yet these men, with Bob to lead them, were ready for any enterprise, provided they could have arms and ammunition. Once more landed on shore, they started with a determination to accomplish the object for which they had been sent. They had not gone far before they were attacked by a scouting-party from the rebel camp, and four of the whites and one of the blacks were killed: one also of the latter was wounded. However, the rebels were put to flight, and the negroes made good their escape. Still bent on obeying the orders of the commander, they took a somewhat different route, and proceeded on their journey. Having finished their mission, which was the destroying of two very large salt-works, breaking up fifty salt-kettles, a large tannery, and liberating twenty-three slaves, some of whom they armed with guns taken in their fight with the rebels, Bob commenced retracing his steps. The return was not so easily accomplished, for the enemy were well distributed on the line between them and the gunboats. After getting within four miles of the fleet, and near Point Rodman, a fight took place between the colored men and the rebels, which lasted nearly an hour. The blacks numbered less than forty; while the whites were more than one hundred. The negroes were called upon to surrender; but Bob answered, " No, I never surrenders." And then he cried out,. " Come on, boys! ef we's captud, we's got to hang; and dat's a fack. And nobly did they fight, whipping their assailants, and reaching the gunboats with but the loss of three men killed and ten wounded. Bob and his companions were greatly praised when once more on the fleet.

But Bob's days were numbered; for the next day a flat full of soldiers, with four blacks, including Bob, attempted to land at Rodman's Point, but were repulsed by a terrible fire of rebel bullets, all tumbling into the boat, and lying flat to escape being shot. Meanwhile the boat stuck fast on the sand-bar, while the balls were still whizzing over and around the flat. Seeing that something must be done at once, or all would be lost, Big Bob exclaimed, "Somebody's got to die to get us out of this, and it may as well be me!" He then deliberately got out, and pushed the boat of, and fell into it, pierced by five bullets.

" The surf with ricochetting balls
    Was churned and splashed around us :
I heard my comrades' hurried calls,
    ' The rebel guns have found us.'

Our vessel shivered!   Far beneath
    The treacherous sand had caught her .
What man will leap to instant death
    To shove her into water ?

Strange light shone in our hero's eye;
    His voice was strong and steady :
' My brothers, one of us must die ;
    And I, thank God! am ready.'

A shell flew toward us, hissing hate,
    Then screaming like a demon :
He calmly faced the awful fate,
    Resolved to die a freeman.

He fell, his heart cut through with shot:
    The true blood of that martyr
Out from his body spurted hot
    To flee the shame of barter.

We lifted up the brave man's corse ;
    We thought him fair and saintly :
The rebel bullets round us hoarse
    We heard, but dull and faintly.

> ' Tis ever so : a great deed wrought,
>   The doer falls that moment,
> As if to save the God-like thought
>   From any human comment.
>
> Heroes are dead men by that fact;
>   Fame haunts our grave-yards, sighing,
> ' Alas ! that man's divinest act
>   Should be the act of dying.' " [1]

CHAPTER XXIX.

The Union Troops decoyed into a Swamp. — They are outnumbered. — Their great Bravery. — The Heroism of the Fifty-fourth Massachusetts. — Death of Col. Fribley.

THE battle of Olustee was fought in a swamp situated thirty-five miles west of Jacksonville, and four miles from Sanderson, in the State of Florida. The expedition was under the immediate command of Gen. C. Seymour, and consisted of the Seventh New Hampshire, Seventh Connecticut (armed with Spencer rifles, which fire eight times without loading), Eighth United-States (colored) Battery, Third United-States Artillery, Fifty-fourth Massachusetts (colored), and First North-Carolina (colored). The command having rested on the night of the 19th of February, 1864, at Barbour's Ford, on the St. Mary's River, took up its line of march on the morning of the 20th, and proceeded to Sanderson, nine miles to the west, which was reached at one o'clock, P.M., without interruption; but, about three miles beyond, the advance drove in the enemy's pickets. The Seventh Connecticut, being deployed as skirmishers, fell in with the enemy's force in the swamp, strengthened still more by rifle-pits. Here they were met by cannon and musketry; but our troops, with their Spencer rifles, played great havoc with the enemy, making an attempt to take one of his pieces of artillery, but

217

failed. However, they held their ground nobly foɪ three-quarters of an hour, and were just about retiring as the main body of our troops came up.

The Eighth (colored), which had never been in battle, and which had been recruited but a few weeks, came up and filed to the right, when they met with a most terrific shower of musketry and shell. Gen. Seymour now came up, and pointing in front, towards the railroad, said to Col. Fribley, commander of the Eighth, "Take your regiment in there," — a place which was sufficiently hot to make the oldest and most field-worn veterans tremble ; and yet these men, who had never heard the sound of a cannon before, rushed in where they commenced dropping like grass before the sickle : still on they went without faltering, until they came within two hundred yards of the enemy's strongest works. Here these brave men stood for nearly three hours before a terrible fire, closing up as their ranks were thinned out, fire in front, on their flank, and in the rear, without flinching or breaking.

Col. Fribley, seeing that it was impossible to hold the position, passed along the lines to tell the officers to fire, and fall back gradually, and was shot before he reached the end. He was shot in the chest, told the men to carry him to the rear, and expired in a very few minutes. Major Burritt took command, but was also wounded in a short time. At this time Capt. Hamilton's battery became endangered, and he cried out to our men for God's sake to save his battery. Our United-States flag, after three sergeants had forfeited their lives by bearing it during the fight, was planted on the battery by Lieut. Elijah Lewis, and the men rallied around it ; but the guns had been jammed up so indiscriminately, and so close to the enemy's lines, that the gunners were shot down as fast as they made their appearance; and the horses, whilst they were wheeling the pieces into position, shared the same fate. They were compelled to leave the battery, and failed to bring the flag away. The battery fell into the enemy's hands. During the excitement, Capt. Bailey took command, and brought out the regiment in good order. Sergt. Taylor, Company D, who carried the battle-flag, had his right hand nearly shot off, but grasped the colors with the left hand, and brought them out.

The Seventh New Hampshire was posted on both sides of the wagon-road, and broke, but soon rallied, and did good execution. The line was probably one mile long, and all along the fighting was terrific.

Our artillery, where it could be worked, made dreadful havoc on the enemy; whilst the enemy did us but very little injury with his, with the exception of one gun, a sixty-four pound swivel, fixed on a truck-car on the railroad, which fired grape and canister. On the whole, their artillery was very harmless; but their musketry fearful.

Up to this time, neither the First North Carolina nor the Fifty-fourth Massachusetts had taken any part in the fight, as they were in the rear some distance. However, they heard the roar of battle, and were hastening to the field, when they were met by an aide, who came riding up to the colonel of the Fifty-fourth, saying, "For God's sake, colonel, double-quick, or the day is lost!" Of all the regiments, every one seemed to look to the Fifty-fourth Massachusetts with the most dependence on the field of battle. This regiment was under the command of Col. E. N. Hallowell, who fell wounded by the side of Col. Shaw, at Fort Wagner, and who, since his recovery, had been in several engagements, in all of which he had shown himself an excellent officer, and had gained the entire confidence of his men, who were willing to follow him wherever he chose to lead. When the aide met these two regiments, he found them hastening on.

The First North Carolina was in light marching order; the Fifty-fourth Massachusetts was in heavy marching order, with knapsacks, haversacks, canteens, and every other appurtenance of the soldier. But off went every thing, and they double-quicked on to the field. At the most critical juncture, just as the rebels were preparing for a simultaneous charge along the whole line, and they had captured our artillery and turned it upon us, Col. James Montgomery, Col. Hallowell, and Lieut.-Col. Hooper formed our line of battle on right by file into line.

The Fifty-fourth Massachusetts went in first, with a cheer. They were followed by the First North Carolina (colored). Lieut.-Col. Reed, in command, headed the regiment, sword in hand, and charged upon the rebels. They broke when within twenty yards of contact with our negro troops. Overpowered by numbers, the First North Carolina fell back in good order, and poured in a destructive fire. Their colonel fell, mortally wounded. Major Bogle fell wounded, and two men were killed in trying to reach his body. The Adjutant, William C. Manning, wounded before at Malvern Hills, got a bullet in his body, but persisted in remaining until another shot struck him. His lieutenant-colonel, learning the fact, embraced him, and implored him to leave the field. The next moment the two friends were stretched side by side: the colonel had received his own death-wound. *But the two colored regiments had stood in the gap, and saved the army!* The Fifty-fourth Massachusetts, which, with the First North Carolina, may be truly said to have saved the forces from utter route, lost eighty men.

There were three color-sergeants shot down: the last one was shot three times before he relinquished the flag of his country. His name was Samuel C. Waters, Company C, and his body sleeps where he fell. The battle-flag carried by Sergt. Taylor was borne through the fight with the left hand, after the right one was nearly shot off. The rebels fired into the place where the wounded were being attended to; and their cavalry was about making a charge on it just as the Fifty-fourth Massachusetts appeared on the field, when they retired.

Had Col. Hallowell not seen at a glance the situation of affairs, the Fifty-fourth Massachusetts Volunteers would have been killed or captured. When they en tered the field with the First North Carolina, which is a brave regiment, they (the First North Carolina) fired well while they remained; but they gave way, thus exposing the right. On the left, the rebel cavalry were posted; and, as the enemy's left advanced on our right, their cavalry pressed the left. Both flanks were thus being folded up, and slaughter or capture would have been the inevitable result. We fell back in good order, and established new lines of battle, until we reached Sanderson. Here a scene that beggars description was presented. Wounded men lined the railroad station; and the roads were filled with artillery, caissons, ammunition and baggage-wagons, infantry, cavalry, and ambulances. The only organized bodies ready to repel attack were a portion of the Fortieth Massachusetts Mounted Infantry, armed with the Spencer repeating-rifle, the Fifty-fourth Massachusetts Volunteers, and the Seventh Connecticut, commanded by Col. Hawley, now governor of Connecticut.

An occurrence of thrilling interest took place during the battle, which I must not omit to mention: it was this : —

Col. Hallowell ordered the color-line to be advanced one hundred and fifty paces. Three of the colored corporals, Pease, Palmer, and Glasgow, being wounded, and the accomplished Goodin killed, there were four only left, — Wilkins the acting sergeant, Helman and Lenox. The colors were perforated with bullets, and the staff was struck near the grasp of the sergeant; but the color-guard marched steadily out, one hundred and fifty paces to the front, with heads erect and square to the front; and the battalion rallied around it, and fought such a fight as made Col. Hallowell shout with very joy, and the men themselves to ring out defiant cheers which made the pines and marshes of Ocean Pond echo again.

The attachment which the colored men form for their officers is very great, often amounting to self-sacrifice. Thus when Major Bogle fell wounded, one of his soldiers sprang forward to rescue him, and bear him to the rear. At that instant a rebel sergeant fired, and wounded the black man in the shoulder. This, however, did not force him to relinquish his purpose, but appeared to add to his determination; and he had his arms around the wounded officer, when a second ball passed through the soldier's head, and he fell and expired on the body of his superior, who was taken prisoner by the enemy.

Although these colored men had never been paid off, and their families at home were in want, they were as obedient and fought as bravely as the white troops, whose pockets contained "greenbacks," and whose wives and children were provided for.

The Fifty-fourth Massachusetts went into the battle with "Three cheers for Massachusetts, and seven dollars a month."

It is well known that the general in command came to the colonel and said, "The day is lost : you must do what you can to save the army from destruction." And nobly did they obey him. They fired their guns till their ammunition was exhausted, and then stood with fixed bayonets till the broken columns had time to retreat, and though once entirely outflanked, the enemy getting sixty yards in their rear, their undaunted front and loud cheering caused the enemy to pause, and allowed them time to change front. They occupied the position as rear guard all the way back to Jacksonville ; and, whereever was the post of danger, there was the Fifty-fourth to be found.

When the forces arrived at Jacksonville, they there learned that the train containing the wounded was at Ten-Mile Station, where it had been left, owing to the breaking down of the engine. The Fifty-fourth Massachusetts, fatigued and worn out as it was, was despatched at once, late at night, to the assistance of the disabled train. Arriving at Ten-Mile Station, they found that the only way to bring the wounded with them was to attach ropes to the cars, and let the men act as motive power. Thus the whole train of cars containing the wounded from the battle of Olustee was dragged a distance of ten miles by that brave colored regiment. All accounts give the ne-

groes great praise for gallantry displayed at this battle.
Even the correspondent of " The New-York Herald "
gives this emphatic testimony : " The First North Carolina and the Fifty-fourth Massachusetts, of the colored
troops, *did admirably.* The First North Carolina *held
the positions it was placed in with the greatest tenacity,
and inflicted heavy loss on the enemy. It was cool and
steady, and never flinched for a moment. The Fifty-
fourth sustained the reputation they had gained at Wagner, and bore themselves like soldiers throughout the battle."*

A letter from Beaufort, dated Feb. 26, from a gentleman who accompanied Gen. Seymour's expedition, has
the following passage relative to the conduct of the
Fifty-fourth in the repulse in Florida : —

" A word about the terrible defeat in Florida. We
have been driven from Lake City to within seven miles
of Jacksonville, — fifty-three miles. The rebels allowed
us to penetrate, and then, with ten to our one, cut us off,
meaning to ' bag ' us ; *and, had it not been for the glorious Fifty-fourth Massachusetts, the whole brigade would
have been captured or annihilated.* This was the only
regiment that rallied, broke the rebel ranks, and saved
us. *The Eighth United-States (colored) lost their flag
twice, and the Fifty-fourth recaptured it each time.* They
had lost, in killed and missing, about three hundred and
fifty. They would not retreat when ordered, but charged
with the most fearful desperation, driving the enemy
before them, and turning their left flank. If this regiment has not won glory enough to have shoulder-straps,
where is there one that ever did ? "

CHAPTER XXX.

BATTLE OF POISON SPRINGS, ARKANSAS.

Hard-fought Battle. — Bravery of the Kansas Colored Troops. — They die but will not yield. — Outnumbered by the Rebels. — Another severe Battle. — The heroic Negro, after being wounded, fights till he dies.

THE battle of Poison Springs, Ark., between one thousand Union and eight thousand rebel troops, was one of the most severe conflicts of the war. Six hundred of the Union forces were colored, and from Kansas, some of them having served under old John Brown during the great struggle in that territory. These black men, as it will be seen, bore the brunt of the fight, and never did men show more determined bravery than was exhibited on this occasion. They went into the battle singing the following characteristic song: —

" Old John Brown's body lies a mouldering in the grave,
While weep the sons of bondage, whom he ventured to save ;
But though he lost his life in struggling for the slave,
       His soul is marching on.
      Glory, glory, Hallelujah !
      Glory, glory, Hallelujah !
      Glory, glory, Hallelujah !
       His soul is marching on !

John Brown was a hero, undaunted, true, and brave,
And Kansas knew his valor, when he fought her rights to save ;
And now, though the grass grows green above his grave,
       His soul is marching on.

He captured Harper's Ferry with his nineteen men so few,
And he frightened ' Old Virginny ' till she trembled through and through :
They hung him for a traitor, themselves a traitor crew,
    For his soul is marching on, &c.

John Brown was John the Baptist, of the Christ we are to see, —
Christ, who of the bondman shall the Liberator be ;
And soon throughout the sunny South the slaves shall all be free,
    For his soul is marching on, &c.

The conflict that he heralded, he looks from heaven to view,
On the army of the Union, with its flag, red, white, and blue ;
And heaven shall ring with anthems o'er the deed they mean to do,
    For his soul is marching on, &c.

Ye soldiers of freedom then strike, while strike ye may,
The death-blow of oppression in a better time and way ;
For the dawn of old John Brown has brightened into day,
    And his soul is marching on.
      Glory, glory, Hallelujah !
      Glory, glory, Hallelujah !
      Glory, glory, Hallelujah !
      And his soul is marching on."

The following graphic description of the battle will be read with thrilling interest : —

"*Official Report of Major Richard G. Ward, commanding First Kansas Colored Regiment at the battle of Poison Springs.*

            " HEADQUARTERS FIRST KANSAS COLORED VOLS.,
                CAMDEN, Ark., April 20, 1864.

"*Col. J. M. Williams, commanding Escort to Forage-train.*

"COLONEL, — In conformity with the requirements of the circular issued by you, April 19, 1864, I submit the following report of the conduct of that portion of the escort which I had the honor to command, and of the part taken by them in the action of the 18th inst : —

"I marched from the camp on White-Oak Creek, with the six companies left with me as rear-guard, about seven o'clock, A.M. When I arrived at the junction of the Washington Road, I found the Eighteenth Iowa Infantry and a detachment of cavalry waiting to relieve me as rear-guard. At this moment I received your order to press forward to the front, as your advance was skirmishing with the enemy. Upon arriving, agreeably to your order, I placed one wing of this regiment on each side of the section of Rabb's Battery, to support it, and awaited further developments.

" After your cavalry had ascertained the position of the enemy's force on our right flank, and Lieut. Haines had planted one of his pieces in a favorable position, I placed Companies A, B, E, and H in position to support it. We had hardly got into position here, before our cavalry were forced back upon our line by an overwhelming force of the enemy. Lieut. Henderson, commanding detachment Sixth Kansas (than whom a braver officer never existed), was severely wounded, and I ordered Corp. Wallahan, Company M, Sixth Kansas, to form his men on my right. He had scarcely formed them, ere Lieut. Mitchell, commanding detachment Second Kansas Cavalry, was also driven in, when he was placed upon the extreme right under your personal supervision.

" The line of battle was now nearly in the form of the segment of a circle, the convex side being outward, or toward the enemy. Companies C and I being on the north side of the road facing toward the east ; Companies D and F on the south side of the road, facing in the same direction, whilst on my extreme right the men were drawn up in line facing due south. It was now about half past eleven o'clock, A.M. These dispositions were scarcely made ere the enemy opened a severe and well-directed fire from a six-gun battery, at the distance of about one thousand yards. This battery was near the road, due east of our line. At the same time a howitzer battery, reported to me as having four guns, opened on the south opposite my right, at a distance of six or seven hundred yards. Although this was much the severest artillery fire that any of the men had ever before been subjected to, and many of the men were thus under fire for the *first time*, they were as cool as veterans, and patiently awaited the onset of the enemy's infantry.

" Just after twelve o'clock, the enemy's batteries slackened their fire, and their infantry advanced to the attack. From the position of the ground, it was useless to deliver a fire until the enemy were within one hundred yards. I therefore reserved my fire until their first line was within that distance, when I gave the order to fire. For about a quarter of an hour, it seemed as though the enemy were determined to break my lines, and capture the guns ; but their attempts were fruitless, and they were compelled to fall precipitately back, not, however, before they had disabled more than half of the gunners belonging to the gun on the right.

" Again they opened their infernal cross-fires with their batteries, and through the smoke I could see them massing their infantry for another attack. I immediately applied to you for more men.

" Companies G and K were sent me. I placed Company K upon the extreme right (where the cavalry had rested, but which had now retired), and Company G upon the left of Company B. Shortly after these dispositions were made, the enemy again advanced, this time in two columns yelling like fiends. Lieut. Macy, of Company C, whom you had sent out with skirmishers from the left, was driven in; and I placed him, with his small command, between Companies G and B. At this moment, yourself and Lieut. Haines arrived on the right, and I reported to you the condition of the gun, only two men being left to man it, when you ordered it to the rear. Just as the boys were preparing to limber, a large body of the enemy was observed making for the gun in close column, whereupon private Alonzo Hendshaw, of the Second Indiana Battery, himself double-loaded the piece with canister, and poured into the advancing column a parting salute at the distance of about three hundred yards, and then limbered. The effect was terrific. Our infantry redoubled their fire, and again the massed columns sullenly retired.

" Three different times the enemy were thus repulsed; and, as they were massing for the fourth charge, I informed you that I believed it would be impossible to hold my position without more men on my right and centre. You replied that I should have them if they could be spared from other points. I held my position until you returned; when, seeing your horse fall, I gave you mine for the purpose of going to the Eighteenth Iowa to form them in a favorable position for my line to fall back upon. Agreeably to your order to hold the ground at any and all events until this could be done, I encouraged the men to renew their exertions, and repel the coming charge, intending, if I succeeded, to take that opportunity of falling back, instead of being compelled to do so under fire. My right succeeded in checking the advance; but, my left being outflanked at the same time that my left-centre was sustaining the attack of ten times their number, I ordered to fall back slowly toward

the train, changing front toward the left, to prevent the
enemy from coming up in my rear. We here made a
stand of about ten minutes, when I perceived that the
enemy had succeeded in flanking my extreme right, and
that I was placed in a position to receive a cross-fire
from their two lines. I was then compelled, in order to
save even a fragment of the gallant regiment which for
nearly two hours had, unaided, sustained itself against
Price's whole army, to order a retreat.

"Although a portion retired precipitately, the greater
portion of them kept up a continued fire the whole
length of the train. I ordered the men to retire behind
the line of the Iowa Eighteenth, and form; but, alas!
four companies had lost their gallant commanders, and
were without an officer. By your aid, and the assistance
of the few unharmed officers, I succeeded in collecting
a few of the command, and placing them on the left of
the Iowa Eighteenth. As they were slowly forced back-
ward, others took position in the line, and did all that
could be done to check the advance of the overwhelming forces of the enemy. I sent a small force to assist
Lieut. Haines in his gallant and manly efforts to save his
guns; and, had it not been for the worn condition of the
horses, I believe he would have succeeded. Accompanying this, I send the reports of company commanders
of the losses sustained by their respective companies.
It will be noticed that the heaviest punishment was inflicted upon Company G, from the fact that it was more
exposed to the galling cross-fires of the enemy.

"You will see that I went into action with about four
hundred and fifty enlisted men, and thirteen officers of
the line. Seven out of that gallant thirteen were killed
or wounded. Five are reported dead on the field: Capt.

A. J. Armstrong, Company D ; Lieut. B. Hitchcock, Company G ; Lieuts. Charles J. Coleman and Joseph B. Samuels, Company H; and Lieut. John Topping, Company B. The cheerful offering of the lives of such noble men needs not the assistance of any studied panegyric to bespeak for it that spirit of lasting admiration with which their memories will ever be enshrined.

" Four companies fought their way to the rear, without a commissioned officer. One hundred and thirteen men are killed, and sixty-nine wounded, — some of them mortally. I cannot refrain from mentioning the names of Capt. B. W. Welch, Company K, and Lieut. E. Q. Macy, Company C, both of whom were wounded, as among the number of sufferers who have earned the thanks and merit the sympathy of the loyal and generous everywhere. Any attempt to mention the names of any soldier in particular would be unjust, unless I mentioned all ; for every one, as far as I could see, did his duty coolly, nobly, and bravely. On the right, where the enemy made so many repeated attempts to break my line, I saw officers and men engaged in taking the cartridges from the bodies of the dead ; and, upon inquiring, found that their ammunition was nearly expended.

" The brave and soldier-like Topping was killed in the first charge ; and the gallant young Coleman, commanding Company H, was shot down in the second charge. At what particular period of the engagement the other officers fell, I am unable to state. To Capt. John R. Gratton, Company C ; Capt. William H. Smallwood, Company G ; Lieut. R. L. Harris, Company I : Lieut. B. G. Jones, Company A ; Lieut. John Overdier, Company E ; Lieut. S. S. Crepps, Company F ; and Adjutant William C. Gibbons, I would tender my heartfelt thanks, for the faithful, efficient, and manly performance of the most arduous duties, while subjected to the hottest fire.

"The loss in arms and clothing is quite serious; but, from the exhausted state of the men, it is strange that as many of them brought in their arms and accoutrements as did. Out of seventy-eight hours preceding the action, sixty-three hours were spent by the entire command on duty, besides a heavy picket-guard having been furnished for the remaining fifteen hours. You are also reminded that the rations were of necessity exceedingly short for more than a week previous to the battle.

"We were obliged to bring our wounded away the best we could, as the rebels were seen shooting those who fell into their hands. The men who brought in the wounded were obliged to throw away their arms; but the most who did so waited till they reached the swamps, and then sunk them in the bayous.

"I am, colonel, very respectfully,
"Your obedient servant,

"R. G. WARD,
"*Major First Kansas Colored Volunteers.*"

"Since this Report was published, official information has been received at Fort Smith, that Capt. Armstrong and Lieut. Hitchcock are prisoners of war in Arkansas, and not killed as reported.

"Yours,

"J. BOWLES,
"*Lieutenant-Colonel First Kansas Volunteers.*"

Eight days later, the same colored regiment had a fight with a superior force in numbers of the rebels; and the subjoined account of the engagement will show with what determination they fought.

"On the 29th, we skirmished in the forenoon. In the afternoon, the venturing-out of a detachment beyond the distance ordered brought on a severe though short general engagement. At least one hundred and twenty of the rebel cavalry made a charge upon this detachment of twenty-four men. Before we could bring up re-enforcements, these fearfully disproportioned parties were engaged in a desperate hand-to-hand encounter. I was on the field, doing, with the other officers, the best we could to bring up re-enforcements. There was no flinching, no hesitation, or trembling limbs among the men; but fierce determination flashing in their eyes, and exhibiting an eager, passionate haste to aid their comrades, and vindicate the manhood of their race. The air was rent with their yells, as they rushed on, and the difficulty manifested was in holding them well in rather than in faltering. Among the detachment cut off, of whom only six escaped unhurt, nothing I have ever seen, read, or heard in the annals of war, surpasses the desperate personal valor exhibited by each and every man. Bayonets came in bloody, as did the stocks of guns; and the last charge was found gone from cartridge-boxes.

"During the fight, one poor fellow received a mortal wound, but would not go to the rear. He told his officer that he could not live, but would die fighting for the flag of liberty; and continued to load and discharge his rifle until he fell dead on the field of glory.

> "The ball had crushed a vital part, —
> He could not long survive;
> But, with a brave and loyal heart,
> For victory still would strive;

His rifle 'gainst the traitor foe
　　With deadly aim would ply ;
And, till his life-blood ceased to flow,
　　Fight on for liberty.

His skin was of the ebon hue,
　　His heart was nobly brave :
To country, flag, and freedom true,
　　He would not live a slave.

His rifle flashed, — a traitor falls :
　　While death is in his eye,
He bravely to his comrades calls,
　　'Fight on for liberty !'

He looked upon his bannered sign,
　　He bowed his noble head, —
'Farewell, beloved flag of mine !'—
　　Then fell among the dead.

His comrades will remember well
　　The hero's battle-cry,
As in the arms of death he fell, —
　　'Fight on for liberty !'

And still for liberty and laws
　　His comrades will contend,
Till victory crowns the righteous cause,
　　And tyrant power shall end.

Though low in earth the martyr lies,
　　Still rings his battle-cry :
From hill to hill the echo flies, —
　　'Fight on for liberty !' "

CHAPTER XXXI.

THE MASSACRE AT FORT PILLOW.

Assault and Capture of the Fort. — "No Quarter." — Rebel Atrocities. — Gens. Forrest and Chalmers. — Firing upon Flags of Truce. — Murder of Men, Women, and Children. — Night after the Assault. — Buried Alive. — Morning after the Massacre.

NOTHING in the history of the Rebellion has equalled in inhumanity and atrocity the horrid butchery at Fort Pillow, Ky., on the 13th of April, 1864. In no other school than slavery could human beings have been trained to such readiness for cruelties like these. Accustomed to brutality and bestiality all their lives, it was easy for them to perpetrate the atrocities which will startle the civilized foreign world, as they have awakened the indignation of our own people.

We have gleaned the facts of the fight from authentic sources, and they may be relied upon as truthful. The rebels, under Forrest, appeared, and drove in the pickets about sunrise on Tuesday morning. The garrison of the fort consisted of about two hundred of the Thirteenth Tennessee Volunteers, and four hundred negro artillery, all under command of Major Booth: the gunboat "No. 7" was also in the river. The rebels first attacked the outer forts, and, in several attempts to charge, were repulsed. They were constantly re-enforced, and extended their lines to the river on both sides of the fort. The garrison in the two outer forts was at length overpowered by superior numbers, and about noon evacuated them, and retired to the fort on the river. Here the fight was maintained with great obstinacy, and continued till about four, P.M. The approach to the fort from the rear is over a gentle declivity, cleared, and fully exposed to a raking fire from two sides of the fort. About thirty yards from the fort is a deep ravine, running all along the front, and so steep at the bottom as to be hidden from the fort, and not commanded by its guns. The rebels charged with great boldness down the declivity, and faced, without blanching, a murderous fire from the guns and small-arms of the fort, and crowded into the ravine; where they were sheltered from fire by the steep bank, which had been thus left by some unaccountable neglect or ignorance. Here the rebels organized for a final charge upon the fort, after sending a flag of truce with a demand for surrender, which was refused. The approach from the ravine was up through a deep, narrow gully, and the steep embankments of the fort. The last charge was made about four, P.M., by the whole rebel force, and was successful after a most desperate and gallant defence. The rebel army was estimated at from two thousand to four thousand, and succeeded by mere force of numbers. The gunboat had not been idle, but, guided by signals from the fort, poured upon the rebels a constant stream of shot and shell. She fired two hundred and sixty shells, and, as testified to by those who could see, with marvellous precision and with fatal effect. Major Booth, who was killed near the close of the fight, conducted the defence with great coolness, skill, and gallantry. His last signal to the boat was, "We are hard pressed and shall be overpowered." He

refused to surrender, however, and fought to the last.
By the uniform and voluntary testimony of the rebel
officers, as well as the survivors of the fight, the negro-
artillery regiments fought with the bravery and coolness of veterans, and served the guns with skill and precision. They did not falter nor flinch, until, at the last
charge, when it was evident they would be overpowered, they broke, and fled toward the river; and here
commenced the most barbarous and cruel outrages that
ever the fiendishness of rebels has perpetrated during
the war.

After the rebels were in undisputed possession of the
fort, and the survivors had surrendered, they commenced the indiscriminate butchery of all the Federal
soldiery. The colored soldiers threw down their guns,
and raised their arms, in token of surrender; but not the
least attention was paid to it. They continued to shoot
down all they found. A number of them, finding no
quarter was given, ran over the bluff to the river, and
tried to conceal themselves under the bank and in the
bushes, where they were pursued by the rebel savages,
whom they implored to spare their lives. Their appeals
were made in vain; and they were all shot down in
cold blood, and, in full sight of the gunboat, chased and
shot down like dogs. In passing up the bank of the
river, fifty dead might be counted, strewed along. One
had crawled into a hollow log, and was killed in it;
another had got over the bank into the river, and had got
on a board that run out into the water. He lay on it on
his face, with his feet in the water. He lay there, when
exposed, stark and stiff. Several had tried to hide in
crevices made by the falling bank, and could not be
seen without difficulty; but they were singled out, and

killed. From the best information to be had, the white soldiers were, to a very considerable extent, treated in the same way. D. W. Harrison, one of the Thirteenth Tennessee on board, says, that, after the surrender, he was below the bluff, and one of the rebels presented a pistol to shoot him. He told him he had surrendered, and requested him not to fire. He spared him, and directed him to go up the bluff to the fort. Harrison asked him to go before him, or he would be shot by others; but he told him to go along. He started, and had not proceeded far before he met a rebel, who presented his pistol. Harrison begged him not to fire; but, paying no attention to his request, he fired, and shot him through the shoulder; and another shot him in the leg. He fell; and, while he lay unable to move, another came along, and was about to fire again, when Harrison told him he was badly wounded twice, and implored him not to fire. He asked Harrison if he had any money. He said he had a little money, and a watch. The rebel took from him his watch and ninety dollars in money, and left him. Harrison is, probably, fatally wounded. Several such cases have been related to me; and I think, to a great extent, the whites and negroes were indiscriminately murdered. The rebel Tennesseeans have about the same bitterness against Tennesseeans in the Federal army, as against the negroes. It was told by a rebel officer that Gen. Forrest shot one of his men, and cut another with his sabre, who were shooting down prisoners. It may be so; but he is responsible for the conduct of his men. Gen. Chalmers stated publicly, while on the Platte Valley, that, though he did not encourage or countenance his men in shooting down negro captives, yet it was right and justifiable.

The negro corporal, Jacob Wilson, who was picked up below Fort Pillow, had a narrow escape. He was down on the river-bank, and, seeing that no quarter was shown, stepped into the water so that he lay partly under it. A rebel coming along asked him what was the matter : he said he was badly wounded; and the rebel, after taking from his pocket all the money he had, left him. It happened to be near by a flat-boat tied to the bank, and about three o'clock in the morning. When all was quiet, Wilson crawled into it, and got three more wounded comrades also into it, and cut loose. The boat floated out into the channel, and was found ashore some miles below. The wounded negro soldiers aboard feigned themselves dead until Union soldiers came along.

The atrocities committed almost exceed belief; and, but for the fact that so many confirm the stories, we could not credit them. One man, already badly wounded, asked of a scoundrel who was firing at him, to spare his life. "No: damn you!" was the reply. "You fight with niggers!" and forthwith discharged two more balls into him. One negro was made to assist in digging a pit to bury the dead in, and was himself cast in among others, and buried. Five are known to have been buried alive : of these, two dug themselves out, and are now alive, and in the hospital. Daniel Tyler, of Company B, was shot three times, and struck on the head, knocking out his eye. After this, he was buried; but, not liking his quarters, dug out. He laughs over his adventures, and says he is one of the best "dug-outs" in the world.

Dr. Fitch says he saw twenty white soldiers paraded in line on the bank of the river; and, when in line, the rebels fired upon and killed all but one, who ran to the

river, and hid under a log, and in that condition was
fired at a number of times, and wounded.   He says that
Major Bradford also ran down to the river, and, after he
told them that he had surrendered, more than fifty shots
were fired at him.   He then jumped into the river, and
swam out a little ways, and whole volleys were fired at
him there without hitting him.   He returned to the
shore, and meeting, as the doctor supposes, some officer,
was protected ; but he heard frequent threats from the
rebels that they would kill him.

"Yesterday afternoon," says "The Cairo News" of
April 16, "we visited the United-States Hospital at
Mound City, and had an interview with the wounded
men from Fort Pillow.

"The Fort-Pillow wounded are doing much better
than could be expected from the terrible nature of their
wounds.   But one, William Jones, had died, though Adjutant Learing and Lieut. John H. Porter cannot possibly long survive.   Of the whole number, — fifty-two, —
all except two were cut or shot after they had surrendered !   They all tell the same story of the rebel bar-
barities ; and listening to a recital of the terrible scenes
at the fort makes one's blood run cold.   They say they
were able to keep the rebels at bay for several hours,
notwithstanding the immense disparity of numbers ; and,
but for their treachery in creeping up under the walls
of the fort while a truce was pending, would have held
out until 'The Olive Branch' arrived with troops, with
whose assistance they would have defeated Chalmers.

" So well were our men protected behind their works,
that our loss was very trifling before the rebels scaled
the walls, and obtained possession.   As soon as they
saw the Rebels inside the walls, the Unionists ceased

firing, knowing that further resistance was useless; but the Rebels continued firing, crying out, ' Shoot them, shoot them! Show them no quarter!'

"The Unionists, with one or two exceptions, had thrown down their arms in token of surrender, and therefore could offer no resistance. In vain they held up their hands, and begged their captors to spare their lives. But they were appealing to fiends; and the butchery continued until, out of near six hundred men who composed the garrison, but two hundred and thirty remained alive: and of this number, sixty-two were wounded, and nine died in a few hours after.

" Capt. Bradford, of the First Alabama Cavalry, was an especial object of rebel hatred, and his death was fully determined upon before the assault was made. After he had surrendered, he was basely shot; but, having his revolver still at his side, he emptied it among a crowd of rebels, bringing three of the scoundrels to the ground. The massacre was acquiesced in by most of the rebel officers, Chalmers himself expressly declaring that ' home-made Yankees and negroes should receive no quarter.'"

The following is an extract from the Report of the Committee on the Conduct of the War on the Fort-Pillow Massacre:

"It will appear from the testimony that was taken, that the atrocities committed at Fort Pillow were not the results of passion elicited by the heat of conflict, but were the results of a policy deliberately decided upon, and unhesitatingly announced. Even if the uncertainty of the fate of those officers and men belonging to colored regiments, who have heretofore been taken prisoners by the rebels, has failed to convince the authorities of our Government of this fact, the testimony herewith submitted must convince even the most sceptical, that it is the intention of the rebel authorities not to recognize the officers and men of our colored regiments as entitled to the treatment accorded by all civilized nations to prisoners of war.

"The declarations of Forrest and his officers, both before and after the capture of Fort Pillow, as testified to by such of our men as have escaped after being taken by him; the threats contained in the various demands for surrender made at Paducah, Columbus, and other places; the renewal of the massacre the morning after the capture of Fort Pillow; the statements made by the rebel officers to the officers of our gunboats who received the few survivors at Fort Pillow, — all this proves most conclusively the policy they have determined to adopt.

" It was at Fort Pillow that the brutality and cruelty of the rebels were most fearfully exhibited. The garrison there, according to the last returns received at headquarters, amounted to ten officers and five hundred and thirty-eight enlisted men, of whom two hundred and sixty-two were colored troops, comprising one battalion of the Sixteenth United-States Heavy Artillery, formerly the First Alabama Artillery of colored troops, under the command of Major L. F. Booth; one section of the Second Light Artillery (colored); and a battalion of the Thirteenth Tennessee Cavalry (white), commanded by Major A. F. Bradford. Major Booth was the ranking officer, and was in command of the fort.

" Immediately after the second flag of truce retired, the rebels made a rush from the positions they had so

treacherously gained, and obtained possession of the
fort, raising the cry of ' No quarter.'   But little opportunity was allowed for resistance.   Our troops, white
and black, threw down their arms, and sought to escape
by running down the steep bluff near the fort, and
secreting themselves behind trees and logs in the
brush, and under the brush ; some even jumping into
the river, leaving only their heads above the water.'
Then followed a scene of cruelty and murder without
parallel in civilized warfare, which needed but the toma-
hawk and scalping-knife to exceed the worst atrocities
ever committed by savages.

"The rebels commenced an indiscriminate slaughter,
sparing neither age nor sex, white nor black, soldier nor
civilian.   The officers and men seemed to vie with each
other in the devilish work.   Men, women, and children,
wherever found, were deliberately shot down, beaten,
and hacked with sabres.   Some of the children not more
than ten years old were forced to stand up by their murderers while being shot.   The sick and wounded were
butchered without mercy ; the rebels even entering the
hospital-buildings, and dragging them out to be shot, or
killing them as they lay there unable to offer the least
resistance.   All over the hillside the work of murder
was going on.   Numbers of our men were collected
together in lines or groups, and deliberately shot.   Some
were shot while in the river ; while others on the bank
were shot, and their bodies kicked into the water, many
of them still living, but unable to make exertions to
save themselves from drowning.

" Some of the rebels stood upon the top of the hill, or a
short distance from its side, and called to our soldiers to
come up to them, and, as they approached, shot them

down in cold blood; and, if their guns or pistols missed fire, forced them to stand there until they were again prepared to fire. All around were heard cries of ' No quarter, no quarter!' 'Kill the d—d niggers, shoot them down!' All who asked for mercy were answered by the most cruel taunts and sneers. Some were spared for a time, only to be murdered under circumstances of greater cruelty.

" No cruelty which the most fiendish malignity could devise was omitted by these murderers. One white soldier who was wounded in the leg so as to be unable to walk was made to stand up while his tormentors shot him. Others who were wounded, and unable to stand up, were held up and again shot. One negro who had been ordered by a rebel officer to hold his horse was killed by him when he remonstrated; another, a mere child, whom an officer had taken up behind him on his horse, was seen by Gen. Chalmers, who at once ordered him to put him down and shoot him, which was done.

" The huts and tents in which many of the wounded sought shelter were set on fire, both on that night and the next morning, while the wounded were still in them; those only escaping who were able to get themselves out, or who could prevail on others less injured to help them out: and some of these thus seeking to escape the flames were met by these ruffians, and brutally shot down, or had their brains beaten out. One man was deliberately fastened down to the floor of a tent, face upwards, by means of nails driven through his clothing and into the boards under him, so that he could not possibly escape; and then the tent was set on fire. Another was nailed to the sides of a building outside of the fort, and then the building was set on fire and burned. The charred remains of five or six bodies were afterwards found, all but one so much disfigured and consumed by the flames, that they could not be identified; and the identification of that one is not absolutely certain, although there can hardly be a doubt that it was the body of Lieut. Albertson, Quartermaster of the Thirteenth Virginia Cavalry, and a native of Tennessee. Several witnesses who saw the remains, and who were personally acquainted with him while living here, testified it to be their firm belief that it was his body that was thus treated.

" These deeds of murder and cruelty closed when night came on, only to be renewed the next morning, when the demons carefully sought among the dead lying about in all directions for any other wounded yet alive; and those they found were deliberately shot. Scores of the dead and wounded were found there the day after the massacre by the men from some of our gunboats, who were permitted to go on shore, and collect the wounded, and bury the dead.

" The rebels themselves had made a pretence of burying a great many of their victims; but they had merely thrown them, without the least regard to care or decency, in the trenches and ditches about the fort, or little hollows and ravines on the hillside, covering them but partially with earth. Portions of heads and faces were found protruding through the earth in every direction; and even when your Committee visited the spot, two weeks afterwards, although parties of men had been sent on shore from time to time to bury the bodies unburied, and re-bury the others, and were even then engaged in the same work, we found the evidences of the murder and cruelty still most painfully apparent.

" We saw bodies still unburied, at some distance from the fort, of some sick men who had been met fleeing from the hospital, and beaten down and brutally murdered, and their bodies left where they had fallen. We could still see the faces and hands and feet of men, white and black, protruding out of the ground, whose graves had not been reached by those engaged in re-interring the victims of the massacre ; and, although a great deal of rain had fallen within the preceding two weeks, the ground, more especially on the side and at the foot of the bluff where most of the murders had been committed, was still discolored by the blood of our brave but unfortunate soldiers ; and the logs and trees showed but too plainly the evidences of the atrocities perpetrated.

" Many other instances of equally atrocious cruelty might be mentioned ; but your Committee feel compelled to refrain from giving here more of the heart-sickening details, and refer to the statements contained in the voluminous testimony herewith submitted. These statements were obtained by them from eye-witnesses and sufferers. Many of them as they were examined by your Committee were lying upon beds of pain and suffering ; some so feeble that their lips could with difficulty frame the words by which they endeavored to convey some idea of the cruelties which had been inflicted on them, and which they had seen inflicted on others."

When the murderers returned, the day after the capture, to renew their fiendish work upon the wounded and dying, they found a young and beautiful mulatto woman searching among the dead for the body of her husband. She was the daughter of a wealthy and influential rebel residing at Columbus. With her husband, this woman was living near the fort when our forces oc-

cupied it, and joined the Union men to assist in holding
the place.   Going from body to body with all the earnestness with which love could inspire an affectionate heart,
she at last found the object of her search.   He was not
dead; but both legs were broken.   The wife had succeeded in getting him out from among the piles of dead,
and was bathing his face, and giving him water to drink
from a pool near by, which had been replenished by the
rain that fell a few hours before.   At this moment she
was seen by the murderous band; and the cry was at
once raised, " Kill the wench, kill her ! "   The next moment
the sharp crack of a musket was heard, and the angel
of mercy fell a corpse on the body of her wounded husband, who was soon after knocked in the head by the
butt-end of the same weapon.   Though these revolting
murders were done under the immediate eye of Gen.
Chalmers, the whole was planned and carried out by Gen.
Forrest whose inhumanity has never been surpassed in
the history of civilized or even barbarous warfare.

CHAPTER XXXII.

INJUSTICE TO COLORED TROOPS.

The Pay of the Men. — Government refuses to keep its Promise. — Efforts of Gov. Andrew to have Justice done. — Complaint of the Men. — Mutiny. — Military Murder. — Everlasting Shame.

WHEN the War Department commenced recruiting colored men as soldiers in Massachusetts, New Orleans, and Hilton Head, it was done with the promise that these men should receive the same pay, clothing, and treatment that white soldiers did. The same was promised at Camp William Penn, at Philadelphia. After several regiments had been raised and put in the field, the War Department decided to pay them but ten dollars per month, without clothing. The Fifty-fourth Massachusetts Volunteers, and the Fifty-fifth, were both in South Carolina when this decision was made; yet the Government held on to the men who had thus been obtained under false pretences. Dissatisfaction showed itself as soon as this was known among the colored troops. Still the blacks performed their duty, hoping that Congress would see that justice was done to them. The men refused to receive less than was their just due when the paymaster came round, as the following will show : —

"HILTON HEAD, S.C., Feb. 6, 1864.

"Samuel Harrison, Chaplain of the Fifty-fourth Regiment Massachusetts Volunteers (colored troops), asks pay at the usual rate of chaplains, — one hundred dollars per month and two rations, which, he being of African descent, I decline paying, under Act of Congress, July 17, 1862, which authorizes the employment of persons of African descent in the army. The chaplain declines receiving any thing less of

" TEN EYKE,
Paymaster, United-States Army."

It was left, however, for Massachusetts to take the lead, both by her governor, and by her colored soldiers in the field, to urge upon the Congress and the Administration the black man's claims. To the honor of John A. Andrew, the patriotic Chief Magistrate of the Bay State during the Rebellion, justice was demanded again and again. The following will show his feelings upon the subject : —

His Excellency Gov. Andrew, in a letter dated Executive Department, Boston, Aug. 24, and addressed to Mr. Frederick Johnson, an officer in the regiment, says, —

" I have this day received your letter of the 10th of August, and in reply desire, in the first place, to express to you the lively interest with which I have watched every step of the Fifty-fourth Regiment since it left Massachusetts, and the feelings of pride and admiration with which I have learned and read the accounts of the heroic conduct of the regiment in the attack upon Fort Wagner, when you and your brave soldiers so well proved their manhood, and showed themselves to be true soldiers of Massachusetts. As to the matter inquired about in your letter, you may rest assured that I shall not rest until you shall have secured all of your rights, and that I have no doubt whatever of ultimate success. I have no doubt, by law, you are entitled to the same pay as other soldiers; and, on the authority of the Secretary of War, I promised that you should be paid and treated in all respects like other soldiers of Massachusetts. Till this is done, I feel that my promise is dishonored by the Government. The whole difficulty arises from a misapprehension, the correction of which will no doubt be made as soon as I can get the subject fully examined by the Secretary of War.

"I have the honor to be your obedient servant,

"JOHN A. ANDREW,
"*Governor of Massachusetts.*"

The subjoined letter, from a soldier of the Fifty-fourth Massachusetts Volunteers, needs no explanation : —

"We are still anticipating the arrival of the day when the Government will do justice to the Fifty-fourth and Fifty-fifth Regiments, and pay us what is justly our due.

"We have fought like men; we have worked like men; we have been ready at every call of duty, and thus have proved ourselves to be men: but still we are refused the thirteen dollars per month.

"Oh, what a shame it is to be treated thus! Some of us have wives and little children, who are looking for succor and support from their husbands and fathers; but, alas! they look in vain. The answer to the question, 'When shall we be able to assist them?' is left wholly to the Congress of the United States.

"What will the families of those poor comrades of ours who fell at James's Island, Fort Wagner, and Olustee, do? They must suffer; for their husbands and fathers have gone the way of all the earth. They have gone to join that number that John saw, and to rest at the right hand of God.

"Our hearts pine in bitter anguish when we look back to our loved ones at home, and we are compelled to shed many a briny tear. We have offered our lives a sacrifice for a country that has not the magnanimity to treat us as men. All that we ask is the rights of other soldiers, the liberty of other free men. If we cannot have these, give us an honorable discharge from the United-States service, and we will not ask for pay.

"We came here to fight for liberty and country, and not for money (we would scorn to do that); but they promised us, if we would enlist, they would give us thirteen dollars per month.

"It was all false. They only wanted to get the halter over our heads, and then say, 'Get out if you can.'

"Sir, the Fifty-fourth and Fifty-fifth Regiments would sooner consent to fight for the whole three years, gratis, than to be put upon the footing of contrabands.

"It is not that we think ourselves any better than they; for we are not. We know that God 'hath made of one blood all nations of men for to dwell on all the face of the earth;' but we have enlisted as Massachusetts Volunteers, and we will not surrender that proud position, come what may."

Sergt. William Walker, of Company A, Third South-Carolina colored troops, feeling that he and his associates were unjustly dealt with, persuaded his company to go to their captain's tent, and stack their muskets, and refuse duty till paid. They did so, and the following was the result : —

CONDEMNED AND SHOT FOR MUTINY.

"Sergt. William Walker, of Company A, Third South-Carolina colored troops, was yesterday killed, in accordance with the sentence of a court-martial. He had declared he would no longer remain a soldier for seven dollars per month, and had brought his company to stack their arms before their captain's tent, refusing to do duty until they should be paid thirteen dollars a month, as had been agreed when they were enlisted by Col. Saxon. He was a smart soldier and an able man, dangerous as leader in a revolt. His last moments were attended by Chaplain Wilson, Twenty-fourth Massachusetts, and Chaplain Moore, of the Second South-Carolina colored troops. The execution took place at Jacksonville, Fla., in presence of the regiments there in garrison. He met his death unflinchingly. Out of eleven shots first fired, but one struck him. A reserve firing-party had been provided, and by these he was shot to death.

"The mutiny for which this man suffered death arose entirely out of the inconsistent and contradictory orders of the Paymaster and the Treasury Department at Washington." — *Beaufort (S.C.) Cor. Tribune.*

The United-States Paymaster visited the Department three times, and offered to pay laborers' wages, of ten dollars per month, to the Massachusetts Fifty-fourth and Fifty-fifth, which to a man they refused, saying, "'Tis an insult, after promising us a soldier's pay, and calling upon us to do a soldier's duty (and faithfully has it been performed), to offer us the wages of a laborer, who is

not called upon to peril his life for his country." Finding that the Government had tried to force them to take
this reduced pay, Massachusetts sent down agents to
make up the difference to them out of the State Treasury, trusting, that, ere long, the country would acknowledge them as on an equality with the rest of the army.
But, in a manner that must redound to their credit, they
refused it. Said they, " 'Tis the principle, not the money,
that we contend for: we will either be paid as soldiers,
or fight without reward." This drew down upon them
the hatred of the other colored troops (for those regiments raised in the South were promised but ten dollars,
as the Government also took care of their families), and
they had to bear much from them; but they did not
falter. Standing by their expressed determination to
have justice done them, they quietly performed their duties, only praying earnestly that every friend of theirs
at the North would help the Government to see what a
blot rests on its fair fame, — a betrayal of the trust
reposed in them by the colored race.

When they rushed forward to save our army from
being slaughtered at Olustee, it was the irrepressible
negro humor, with something more than a dash of sarcasm, that prompted the battle-cry, " Three cheers for
Old Massachusetts, and seven dollars a month!" (Three
dollars were reserved by Government for clothes.)

Another soldier, a member of the Fifty-fifth Massachusetts, complains as follows: —

" Eleven months have now passed away, and still we
are without our pay. How our families are to live and
pay house-rent I know not. Uncle Sam has long wind,
and expects as much of us as any soldiers in the field;
but, if we cannot get any pay, what have we to stimu-
late us?

"To work the way this regiment has for days, weeks, nay, months, and yet to get no money to send to our wives, children, and mothers, who are now suffering, would cause the blush of shame to mantle the cheek of a cannibal, were he our paymaster.

"But we will suffer all the days of our appointed time with patience, only let us know that we are doing some good, make manifest, too, that we are making men (and women) of our race; let us know that prejudice, the curse of the North as slavery is the curse of the South, is breaking, slowly but surely; then we will suffer more, work faster, fight harder, and stand firmer than before."

CHAPTER XXXIII.

BATTLE OF HONEY HILL, SOUTH CAROLINA.

Union Troops. — The March. — The Enemy. — The Swamp. — Earth
works. — The Battle. — Desperate Fighting. — Great Bravery. — Col.
Hartwell. — Fifty-fifth Massachusetts. — The Dying and the Dead. —
The Retreat. — The Enemy's Position. — Earthworks. — His Advan-
tages. — The Union Forces. — The Blacks. — Our Army outnumbered
by the Rebels. — Their concealed Batteries. — Skirmishing. — The
Rebels retreat to their Base. — The Battle. — Great Bravery of our
Men. — The Fifty-fifth Massachusetts saves the Army.

HONEY HILL is about two and a half miles east of the
village of Grahamville, Beaufort District. On the crest
of this, where the road or the highway strikes it, is a
semicircular line of earthworks, defective, though, in
construction, as they are too high for infantry, and have
little or no exterior slope. These works formed the
centre of the rebel lines; while their left reached up
into the pine-lands, and their right along a line of fence
that skirted the swamp below the batteries. They commanded fully the road in front as it passes through the
swamp at the base of the hill, and only some fifty or
sixty yards distant. Through the swamp runs a small
creek, which spreads up and down the roads for some
thirty or forty yards, but is quite shallow the entire distance. Some sixty yards beyond this creek, the main
road turns off to the left, making an obtuse angle; while
another and smaller road makes off to the right from the
same point.

255

The Union forces consisted of six thousand troops, artillery, cavalry, and infantry, all told, under the command of Major-Gen. J. G. Foster; Gen. John P. Hatch having the immediate command. The First Brigade, under Gen. E. E. Potter, was composed of the Fifty-sixth and One Hundred and Forty-fourth United-States, Twenty-fifth Ohio, and Thirty-fourth and Thirty-fifth United-States (colored). The Second Brigade, under Col. A. S. Hartwell, was composed of the Fifty-fourth and Fifty-fifth Massachusetts, and Twenty-sixth and Thirty-second United-States (colored). Col. E. P. Hallowell, of the Fifty-fourth Massachusetts, had, in spite of his express desire, been left behind in command of Morris and Folly Islands. As at the battle of Olustee, the enemy was met in small numbers some three or four miles from his base, and, retreating, led our army into the swamp, and up to his earthworks. So slight was the fighting as our troops approached the fort, that all the men seemed in high glee, especially the colored portion, which was making the woods ring with the following song : —

" Ho, boys, chains are breaking ;
    Bondsmen fast awaking ;
    Tyrant hearts are quaking ;
    Southward we are making.
        Huzza ! Huzza !
        Our song shall be
        Huzza ! Huzza !
        THAT WE ARE FREE !

For Liberty we fight, —
    Our own, our brother's, right :
    We'll face Oppression's blight
    In Freedom's earnest might.
        Huzza ! Huzza ! &c.

For now as men we stand
Defending Fatherland :
With willing heart and hand,
In this great cause we band.
            Huzza! Huzza! &c.

Our flag's Red, White, and Blue:
We'll bear it marching through,
With rifles swift and true,
And bayonets gleaming too.
            Huzza! Huzza! &c.

Now for the Union cheers,
            Huzza! Huzza! Huzza!
For home and loved ones tears,
For rebel foes no fears.
            Huzza! Huzza! Huzza!
And joy that conflict nears.
            Huzza! Huzza!
            Our song shall be
            Huzza! Huzza!
            THAT WE ARE FREE!

No more the driver's horn
Awakes us in the morn ;
But battle's music borne,
Our manhood shall adorn.
            Huzza! Huzza! &c.

No more for trader's gold
Shall those we love be sold ;
Nor crushed be manhood bold
In slavery's dreaded fold.
            Huzza! Huzza! &c.

But each and all be free
As singing-bird in tree,
Or winds that whistling flee
O'er mountain, vale, and sea.
            Huzza! Huzza! &c.

The Union forces approached the fort by the left road,
which brought them in front of the enemy's guns pointing

down the hill, which was also down the road.   An eye-witness of the battle gives the following account of it : —

"The Thirty-second United-States colored troops were ordered to charge the rebel fort as soon as we had got in position at the head of the road.   They attempted, but got stuck in the marsh, which they found impassable at the point of their assault ; and a galling fire of grape, canister, and musketry, being opened on them, they were forced to retire.

The Thirty-fourth United-States colored troops also essayed an assault, but could not get near enough to produce any effect upon it.   These regiments, however, only fell back to the line of battle, where they remained throughout the entire fight.

"The Fifty-fifth Massachusetts (colored) went into the fight on the right of the brigade, commanded by Col. Hartwell.   The fire became very hot; but still the regiment did not waver, — the line merely quivered.   Capt. Goraud, of Gen. Foster's staff, whose gallantry was conspicuous all day, rode up just as Col. Hartwell was wounded in the hand, and advised him to retire; but the colonel declined.

" Col. Hartwell gave the order: the colors came to the extreme front, when the colonel shouted, 'Follow your colors!' The bugle sounded the charge, and then the colonel led the way himself.

"After an unsuccessful charge in line of battle by the Fifty-fourth and Fifty-fifth Massachusetts, the Fifty-fifth was formed in column by company, and again thrice marched up that narrow causeway in the face of the enemy's batteries and musketry.

" Capt. Crane, of the Fifty-fifth Massachusetts, whose

company had been left in charge of Fort Delafield, at Folly Island, but who, at his own request, had gone as aide to Col. Hartwell, was, as well as the colonel, mounted.

"Just as they reached the marsh in front of the turn in the road, and within a short distance of the rebel works, the horse of brave Col. Hartwell, while struggling through the mud, was literally blown in pieces by a discharge of canister.

"The colonel was wounded at the same time, and attempted to jump from his horse; but the animal fell on him, pressing him into the mud. At this time, he was riding at the side of the column, and the men pressed on past; but, as they neared the fort, they met a murderous fire of grape, canister, and bullets at short range. As the numbers of the advance were thinned, the few who survived began to waver, and finally the regiment retreated.

"In retiring, Lieut. Ellsworth, and one man of the Fifty-fifth Massachusetts, came to the rescue of Col. Hartwell, and in spite of his remonstrance that they should leave him to his fate, and take care of themselves, released him from his horse, and bore him from the field. But, before he was entirely out of range of the enemy's fire, the colonel was again wounded, and the brave private soldier who was assisting was killed; and another heroic man lost.

"The Twenty-fifth Ohio, soon after the commencement of the engagement, were sent to the right, where they swung round, and fought on a line nearly perpendicular to our main front. A portion of the Fifty-fifth Massachusetts were with them. One or two charges were essayed, but were unsuccessful; but the front was maintained there throughout the afternoon. The Twenty-fifth had the largest loss of all the regiments.

" The colored troops fought well throughout the day. Countercharges were made at various times during the fight by the enemy; but our infantry and artillery mowed them down, and they did not at any time get very near our lines. Whenever a charge of our men was repulsed, the rebels would flock out of their works, whooping like Indians; but Ames's guns and the terrible volleys of our infantry would send them back. The Naval Brigade behaved splendidly.

"The Fifty-fourth Massachusetts, heroes of all the hard fights that have occurred in the department, were too much scattered in this battle to do full justice to themselves. Only two companies went into the fight at first, under Lieut.-Col. Hooper. They were posted on the left. Subsequently they were joined by four more companies, who were left on duty in the rear.

" Many scenes transpired in this battle which would furnish rich material for the artist. In the midst of the engagement, a shell exploded amongst the color-guard, severely wounding the color-sergeant, Ring, who was afterwards killed by a bullet. Private Fitzgerald, of Company D, Massachusetts Fifty-fifth, was badly wounded in the side and leg, but remained at his post. Major Nutt, seeing his condition, ordered him to the rear. The man obeyed; but soon the major saw that he had returned, when he spoke sharply, ' Go to the rear, and have your wounds dressed.' The man again obeyed the order; but in a few minutes more was seen by the major, with a handkerchief bound around the leg, and loading and firing. The major said to our informant, ' I thought I would let him stay.' "

Like the Fifty-fourth at Olustee, the Fifty-fifth was the last regiment to leave the field, and cover the retreat at Honey Hill. The following account of the battle is from "The Savannah Republican" (rebel), published a few days after the fight: —

"The negroes, as usual, formed the advance, and had nearly reached the creek, when our batteries opened upon them down the road with a terrible volley of spherical case. This threw them into temporary confusion; but the entire force, estimated at five thousand, was quickly restored to order, and thrown into a line of battle parallel with our own, up and down the margin of the swamp. Thus the battle raged from eleven in the morning till dark. The enemy's centre and left were most exposed, and suffered terribly. Their right was posted behind an old dam that ran through the swamp, and.it maintained its position till the close of the fight. Our left was very much exposed, and an attempt was once or twice made by the enemy to turn it by advancing through the swamp, and up the hill; but they were driven back without a prolonged struggle.

"The centre and left of the enemy fought with a desperate earnestness. Several attempts were made to charge our batteries, and many got nearly across the swamp, but were, in every instance, forced back by the galling fire poured into them from our lines. We made a visit to the field the day following, and found the road literally strewn with their dead. Some eight or ten bodies were floating in the water where the road crosses; and in a ditch on the roadside, just beyond, we saw six negroes piled one on top of the other. A colonel of one of the negro regiments, with his horse, was killed while fearlessly leading his men across the creek in a charge.

With that exception, all the dead and wounded officers were carried off by the enemy during the night. Many traces were left where they were dragged from the woods to the road, and thrown into ambulances or carts. We counted some sixty or seventy bodies in the space of about an acre, many of which were horribly mutilated by shells ; some with half their heads shot off, and others completely disembowelled. The artillery was served with great accuracy, and we doubt if any battle-field of the war presents such havoc among the trees and shrubbery. Immense pines and other growth were cut short off or torn into shreds."

It is only simple justice to the Fifty-fifth Massachusetts Regiment, to say, that at Honey Hill it occupied the most perilous position throughout nearly the entire battle.

Three times did these heroic men march up the hill nearly to the batteries, and as many times were swept back by the fearful storm of grape-shot and shell; more than one hundred being cut down in less than half an hour. Great was its loss; and yet it remained in the gap, while our outnumbered army was struggling with the foe on his own soil, and in the stronghold chosen by himself.

What the valiant Fifty-fourth Massachusetts had been at the battle of Olustee, the Fifty-fifth was at Honey Hill.

Never was self-sacrifice, by both officers and men, more apparent than on this occasion ; never did men look death more calmly in the face. See the undaunted and heroic Hartwell at the head of his regiment, and hear him shouting, " Follow your colors, my brave men ! " and with drawn sword leading his gallant band. His horse

is up to its knees in the heavy mud. The rider, already
wounded, is again struck by the fragment of a shell, but
keeps his seat; while the spirited animal struggling in
the mire, and plunging about, attracts the attention of the
braves, who are eagerly pressing forward to meet the enemy, to retake the lost ground, and gain a victory, or at
least save the little army from defeat.   A moment more he
is killed; and the brave Hartwell attempts to jump from
his charger, but is too weak.   The horse falls with fearful struggles upon its rider, and both are buried in the
mud.   The brave Capt. Crane, the Adjutant, is killed,
and falls from his horse near his colonel.   Lieut. Boynton,
while urging his men, is killed.   Lieut. Hill is wounded,
but still keeps his place.   Capts. Soule and Woodward
are both wounded, and yet keep their command.   The
blood is running freely from the mouth of Lieut. Jewett;
but he does not leave his company.   Sergeant-major
Trotter is wounded, but still fights.   Sergt. Shorter is
wounded in the knee, yet will not go to the rear. A shell
tears off the foot of Sergeant-major Charles L. Mitchel;
and, as he is carried to the rear, he shouts, with uplifted
hand, " Cheer up, boys: we'll never surrender ! "   But
look away in front: there are the colors, and foremost
amongst the bearers is Robert M. King, the young, the
handsome, and the gentlemanly sergeant, whose youth
and bravery attract the attention of all.   Scarcely more
than twenty years of age, well educated, he has left a
good home in Ohio to follow the fortunes of war, and to
give his life to help redeem his race.   The enemy train
their guns upon the colors, the roar of cannon and crack‘
of rifle is heard, the advanced flag falls, the heroic King
is killed : no, he is not dead, but only wounded.   A fellow sergeant seizes the colors; but the bearer will not

give them up. He rises, holds the old flag aloft with
one hand, and presses the other upon the wound in his
side to stop the blood. " Advance the colors ! " shouts
the commander. The brave King, though saturated with
his own blood, is the first to obey the order. As he
goes forward, a bullet passes through his heart, and he
falls. Another snatches the colors ; but they are fast, the
grasp of death holds them tight. The hand is at last
forced open, the flag is raised to the breeze ; and the
lifeless body of Robert M. King is borne from the field.
This is but a truthful sketch of the part played by one
heroic son of Africa, whose death was lamented by all
who knew him.   This is only one of the two hundred and
forty-nine that fell on the field of Honey Hill. With a
sad heart, we turn away from the picture.

But shall we weep for the sleeping braves, who, turning their backs upon the alluring charms of home-life,
went forth at the call of country and race, and died, noble
martyrs to the cause of liberty ? 'Tis noble to *live* for
freedom ; but is it not nobler far to *die* that those coming
after you may enjoy it ?

> " Dear is the spot where Christians weep ;
>   Sweet are the strains which angels pour :
> Oh ! why should we in anguish weep ?
>   They are not lost, but gone before."

CHAPTER XXXIV.

BEFORE PETERSBURG AND RICHMOND.

Assault and Failure. — Who to Blame. — Heroic Conduct of the Blacks.
— The Mine. — Success at the Second Attack. — Death of a Gallant
Negro. — A Black Officer.

WHEN the mining assault on Petersburg failed, with
such fearful loss in killed and wounded, the cry went
through the land that it was owing to the cowardice of the negro troops; but this falsehood was very
soon exploded. However, it will be well to state the
facts connected with the attempt. A writer in "The
New-York Evening Post" gave the following account
of the preparation, attack, and failure, a few days after
it occurred: —

"We have been continually notified for the last fort-
night, that our sappers were mining the enemy's position. As soon as ready, our division was to storm the
works on its explosion. This rumor had spread so wide,
we had no faith in it. On the night of the 29th, we
were in a position on the extreme left. We were drawn
in about nine, P.M., and marched to Gen. Burnside's
headquarters, and closed in mass by division, left in
front. We there received official notice that the long-
looked-for mine was ready charged, and would be fired
at daylight next morning. The plan of storming was
as follows: One division of white troops was to charge
the works immediately after the explosion, and carry

the first and second lines of rebel intrenchments. Our division was to follow immediately, and push right into Petersburg, take the city, and be supported by the remainder of the Ninth and the Twenty-eighth corps. We were up bright and early, ready and eager for the struggle to commence. I had been wishing for something of this sort to do for some time, to gain the respect of the Army of the Potomac. You know their former prejudices. At thirty minutes after five, the ball opened. The mine, with some fifty pieces of artillery, went off almost instantaneously: at the same time, the white troops, according to the plan, charged the fort, which they carried, for there was nothing to oppose them; but they did not succeed in carrying either of the lines of intrenchments.

"We were held in rear until the development of the movement of the white troops; but, on seeing the disaster which was about to occur, we were pushed in by the flank (for we could go in in no other way to allow us to get in position): so you see on this failure we had nothing to do but gain by the flank. A charge in that manner has never proved successful, to my knowledge: when it does, it is a surprise.

"Our men went forward with enthusiasm equal to any thing under different circumstances; but, in going through the fort that had been blown up, the passage was almost impeded by obstacles thrown up by the explosion. At the same time, we were receiving a most deadly cross-fire from both flanks. At this time, our lieutenant-colonel (E. W. Ross) fell, shot through the left leg, bravely leading the men. I immediately assumed command, but only to hold it a few minutes, when I fell, struck by a piece of shell in the side.

Capt. Robinson, from Connecticut, then took command; and, from all we can learn, he was killed. At this time, our first charge was somewhat checked, and the men sought cover in the works. Again our charge was made, but, like the former, unsuccessful. This was followed by the enemy making a charge. Seeing the unorganized condition and the great loss of officers, the men fell back to our own works. Yet a large number still held the fort until two, P.M.; when the enemy charged again, and carried it. That ended the great attempt to take Petersburg.

"It will be thus seen that the colored troops did not compose the first assaulting, but the supporting column; and they were not ordered forward until white troops in greater numbers had made a desperate effort to carry the rebel works, and had failed. Then the colored troops were sent in; moved over the broken ground, and up the slope, and within a short distance of the parapet, in order, and with steady courage; but finally broke and retreated under the same fire which just before had sent a whole division of white regiments to the right-about. If there be any disgrace in that, it does not belong exclusively nor mainly to the negroes. A second attack is far more perilous and unlikely to succeed than a first; the enemy having been encouraged by the failure of the first, and had time to concentrate his forces. And, in this case, there seems to have been a fatal delay in ordering both the first and second assault."

An officer in the same engagement said, —

"In regard to the bravery of the colored troops, although I have been in upwards of twenty battles, I never saw so many cases of gallantry. The 'crater,' where we were halted, was a perfect slaughter-pen.

Had not 'some one blundered,' but moved us up at
daylight, instead of eight o'clock, we should have been
crowned with success, instead of being cut to pieces by
a terrific enfilading fire, and finally forced from the field
in a panic. We had no trouble in rallying the troops,
and moving them into the rifle-pits ; and, in one hour
after the rout, I had nearly as many men together as
were left unhurt.

"I was never under such a terrific fire, and can
hardly realize how any escaped alive. Our loss was
heavy. In the Twenty-eighth (colored), for instance,
commanded by Lieut.-Col. Russell (a Bostonian), he lost
seven officers out of eleven, and ninety-one men out of
two hundred and twenty-four ; and the colonel himself
was knocked over senseless, for a few minutes, by a
slight wound in the head : both his color-sergeants and
all his color-guard were killed. Col Bross, of the Twenty-ninth, was killed outright, and nearly every one of
his officers hit. This was nearly equal to Bunker Hill.
Col. Ross, of the Thirty-first, lost his leg. The Twenty-eighth, Twenty-ninth, and Thirtieth (colored), all
charged over the works ; climbing up an earthwork six
feet high, then down into a ditch, and up on the other
side, all the time under the severest fire in front and
flank. Not being supported, of course the storming-
party fell back. I have seen white troops run faster
than these blacks did, when in not half so tight a
place. Our brigade lost thirty-six prisoners, all cut off
after leaving the 'crater.' My faith in colored troops
is not abated one jot."

Soon after the failure at Petersburg, the colored
troops had a fair opportunity, and nobly sustained their
reputation gained on other fields. At the battle of New-

Market Heights, Va., the Tenth Army Corps, under Major-Gen. Birney, met a superior number of the enemy, and had a four-hours' fight, Sept. 29, in which our men came off victorious. The following order, issued on the 8th of October, needs no explanation : —

"HEADQUARTERS, 3D DIVISION, 18TH ARMY CORPS,
Before Richmond, Va., Oct. 7, 1864.

"GENERAL ORDERS No. 103.

" OFFICERS AND SOLDIERS OF THIS DIVISION, — Major-Gen. D. B. Birney, commanding the Tenth Army Corps, has desired me to express to you the high satisfaction he felt at your good conduct while we were serving with the Tenth Corps, Sept. 29 and 30, 1864, and with your gallantry in storming New-Market Heights.

" I have delayed issuing this order, hoping for an opportunity to say this to you in person.

" Accept, also, my own thanks for your gallantry on Sept. 29, and your good conduct since. You have won the good opinion of the whole Army of the James, and every one who knows your deeds.

" Let every officer and man, on all occasions, exert himself to increase your present deserved reputation.

" C. J. PAINE, *Brigadier-General.*

"(Signed)   S. A. CARTER, *A. A.G.*"

"HEADQUARTERS TENTH ARMY CORPS,
Aug. 19, 1864.

" *Major-Gen. Butler commanding Department.*

" The enemy attacked my lines in heavy force last night, and were repulsed with great loss. In front of one colored regiment, eighty-two dead bodies of the enemy are already counted. The colored troops behaved handsomely, and are in fine spirits. The assault was in columns a division strong, and would have carried any works not so well defended.   The enemy's loss was at least one thousand.

    " (Signed)   Respectfully,

                " D. B. BIRNEY, *Major-General.*"

    " Seventy-five of our Black Virginia Cavalry were surrounded by three regiments of rebel infantry, and gallantly cut through them ; and an orderly-sergeant killed with his sabre six of the enemy, and escaped with the loss of an arm by grape-shot.   He lies in an adjoining room, and is slowly recovering."

> " Brave man, thy deeds shall fill the trump of fame,
>   And wake responsive echoes far and wide,
> And on contemners of thy race cast shame ;
>   For thou hast nobly with the noblest vied.
>
> Thy deeds recall the charge at Balaklava,
>   Wherein six hundred were immortalized :
> Not any hero of that charge was braver ;
>   And thy great valor shall be recognized.
>
> No wolf, pursued by hounds o'er hill and plain,
>   At last more savagely stands up at bay,
> Finding past efforts to escape all vain,
>   Then cleaves through dying hounds his bloody way.
>
> Thine was the task, amid war's wild alarm,
>   The valor of thy race to vindicate :
> Now admiration all true bosoms warm,
>   And places thee among the gallant great.
>
> It thrills our hearts to think upon the strife
>   In which, surrounded by the rebel host,
> Thou didst deal death for liberty and life,
>   And freedom win, although an arm was lost.
>
> O lion-hearted hero ! whose fierce sword
>   Made breathless thy oppressors, bravely bear
> Thy sufferings ; for our sympathies are poured
>   For thee, and gladly would relieve or share."

At the second attack on Petersburg, the colored troops did nobly. A correspondent of " The New-York Times " wrote as follows : —

" As everybody seems to have negro on the brain in the army, I may be pardoned for again alluding to the colored troops in this letter. A single day's work has wiped out a mountain of prejudice, and fairly turned the popular current of feeling in this army in favor of the down-trodden race ; and every one who has been with them on the field has some story to relate of their gallant conduct in action, or their humanity and social qualities. The capture of the fort before referred to is related, among other things, in evidence of their manhood and gallantry ; taking prisoners in the exciting moment of actual hand-to-hand fighting, in face of the Fort-Pillow and other similar rebel atrocities perpetrated elsewhere, upon their colored companions-in-arms as evidence of their humanity, — that they are really something more than the stolid brutes, such as some people profess to believe. But, next to bravery, one impromptu act of theirs has done more than all else to remove a supposed natural prejudice against them. Wounded officers of two different brigades in the Second Corps tell me, that, when they relieved the colored troops in front Wednesday night, their men had been out of rations all day, and were very hungry, as may well be supposed. When this fact became known to the negroes, to use the expressive language of a wounded officer, ' They emptied their haversacks, and gave the contents to our boys.' The colored troops, I have had opportunity to know, bear their honors meekly, as become men. Hereafter, the vile oath and offensive epithet will not be blurted out against the negro soldier, and in his presence, upon every favorable opportunity, as has too generally heretofore been the practice. This will be exclusively confined to the professional stragglers, who are never at the front when danger is there."

Sergt. Peter Hawkins, of the Thirty-first United-States, exhibited in the attack upon Petersburg marked abilities as a soldier. All the officers of Company A being killed or wounded, he took command, and held it for fourteen days. An eye-witness said, —

"He appointed men for guard and picket duty, made out his regular morning report, issued rations, drilled his men, took them out on dress-parade, or on fatigue-duty. Whatever important duty was devolved upon him, he was the man to perform without murmuring. He is fully competent to fill the office of a lieutenant or captain. He has clearly proven on the field his unflinching courage and indomitable will."

CHAPTER XXXV.

WIT AND HUMOR OF THE WAR.

Negro Wit and Humor. — The Faithful Sentinel. — The Sentinel's Respect for the United-States Uniform. — The " Nail-kag." — The Poetical Drummer-boy. — Contrabands on Sherman's March. — Negro Poetry on Freedom. — The Soldier's Speech. — Contraband capturing his Old Master.

WITH all the horrors of the Rebellion, there were occasions when these trying scenes were relieved by some amusing incident. Especially was this true with regard to the colored people. Thus when Adjutant-Gen. Thomas first announced the new policy in Mississippi, and they began enlisting freedmen, one was put on guard at night, at Lake Providence, and was instructed not to allow any one to pass without the countersign. He was, however, told not to fire upon a person until he had called out, " One, two, three." The negro seemed not to understand it, and asked to have the instructions repeated. " You are to walk from here to that tree, and back," continued the white sergeant, " and, if you see or hear any one, call out, ' Who comes there? Give the countersign. One, two, three.' And, if you receive no reply, shoot." — " Yes, massa," said Sam. " I got it dis time, and no mistake." After an hour or more on duty, Sam thought he heard the tramp of feet, and began a sharp lookout. Presently bringing his gun to his shoulder, and taking sight, he called out in quick succession, " Who comes dar? Give de countersign. One, two, three !" And " bang " went the gun. Fortunately, the negro's aim was not as reliable as was his determination to do his whole duty ; and the only damage done was a bullet-hole through the intruder's hat. When admonished by the officer for not waiting for the man's answer, the negro said, "Why, massa, I was afraid dat ef I didn't shoot quick, he'd run."

A colored sentinel was marching on his beat in the streets of Norfolk, Va., when a white man, passing by, shouldered him insolently off the sidewalk, quite into the street. The soldier, on recovering himself, called out, —

"White man, halt ! "

The white man, Southerner like, went straight on. The sentinel brought his musket to a ready, cocked it, and hailed again, —

"White man, HALT, or I'll fire ! "

The white man, hearing *shoot* in the tone, halted, and faced about.

"White man," continued the sentry peremptorily, " come here ! "

He did so.

"White man," said the soldier again, " me no care one cent 'bout this particklar Cuffee ; but white man bound to respeck this uniform (striking his breast). White man, move on ! "

A Virginia rebel, who has issued a book giving his experience as a prisoner in the hands of the Federals at Point Lookout and Elmira, tells the following story : —

" The boys are laughing at the summons which S., one of my fellow-Petersburgers, got to-day from a negro sentinel. S. had on when captured, and I suppose still possesses, a tall beaver of the antique pattern considered inseparable from extreme respectability in the last dec-

ade and for many a year before. While wandering
around the enclosure, seeking, I suspect, ' what he might
devour,' he accidentally stepped beyond the ' dead line,'
and was suddenly arrested by a summons from the nearest negro on the parapet, who seemed to be in doubt
whether so well-dressed a man could be a ' reb,' and
therefore whether he should be shot at once.

" White man, you b'long in dar ? "

" Yes."

" Well, ain't you got no better sense dan to cross dat
line ? "

" I did not notice the line."

" Well, you had better notice it, and dat quick, or I'll
blow half dat *nail-kag* off ! "

The following doggerel was composed by a drummer-
boy, aged thirteen, who had been a slave, and was without education. He sung it to the One Hundred and
Seventh Regiment United-States colored troops, to which
he was attached : —

> " Captain Fiddler's come to town
>   With his abolition triggers :
> He swears he's one of Lincoln's men,
>   ' Enlisting all the niggers.'
>
> You'll see the citizens on the street
>   Whispering in rotation :
> What do they seem to talk about ?
>   Lincoln's proclamation.
>
> Some get sick, and some will die,
>   Be buried in rotation :
> What was the death of such a man ?
>   Lincoln's proclamation.
>
> You'll see the rebels on the street,
>   Their noses like a bee gum ;
> I don't care what in thunder they say,
>   I'm fighting for my freedom !

Richmond is a mighty place,
  And Grant's as sound as a dollar;
And every time he throws a shell,
  Jeff begins to holler.

My old massa's come to town,
  Cutting a Southern figure:
What's the matter with the man?
  Lincoln's got his niggers.

Some folks say this ' almighty fuss
  Is getting worse and bigger ; '
Some folks say ' it's worse and worse,'
  Because I am ' a nigger.'

We'll get our colored regiments strung
  Out in a line of battle :
I'll bet my money agin the South
  The rebels will skedaddle."

In his march, Gen. Sherman was followed by large numbers of contrabands. They were always the first to welcome our troops. On entering Fayetteville, the general was met by slaves, old and young; and a man of many years exclaimed, —·

"Tank de Almighty God, Mr. Sherman has come at last! We knew it, we prayed for de day, and de Lord Jesus heard our prayers. Mr. Sherman has come wid his company."

One fat old woman said to him, while shaking him by the hand, which he always gladly gives to those poor people, " I prayed dis long time for yer, and de blessing ob de Lord is on yer. But yesterday afternoon, when yer stopped trowing de shells into de town, and de soldiers run away from de hill ober dar, I thout dat Gen. Burygar had driven you away, for dey said so ; but here yer am dun gone. Bress de Lord, yer will hab a place in heaben : yer will go dar sure."

Several officers of the army, among them Gen. Slocum, were gathered round, interested in the scene. The general asked them : —

" Well, men, what can I do for you? Where are you from ? "

" We's jus come from Cheraw. Massa took us with him to carry mules and horses away from youins."

" You thought we would get them. Did you wish us to get the mules ? "

" Oh, yes, massa! dat's what I wanted. We knowed youins cumin', and I wanted you to hav dem mules ; but no use: dey heard dat youins on de road, and nuthin' would stop dem. Why, as we cum along, de cavalry run away from the Yanks as if they fright to deth. Dey jumped into de river, and some of dem lost dere hosses. Dey frightened at the very name ob Sherman."

Some one at this point said, " That is Gen. Serman who is talking to you."

" God bress me ! is you Mr. Sherman ? "

" Yes : I am Mr. Sherman."

" Dats him, su' nuff," said one.

" Is dat de great Mr. Sherman that we's heard ob so long ? " said another.

" Why, dey so frightened at your berry name, dat dey run right away," shouted a third.

" It is not me that they are afraid of," said the general: " the name of another man would have the same effect with them if he had this army. It is these soldiers that they run away from."

" Oh, no ! " they all exclaimed. " It's de name of Sherman, su' ; and we hab wanted to see you so long while you trabbel all roun jis whar you like to go. Dey said dat dey wanted to git you a little furder on, and den dey

whip all your soldiers ; but, God bress me, you keep
cumin' and a cumin' and dey allers git out."

"Dey mighty 'fraid ob you, sar ; day say you kill de
colored men, too," said an old man, who had not heretofore taken part in the conversation.

With much earnestness, Gen. Sherman replied, —

"Old man, and all of you, understand me. I desire
that bad men should fear me, and the enemies of the
Government which we are all fighting for. Now we are
your friends ; you are now free." ("Thank you, Massa
Sherman," was ejaculated by the group.) "You can go
where you please ; you can come with us, or go home to
your children. Wherever you go, you are no longer
slaves. You ought to be able to take care of yourselves."
("We is ; we will.") "You must earn your freedom,
then you will be entitled to it, sure ; you have a right to
be all that you can be, but you must be industrious, and
earn the right to be men. If you go back to your families, and I tell you again you can go with us if you wish,
you must do the best you can. When you get a chance,
go to Beaufort or Charleston, where you will have a
little farm to work for yourselves."

The poor negroes were filled with gratitude and hope
by these kind words, uttered in the kindest manner, and
they went away with thanks and blessings on their
lips.

During the skirmishing, one of our men who, by the
way, was a forager, was slightly wounded. The most serious accident of the day occurred to a negro woman,
who was in a house where the rebels had taken cover.
When I saw this woman, who would not have been selected as a type of South-Carolina female beauty, the
blood was streaming over her neck and bosom from a

wound in the lobe of her ear, which the bullet had just clipped and passed on.

" What was it that struck you, aunty ? " I asked her.

"Lor bress me, massa, I dun know, I jus fell right down."

" Didn't you feel any thing, nor hear any sound ? "

" Yes, now I 'member, I heerd a s-z-z-z-z, and den I jus knock down. I drap on de groun'. I'se so glad I not dead, for if I died den de bad man would git me, cos 1 dance lately a heap."

A contraband's poetical version of the President's Emancipation Proclamation.

> " I'se gwine to tell ye, Sambo,
> What I heard in town to-day, —
> I listened at the cap'n's tent:
> I'll tell ye what he say.
>
> He say dat Massa Linkum,
> Way yonder Norf, ye see, —
> Him write it in de Yankee book,
> ' De nigger gwine for free.'
>
> And now, ye see, I tell ye
> What Massa Linkum done :
> De secesh can't get way from dat
> No more'n dey dodge a gun.
>
> It's jes' as sure as preachin',
> I tell ye, Sambo, true, —
> De nigger's trouble ober now,
> No more dem lash for you.
>
> I 'spected dat would happen :
> I had a sense, ye see,
> Of something big been gwine to come
> To make de people free.
>
> I t'ought de flamin' angel
> Been gwine for blow de trump ;
> But Massa Linkum write de word
> Dat make de rebel jump.

So now we'll pick de cotton,
So now we'll broke de corn :
De nigger's body am his own
De bery day he born.

He grind de grits in safety,
He eat de yams in peace ;
De Lord, him bring de jubilee,
De Lord, him set de feas'.

So now, I tell ye, Sambo,
Ye're born a man to-day :
Nobody gwine for contradic'
What Massa Linkum say.

Him gwine for free de nigger :
De Lord, him gib de word ;
And Massa Linkum write 'em down,
O Sambo ! praise de Lord ! "

When the teachers were introduced into Jackson, Miss., soon after the Union forces occupied the place, they found some very ignorant material to work upon. One old woman, while attending the Sabbath school, being asked who made her, replied, "I don't know, 'zacly, sir. I heard once who it was ; but I done forgot de gentmun's name." The teacher thought that the Lord's name had been rather a stranger in that neighborhood. During the siege of Port Hudson, a new schoolhouse was erected for the black soldiers who had been enlisted in that vicinity ; and, when it was opened, the following speech was made by a colored soldier, called Sergt. Spencer : —

"I has been a-thinkin' I was old man ; for, on de plantation, I was put down wid de old hands, and I quinsicontly feeled myself dat I was a old man. But since I has come here to de Yankees, and been made a soldier for de Unite States, an' got dese beautiful clothes on,

I feels like one young man; and I doesn't call myself a old man nebber no more. An' I feels dis ebenin' dat, if de rebs came down here to dis old Fort Hudson, dat I could jus fight um as brave as any man what is in the Sebenth Regiment. Sometimes I has mighty feelins in dis ole heart of mine, when I considers how dese ere ossifers come all de way from de North to fight in de cause what we is fighten fur. How many ossifers has died, and how many white soldiers has died, in dis great and glorious war what we is in! And now I feels dat, fore I would turn coward away from dese ossifers, I feels dat I could drink my own blood, and be pierced through wid five thousand bullets. I feels sometimes as doe I ought to tank Massa Linkern for dis blessin' what we has; but again I comes to de solemn conclusion dat I ought to tank de Lord, Massa Linkern, and all dese ossifers. 'Fore I would be a slave 'gain, I would fight till de last drop of blood was gone. I has 'cluded to fight for my liberty, and for dis eddication what we is now to receive in dis beautiful new house what we has. Aldo I hasn't got any eddication nor no book-learnin', I has rose up dis blessed ebenin' to do my best afore dis congregation. Dat's all what I has to say now; but, at some future occasion, I may say more dan I has to say now, and edify you all when I has more preparation. Dat's all what I has to say. Amen."

After the fall of Port Hudson, Sergt. Spencer was sent with his company into the interior; and, while in a skirmish, he captured his old master, who was marched off by the chattel to headquarters, distant about six miles. The master, not liking the long walk and his heavy gun, began upbraiding his slave for capturing him, and, complaining of his misfortune, stopped, laid down his gun, seated himself on an old log, lighted his pipe, and said he could walk no farther.

However, old Spencer soon told the prisoner a different tale. Waiting a reasonable time for resting, the sergeant said, " Come, boss, you's smoked enough dar : come, I is in a hurry. I can't wait no longer." The rebel still remonstrated with his slave, reminding him of what he once was, and the possibility of his being again in his power. But these admonitions made little or no impression on the sergeant, who resumed, " Come, boss, come : dis is no time to tell 'bout what you's been or what you's gwine to be. Jes git right up and come long, or I'll stick dis bayonet in you."—" Well, Spencer," said the master, " you carry my gun."—" No, boss ; you muss tote your own gun. I is bin toting you an' all your chilen des forty years, and now de times is changed. Come, now, git up an move on, or I'll stick you wid dis bayonet " (at the same time drawing the bayonet from its scabbard). " Massa reb " shouldered his unloaded shooter, and reluctantly continued his journey.

CHAPTER XXXVI.[1]

A THRILLING INCIDENT OF THE WAR.

Heroic Escape of a Slave. — His Story of his Sister. — Resides North. —
Joins the Army and returns to the South during the Rebellion. —
Search for his Mother. — Finds her. — Thrilling Scene. — Truth
stranger than Fiction.

IT was in the month of December, 1832, while Col.
Rice and family were seated around a bright wood-fire,
whose blaze lighted up the large dining-room in their
old mansion, situated ten miles from Drayton, in the State
of Ohio, that they heard a knock at the door, which was
answered by the familiar " Come in," that always greets
the stranger in the Western States. Squire Loomis
walked in, and took a seat in one of the three rocking-
chairs which had been made vacant by the young folks,
who rose to give place to their highly influential and
wealthy neighbor. It was a beautiful night : the sky
was clear, the wind had hushed its deep moanings. The
most brilliant of the starry throng stood out in bold relief, despite the superior light of the moon. " I see
some one standing at the gate," said Mrs. Rice, as she
left the window, and came nearer the fire. " I'll go
out and see who it is," exclaimed George, as he quitted
his chair, and started for the door. The latter soon
returned, and whispered to his father ; and both left the
room, evincing that something unusual was at hand.
Not many minutes elapsed, however, before the father
and son entered, accompanied by a young man, whose

complexion showed plainly that other than Anglo-Saxon blood coursed through his veins. The whole company rose, and the stranger was invited to draw near to the fire. Question after question was now pressed upon the new-comer by the colonel and squire, but without eliciting satisfactory replies. " You need not be afraid, my friend," said his host, as he looked intently in the colored man's face, " to tell where you are from, and to what place you are going. If you are a fugitive, as I suspect, give us your story, and we will protect and defend you to the last." Taking courage from these kind remarks, the mulatto said, " I was born, sir, in the State of Kentucky, and raised in Missouri. My master was my father : my mother was his slave. That, sir, accounts for the fairness of my complexion. As soon as I was old enough to labor, I was taken into my master's dwelling as a servant, to attend upon the family. My mistress, aware of my near relationship to her husband, felt humiliated ; and often, in her anger, would punish me severely for no cause whatever. My near approach to the Anglo-Saxon aroused the jealousy and hatred of the overseer ; and he flogged me, as he said, to make me know my place. My fellow-slaves hated me because I was whiter than themselves. Thus my complexion was construed into a crime, and I was made to curse my father for the Anglo-Saxon blood that courses through my veins.

" My master raised slaves to supply the Southern market ; and every year some of my companions were sold to the slave-traders, and taken farther South. Husbands were separated from wives, and children torn from the arms of their agonized mothers. These outrages were committed by the man whom nature compelled me to look upon as my father. My mother and brothers were sold, and taken away from me: still I bore all, and made no attempt to escape; for I yet had near me an only sister, whom I dearly loved. At last the negro-driver attempted to rob my sister of her virtue. She appealed to me for protection. Her innocence, beauty, and tears were enough to stir the stoutest heart. My own, filled with grief and indignation, swelled within me as though it would burst, or leap from my bosom. My tears refused to flow: the fever in my brain dried them up. I could stand it no longer. I seized the wretch by the throat, and hurled him to the ground; and, with this strong arm, I paid him for old and new. The next day I was tried by a jury of slaveholders for the crime of having within me the heart of a man, and protecting my sister from the licentious embrace of a libertine. And, would you believe it, sir? that jury of enlightened Americans, — yes, sir, Christian Americans, — after grave deliberation, decided that I had broken the laws, and sentenced me to receive five hundred lashes upon my bare back. But, sir, I escaped from them the night before I was to have been flogged. Afraid of being arrested and taken back, I remained the following day hid away in a secluded spot on the banks of the Mississippi River, protected from the gaze of man by the large trees and thick canebrakes that sheltered me. I waited for the coming of another night. All was silent around me save the sweet chant of the feathered songsters in the forest, or the musical ripple of the eddying waters at my feet. I watched the majestic bluffs as they gradually faded away through the gray twilight from the face of day into the darker shades of night. I then turned to the rising moon as it peered above, ascending the deep-blue ether, high in the heavens, casting its mellow rays over the surrounding landscape, and gilding the smooth surface of the noble river with its silvery hue. I viewed with interest the stars as they appeared one after another in the firmament. It was then and there that I studied nature in its lonely grandeur, and saw in it the goodness of God, and felt that he who created so much beauty, and permitted the fowls of the air and beasts of the field to roam at large, and be free, never intended that man should be the slave of his fellow-man. I resolved that I would be a bondman no longer; and, taking for my guide the *north star*, I started for Canada, the negro's land of liberty. For many weeks, I travelled by night, and lay by during the day. Oh! how often, while hid away in the forest, waiting for nightfall, have I thought of the beautiful lines I once heard a stranger recite! —

> " ' Oh hail, Columbia! happy land, —
>   The cradle-land of liberty!
> Where none but negroes bear the brand,
>   Or feel the lash, of slavery.
>
> Then let the glorious anthem peal,
>   And drown " Britannia rules the waves : "
> Strike up the song that men can feel, —
>   " Columbia rules four million slaves ! " '

" At last I arrived at a depot of the underground railroad, took the *express* train, and here I am." — " You are welcome," said Col. Rice, as he rose from his chair, walked to the window, and looked out, as if apprehensive that the fugitive's pursuers were near by. " You are welcome," continued he; " and I will aid you on your way to Canada, for you are not safe here."

" Are you not afraid of breaking the laws by assisting
this man to escape?" remarked Squire Loomis. " I care
not for laws when they stand in the way of humanity,"
replied the colonel. " If you aid him in reaching Canada, and we should ever have a war with England, may-
be he'll take up arms, and fight against his own country,"
said the squire. The fugitive eyed the law-abiding
man attentively for a moment, and then exclaimed,
" Take up arms against my country? What country,
sir, have I? The Supreme Court of the United States,
and the laws of the South, doom me to be the slave of
another. There is not a foot of soil over which the *stars
and stripes* wave, where I can stand, and be protected
by law. I've seen my mother sold in the cattle-market :
I looked upon my brothers as they were driven away in
chains by the slave-speculator. The heavy negro-whip
has been applied to my own shoulders, until its biting
lash sunk deep into my quivering flesh. Still, sir, you
call this my country. True, true, I was born in this
land. My grandfather fought in the Revolutionary War :
my own father was in the war of 1812. Still, sir, I am
a slave, a chattel, a thing, a piece of property. I've
been sold in the market with horses and swine. The
initials of my master's name are branded on this arm.
Still, sir, you call this my country. And, now that I am
making my escape, you feel afraid if I reach Canada,
and there should be war with England, that I will take
up arms against my country. Sir, I have no country
but the grave ; and I'll seek freedom there before I
will be taken back to slavery. There is no justice for
me at the South: every right of my race is trampled in
the dust, until humanity bleeds at every pore. I am
bound for Canada, and woe to him that shall attempt to

arrest me! If it comes to the worst, I will die fighting for freedom."—" I honor your courage," exclaimed Squire Loomis, as he sprang from his seat, and walked rapidly to and fro the room. "It is too bad," continued he, "that such men should be enslaved in a land whose Declaration of Independence proclaims all men to be free and equal. I will aid you in any thing that I can. What is your name?"—" I have no name," said the fugitive. "I once had a name,—it was William,—but my master's nephew came to live with him; and as I was a house-servant, and the young master and I would, at times, get confused in the same name, orders were given for me to change mine. From that moment, I resolved, that, as slavery had robbed me of my liberty and my name, I would not attempt to have another till I was free. So, sir, for once, you have a man standing before you without a name."—" I will name you George Loomis," said the squire. "I accept it," returned the fugitive, and shall try never to dishonor it."

True to their promises, his new friends provided for his immediate wants, and, as soon as a favorable opportunity occurred, started him on his journey north. George reached Canada in a few weeks without further adventure, and settled near the city of Toronto, where he resided, engaged in honest labors and enjoying the fruits of his industry, until the breaking-out of the Rebellion, when he returned to the United States, eager to take part in the struggle. Owing to the fairness of his complexion, he readily passed for a white man, and enlisted as such in a Michigan regiment in 1863. He was with Gen. Grant's army at the siege of Vicksburg; and, after the surrender of that stronghold, the regiment to which George belonged was

stationed in the town. Here the quadroon had ample
opportunity of conversing with the freedmen, which he
often did, for he had not lost his interest in the race.
Going into a negro cabin one day, and getting into conversation with an old woman, he found that she was
originally from the state of Kentucky, and lastly from
Missouri, and that they were from the same neighborhood. As each related the experience through which
they had passed, the interview became more and more
interesting. Often they eyed each other, but there was
nothing to indicate that they had ever met before.

However, this was not to last long, for George, in
describing the parting scene with his mother, riveted
the attention of the old woman, who, at its close, said,
" Dat scripshun peers like my gal, but you can't
be no kin to her. But what's your name ? " eagerly
asked the woman. " William was my name, but
I adopted the one I am known by now," replied
he. " You don't mean to say dat you is William ? "
"Yes: that was the name I was known by."—" Well,"
continued she, " I had a son named William ; but he
run away, and massa went arter him, and catched him,
and sold him down the riber to de cotton-planter. So
he said when he came back." The features of the two
had changed so much in thirty years, that they could not
discover in each other any traces whatever of former ac-
quaintance. " My son," said the old woman, " had a scar
on his right hand." George sprang from his seat, and held
out the right hand. Tremblingly she put on her glasses,
seized the hand, and screamed, " Oh, oh, oh ! I can't
'blieve dis is you. My son had a scar, a deep scar, on the
side of the left foot." Quick as thought, George took off
the boot, and held up his foot, while the old woman was

wiping her glasses; for they were wet with tears. A
moment more, and mother and son were locked in each
other's arms. The dead was alive, the lost was found.
God alone knew the sorrow that had visited the two
since they had last met. Great was the rejoicing at this
unexpected meeting; and the old woman would, for several days, cause Loomis to take off his boot, and show
her the scar ; and she would sit, hold the hand, and view
the unmistakable cut which helped her to identify her
long-lost son. And she would weep, and exclaim, " Dis
is de doins ob de Lord ! "

CHAPTER XXXVII.

PROGRESS AND JUSTICE.

Great Change in the Treatment of Colored Troops. — Negro Appoint-
ments. — Justice to the Black Soldiers. — Steamer "Planter." — Progress. — The Paymaster at last. — John S Rock.

THE month of May, 1864, saw great progress in the
treatment of the colored troops by the Government of
the United States. The circumstances were more favorable for this change than they had hitherto been. Slavery
had been abolished in the District of Columbia, Maryland, and Missouri : the heroic assault on Fort Wagner,
the unsurpassed bravery exhibited at Port Hudson, the
splendid fighting at Olustee and Honey Hill, had raised
the colored men in the estimation of the nation. President Lincoln and his advisers had seen their error, and
begun to repair the wrong. The year opened with the
appointment of Dr. A. T. Augusta, a colored gentleman,
as surgeon of colored volunteers, and he was at once assigned to duty, with the rank of major. Following this,
was the appointment, by Gov. Andrew of Massachusetts, of Sergt. Stephen A. Swailes, of Company F, Fifty-
fourth Massachusetts Regiment, as second lieutenant.

M. R. Delany, M.D., was soon after appointed a major
of negro volunteers, and assigned to duty at Charleston, S.C. W. P. Powell, jun., received an appointment as
surgeon, about the same time.

The steamer "Planter," since being brought out of

Charleston by Robert Small, was under the command of a Yankee, who, being ordered to do service where the vessel would be liable to come under the fire of rebel guns, refused to obey: whereupon Lieut.-Col. Elwell, without consultation with any higher authority, issued the following order, which, for simple justice to a brave and loyal negro, officially acknowledged, has seldom been equalled in this or any other department. It is unnecessary to say that Robert Small took command of the vessel, and faithfully discharged the duty required of him.

" OFFICE OF CHIEF QUARTERMASTER,
PORT ROYAL, S.C., Nov. 26, 1863.

"*Capt. A. T. Dutton, Chief Assistant Quartermaster, Folly and Morris Islands.*

" SIR, — You will please place Robert Small in charge of the United-States transport 'Planter,' as captain. He brought her out of Charleston Harbor more than a year ago, running under the guns of Sumter, Moultrie, and the other defences of that stronghold. He is an excellent pilot, of undoubted bravery, and in every respect worthy of the position. This is due him as a proper recognition of his heroism and services. The present captain is a coward, though a white man. Dismiss him, therefore, and give the steamer to this brave black Saxon.

"Respectfully, your obedient servant,

" J. J. ELWELL.
" *Chief Quartermaster Department South.*

It may interest some to know that the above order was immediately approved by Gen. Gillmore.

The following is very complimentary to Capt. Small : —

" It was indeed a privilege to enter Charleston, as we

did recently through the courtesy of Major-Gen. Saxton, in such a steamer as 'The Planter,' and with such a captain as Robert Small. It was their first appearance in the harbor since the memorable morning of their departure in 1862. The fog detained us for a few hours on our arrival at the bar. When it cleared away, you can imagine with what cheer our anchor came up, and with what smiles and satisfaction the vessel and her commander swept by the silenced and dismantled Sumter, and hauled in to the waiting, wondering wharves of the ruined city. Wherever we went on shore, we had only to say to the colored people, 'The Planter and Capt. Small are at the dock ; ' and away they all hurried to greet the well-known, welcome guests. ' Too sweet to think of,' cried one noble-looking old man, who had evidently waited long for the good news of our day, as he hastened to join the crowd.

" We met Small afterwards, walking in the streets in peace and safety. When our rambles about the humble place were over, and we prepared to depart, the scene about the steamer was one that we can never forget. A goodly company of the leading colored people were arranging for a public meeting with Gen. Saxton in the largest hall of the city, to learn from his lips the purposes of our Government on the following week. Their interview over, they joined a large crowd of their own color upon the pier. Small was in the midst of them, with a couple of white men in conversation with him. Curiosity led us near. He introduced us to the builder of the vessel, and the maker of the engine and boilers. ' I put the polish on,' he added laughingly. They withdrew towards a couple of their own complexion. He pointed out the principal person in the group,

to the general, as Col. Ferguson, the original owner of
'The Planter,' and of all her old hands, except Small.
His owner did not show himself.

" Upon our casting off, the colored folks raised at first
a few feeble cheers, from a lurking regard to the pale
listeners behind them ; but, when the general before them
called for three more for Capt. Small, every arm was
swung, and every voice was raised till the welkin rang.
'The Planter' has been placed under Gen. Saxton's orders. She will be often seen in these waters. Her new
claims to her name are to be manifested in her *planting*
the freedmen of the captured city upon the neighboring
sea-islands and the mainland, on their own homesteads,
for the cultivation of their own crops of cotton, rice,
corn, and whatever else they and their families, or
the world, may need. A great price was once put upon
Small's head. He and all his crew, white and black
alike, will be worth their weight in gold if they but continue to serve the general and the Government as we
were sure they did on their first return-trip to Charleston Harbor."

There was one step more which the Government had
taken, that sent a thrill of joy to many hearts. It was
paying the men on the battle-field what it promised. The
following announcement was made by Gen. Saxton, at
Beaufort, S.C., May 22 : —

" Colored soldiers, I have just received intelligence
that the National Government, after a long and desperate
struggle, has decided to put you on an equality with her
white troops, making your pay equal with theirs. Now
that she has done justice to you, I want you to do justice to her and justice to yourselves. Show yourselves
men ; and the way to show yourselves men is to be brave

and stout-hearted. I want you to be particular in the execution of your ' Shoulder arms,' your ' Charge bayonets.' Learn to shoot well at your enemies. You can do it, can't you ? " (" Yes, sir ! " was the answer from the columns.) "Well, do it, then. There is no reason why you should not make just as good soldiers as the whites. Do it, then ; hold your heads up, and be fearless and brave men. Two years ago, when I came here, I was the first to organize a colored regiment into the United-States service; viz., the First South-Carolina Regiment. The first lesson I taught them was to hold up their heads before white men, and to say No. And now they are good soldiers. I would just as soon have the First South-Carolina Regiment to-day with which to go into the field and face the enemy as any white soldiers in the service."

The paymaster shortly after made his appearance, and paid off the men; and thus justice, though long kept back, at last came. Great was the rejoicing, both in the army by the men, and at their homes by their families and friends. Progress is slow, but sure. Everywhere the colored population appeared to be gaining their equality, and rising to a higher level of humanity. The acknowledgment of the civil rights of the negro had already been granted in the admission of John S. Rock, a colored man, to practise law in all the courts within the jurisdiction of the United States. The Supreme Court at Washington, Chief-Justice Chase presiding, did not heap any more honor on Mr. Rock, by this admission, than they gained by having so distinguished a scholar as a member of the bar. Mr. John F. Shorter, who was promoted to a lieutenancy in Company D, Fifty-fifth Massachusetts Regiment, was by trade a carpenter, and was residing in Delaware County, O., when the call was

made for colored troops. Severely wounded at the battle of Honey Hill, S.C., on the 30th of November, 1864, he
still remained with his regiment, hoping to be of service.
At the conclusion of the war, he returned home, but never
recovered from his wound, and died a few days after his
arrival. James Monroe Trotter, promoted for gallantry,
was wounded at the battle of Honey Hill. He is a native
of Grand Gulf, Miss ; removed to Cincinnati, O ; was educated at the Albany (O.) Manual Labor University, where
he distinguished himself for his scholarly attainments.
He afterwards became a school-teacher, which position
he filled with satisfaction to the people of Muskingum
and Pike Counties, O., and with honor to himself. Enlisting as a private in the Fifty-fifth Massachusetts Regiment, on its organization, he returned with it to Boston
as a lieutenant, an office honorably earned.

William H. Dupree, a native of Petersburg, Va., was
brought up and educated at Chillicothe, O. He enlisted in the Fifty-fifth Massachusetts Regiment, on its
formation, as a private, was soon made orderly-sergeant,
and afterwards promoted to a lieutenancy for bravery
on the field of battle.

Charles L. Mitchel, promoted to a lieutenancy in the
Fifty-fifth Massachusetts Regiment for gallantry at the
battle of Honey Hill, where he was severely wounded
(losing a limb), is a native of Hartford, Conn., and son
of Mr. William A. Mitchel of that city. Lieut.
Mitchel served an apprenticeship to William H. Bur-
leigh, in the office of the old " Charter Oak," in Hartford,
where he became an excellent printer. For five or six
years previous to entering the army, he was employed
in different printing-offices in Boston, the last of which
was " The Liberator," edited by William Lloyd Garrison,

who never speaks of Lieut. Mitchel but in words of the highest commendation.   Gen. A. S. Hartwell, late colonel of the Fifty-fifth Massachusetts Regiment, makes honorable mention of Lieut. Mitchel.

The citizens of Boston in Ward Six, where he has so long resided, and who know him well, have shown their appreciation of Lieut. Mitchel's worth by electing him to represent them in the Massachusetts Legislature, — an office which he is every way qualified to fill.

CHAPTER XXXVIII.

FOURTH–OF–JULY CELEBRATION AT THE HOME OF JEFF. DAVIS.

By invitation of the Committee of Arrangements, a party of teachers and their escorts, and other friends of the freedmen, embarked on board "The Diligent," on the morning of the 4th inst. "The Diligent" left the levee at Vicksburg soon after seven o'clock, A.M., and made a pleasant trip in about three hours, down the river, stopping at the landing at Davis's Bend; whence the party were conveyed in ambulances, wagons, buggies, and other vehicles, to the late residence of Jefferson Davis, about two miles from said landing.

DAVIS'S BEND.

This is one of the most extraordinary bends of the wonderful Mississippi River, and has received its name from the fact of the settlement, on the peninsula formed by the bend, of two members of the Davis Family, known as "Jeff." and "Joe." This peninsula is some twelve miles in length; and, at the point where it is attached to the main land of the State of Mississippi, it is so narrow, that the enterprising planters have dug a canal across,

not unlike the celebrated Butler Canal of Petersburg
fame, although not near so long. This canal is called
the "cut-off;" and, in high water, the peninsula becomes,
in fact, an island. This tract of land is of great fertility,
being entirely a deposit of the rich soil washed from the
prairies of the Great West. On this tract are some six
plantations, of from eight hundred to twelve hundred
acres each. Two of the largest and best of these were
owned by Jeff. and Joe Davis, and are known now as
"The Jeff. and Joe places." The form of this peninsula
is such that a few companies of soldiers, with one or two
stockades, can keep out an army of rebels; and the inhabitants, although frequently surrounded by the hordes
of Southern murderers and thieves on the opposite banks
of the river and canal, dwell in peace and comparative
security. In fact, this site, from being the home of
traitors and oppressors of the poor, has become a sort
of earthly paradise for colored refugees. There they
flock in large numbers, and, like Lazarus of old, are permitted as it were, to repose in "Father Abraham's
bosom." The rich men of the Southern Confederacy,
now homeless wanderers, occasionally cry across for the
Lazarus whom they have oppressed and despised; but
he is not sent unto them, because, between the two
parties, "there is a great gulf fixed; so that they which
would pass from hence cannot." On this freedman's
paradise, parties for cultivating the soil are organized
under the superintendence of missionaries; each party
cultivating from ten to one hundred acres, with a fair
prospect of realizing handsomely. These efforts are
aided by the Government; rations, teams, &c., being
supplied and charged to each party, to be deducted
from the proceeds of their crops. Cotton is chiefly cultivated, and some very handsome stands appear.

THE "JOE PLACE."

The "Joe Place" is nearest the landing. The fine brick house, however, is nearly demolished; but the cottage used as a sort of law library and office is remaining uninjured. The negro-quarters also remain.

THE "JEFF. PLACE."

The "Jeff. place" is also a very fine plantation. The residence has not been injured, except the door-locks, and one or two marble mantels broken up, apparently for trophies. The Jeff. furniture has been removed; but the rooms are still furnished with furniture brought here.

THE HOUSE THAT JEFF. BUILT.

The house is, in its ground-plan, in the form of a cross, — but one floor, with large rooms and ample verandas. The portico in front is supported with pillars, and these form the only ornamental features of the house, except such as were added for this occasion by the artistic touches of our Northern sisters. Of these were festoons, wreaths, stars, and garlands mysteriously wóven in evergreens and flowers. Over the portico entrance outside were the following inscriptions, the letters being formed by cedar foliage : —

"THE HOUSE THAT JEFF. BUILT."
" WELCOME."

The latter motto was arched, and, with the festoons, made a beautiful appearance.

Inside were beautiful stars and garlands of flowers;
and over the exit at the back-door, the following
inscription, surmounted by a star: —

"EXIT TRAITOR."

It was facetiously remarked by an observer, that the
moral was, —

"Down with the traitor,
And up with the star."

We understood that to Miss Lee, of Pennsylvania, and
Miss Jennie Huddleson, of Indiana, the party was indebted for those ingenious and appropriate devices.
Very likely; for wit and satire for traitors, and a cordial
welcome to the loyal and patriotic, are characteristics of
these whole-souled missionaries.

The reception-rooms were also decorated with flowers;
and every thing around showed that "gentle hands"
had laid on "the last touches" of fragrance, grace, and
beauty.

These "ladies of the Management" were dressed in
neat "patriotic prints;" they needed no addition to
their toilets to add to the charming air of comfort which
they so appropriately infused. Their smiles of welcome
needed no verbal explanation; and the heartiness with
which they were engaged in their labors of love, and
the evidence of their success in all the surroundings,
showed that they perfectly understood the science of
making home happy. Whether they have read Mrs.
H. B. Stowe's "House and Home Papers" in "The
Atlantic," we know not, but there are many others,
besides that literary lady (Mrs. Stowe), who understand
how to keep house; by magic touches to turn the

most simple objects into luxuries of ornamentation.
We suspect also that Mrs. M. Watson and Miss Lizzie
Findley had been engaged in these preparations, although appearing more in the character of guests.
There were some other ladies, to whom we had not the
honor of an introduction, who, doubtless, deserve particular mention; but your reporter, as the sequel of his
story will show, only received his appointment as a publication committee *after all was over*, and, consequently,
if he should omit anybody's name that deserves mention,
this must be his apology. He now declares his desire
to be just to all, and especially to those whose devotion
and patriotism rendered the 4th of July, 1864, the hap-
piest day of the year.

THE GROUNDS.

On the grounds in front of the residence, the gunboat
crew suspended a string of signal colors, on each side
of the "starry banner," presenting an effect amid
the dense foliage of the live-oaks, and the gray moss,
"altogether beauteous to look upon;" while on the
tables under the trees were spread things not only
"pleasant to the sight," but "good for food." And
when we saw these pleasing objects, the "work of
their hands," and the merry, happy faces of the guests
and their "escorts," and reflected that the sable sons,
by a guard of whom we were surrounded, were "no
longer slaves;" that they had, with thousands of their
brethren, been brought out from the house of bondage,
by the "God of Abraham;" that the very house now
occupied by missionaries and teachers had, but a year
ago, been in the service of despotism, built, in fact, as

a temple of slavery by the great chief, who preferred to rule in a miserable petty despotism to serving in a great and magnanimous republic, — we could but think that Heaven looked approvingly upon the scene; that "God saw every thing that he had made, and behold! it was very good."

THE EXERCISES.

Rev. Dr. Warren conducted the exercises as president of the occasion; and he did it with that ease, freedom, and regard for the rights and interests of all, which usually characterize his public and social conduct. He opened the proceedings, under a grove of trees in front of the house, with an appropriate prayer, and then called upon those appointed to take part.

Mr. Roundtree read the Declaration of Independence in a clear, emphatic, and impressive manner. It was listened to with becoming reverence for the great truths it contains, by both the white and colored races. It is quite improbable that these self-evident truths were ever expressed before publicly in this locality, and within hearing of every one within the "house that Jeff. built."

When this place was first taken by our troops, the following verse was found written on the wall: —

> "Let Lincoln send his forces here!
> We'll lick 'em like blue blazes,
> And send them yelping back to where
> They sung their nigger praises."

Rev. Mr. Livermore, of Wisconsin, delivered an appropriate oration.

The meeting then adjourned for dinner.

A gentle shower at this time rendered the air cool and pleasant, but made it necessary to remove the dining-tables to the house.

THE DINNER.

A sumptuous dinner was served on the veranda at the back of the mansion. There was an abundance of all that could be desired. This being concluded, the following sentiments were presented, and responded to in an impromptu but appropriate manner by the various speakers : —

REGULAR TOASTS.

1. The Day we celebrate : The old ship was launched in '76, the bow-anchors cast out last year at Vicksburg and Gettysburg : may the storm-anchors be dropped to-day at Richmond and Atlanta !

Response by Mr. Israel Lombard.

2. The President : Proved honest and wise by four years of unprecedented trial : we shall keep him there.

Responded to by Dr. Wright.

3. Lieut.-Gen. Grant : We can tie to him in a gale.

Responded to by Col. Clark.

4. The house that Jeff. built.

Responded to by Capt. Powell.

The following song composed for the occasion was led by Mr. McConnell : —

"THE HOUSE THAT JEFF. BUILT."

" Air. — 'Auld Lang Syne.'

" How oft within these airy halls
The traitor of the day
Has heard ambition's trumpet-calls,
Or dreamed of war's array !

Or of an empire dreamed, whose base
Millions of blacks should be !
Aha ! before this day's sweet face
Where can his visions be ?

Those empire dreams shall be fulfilled,
But not as rebels thought :
Like water at the cistern spilled,
Their boasts shall come to nought.
From gulf to lake, from sea to sea,
Behold our country grand !
The very home of Liberty,
And guarded by her hand.

We revel in his halls to-day :
Next year where will he be ?
A dread account he has to pay :
May we be there to see !
And now for country, truth, and right,
Our heritage all free ;
We'll live and die, we'll sing and fight :
THE UNION ! three times three.

5. The Army and Navy: Veterans of three years. The heart of the nation beats anxiously at the cry, " Onward to victory ! "

Response by Dr. Foster.

6. Our Patriot Dead : Silence their most speaking eulogy.

7. The Union : The storm will but root it the more firmly.

Response by Rev. A. J. Compton.

" The Star-spangled Banner," — sung by the whole company, led by Mr. McConnell.

8. Missionaries to Freedmen : Peace has its heroes.

Response by Rev. Mr. Buckley, chaplain Forty-seventh United-States Colored Infantry.

9. Gen Sherman, second in command: " All I am I owe to my Government, and nothing could tempt me to sacrifice my honor or my allegiance."

Response by Capt. Gilpin, Commissary of Subsistence.

10. The Freedmen : Slaves yesterday, to-day free : what shall they be to-morrow ?

The freedmen sung the following song : —

" De Lord he makes us free indeed
    In his own time an' way.
We plant de rice and cotton seed,
    And see de sprout some day :
We know it come, but not de why, —
    De Lord know more dan we.
We 'spected freedom by an' by ;
    An' now we all are free.
            Praise de Lord !   Praise de Lord !
            For now we all are free.

De Norf is on de side of right,
    An' full of men, dey say ;
An' dere, when poor man work, at night
    He sure to get his pay.
De Lord he glad dey are so good,
    And make dem bery strong ;
An' when dey called to give deir blood
    Dey all come right along.
            Praise de Lord !   Praise de Lord !
            Dey all come right along.

Deir blue coats cover all de groun',
    An' make it like de sky ;
An' every grayback loafin' round
    He tink it time to fly.
We not afraid : we bring de child,
    An' stan' beside de door,
An,' oh ! we hug it bery wild,
    An' keep it ebermore.
            Praise de Lord !   Praise de Lord !
            We keep it ebermore.

De massa's come back from his tramp ;
    'Pears he is broken quite :
He takes de basket to de camp
    For rations ebery night.

Dey fought him when he loud and strong,
Dey fed him when he low :
Dey say dey will forgive the wrong,
An' bid him 'pent an' go.
Praise de Lord ! Praise de Lord !
Dey bid him 'pent an' go.

De rice is higher far dis year,
De cotton taller grow ;
De lowest corn-silk on de ear
Is higher than de hoe.
De Lord he lift up every ting
'Cept rebel in his grave ;
De negro bress de Lord, an' sing :
He is no longer slave.
Praise de Lord ! Praise de Lord !
De negro no more slave."

13. Our Colored Troops : Deserving of freedom because they fight like ·men.

Response by Lieut. Wakeman.

Song : "Babylon is fallen."

The party, after selecting a few simple trophies, such as fig-branches for walking-canes, large pond-lilies, flowers, wreaths, and bouquets, returned to the landing, and re-embarked for Vicksburg.

CLOSING EXERCISES.

On the boat, the following business was transacted : —
Vote of thanks to Col. Thomas and staff for getting up the celebration ; to the Orator of the Day, Parson Livermore ; to the President, Rev. Dr. Warren, who made a brief response ; and also to Capt. Wightman and officers of " The Diligent."

The following song was then sung by a young contraband : —

" We heard de proclamation, massa hush it as he will :
   De bird he sing it to us, hoppin' on de cotton-hill ;
   And de possum up de gum-tree he couldn't keep it still.

Father Abraham has spoken, and de message has been sent :
   De prison-doors he opened, and out de prisoners went
   To join de sable army of de ' African descent.'

Dey said, ' Now colored bredren, you shall be forever free,
   From the first of January, eighteen hundred and sixty-three : '
   We heard it in de riber goin' rushin' to de sea.

Den fall in, colored bredren, you'd better do it soon ;
   Don't you hear de drum a-beatin' de Yankee Doodle tune ?
   We are wid you now dis mornin' ; we'll be far away at noon."

Cheers were given for Abraham Lincoln, and groans for Jeff. Davis.

The song, " The House that Jeff. Built," was again sung ; and Capt. Gilpin, Commissary of Subsistence, appointed a committee to furnish a copy of the same to " The New-York Tribune," and also to Jeff. Davis.

Capt. Henry S. Clubb, Assistant Quartermaster, was appointed a committee to furnish a report of the proceedings of the day to " The Vicksburg Daily Herald."

CHAPTER XXXIX.

GALLANTRY, LOYALTY, AND KINDNESS OF THE NEGRO.

The Nameless Hero at Fair Oaks. — The Chivalry whipped by their Former Slaves. — Endurance of the Blacks. — Man in Chains. — One Negro whips Three Rebels. — Gallantry. — Outrages on the Blacks. — Kindness of the Negroes. — Welcome.

THE gallantry and loyalty of the blacks during the Rebellion is a matter of history, and volumes might be written upon that subject.   I give here a few instances out of the many I have gathered : —

" At the bloody battle of Fair Oaks, Va., the rebels, during the first day's fight, drove Gen. Casey's division from their camping-ground, and rested for the night, confident that the morrow would give them a chance to drive the Yankee invaders beyond the Chickahominy ; but, just at daylight that morning, Heintzelman's corps re-enforced our line, and at daybreak were hurled against the rebel foe.   For a long time, the issue was doubtful ; the line swayed to and fro ; but at last the Excelsior Brigade — the heroes of Williamsburg — were ordered to charge. That charge is a matter of history.   It gave us the battle-ground of Fair Oaks.

" During the month of June, that brigade held the ground they won, and skirmishes with the rebels were of daily occurrence.   One afternoon, word was sent to Gen. Sickles that the enemy was advancing in force, and every preparation was at once made for battle.   A few shots were heard from pickets but a few hundred

yards in advance of our battery, and then all was quiet.
What meant that quietness ? What were the rebels do
ing ? Several orderlies sent out to the pickets failed
to bring any satisfactory intelligence. Gen. Sickles
turned to Lieut. Palmer, one of his aides, and acting
assistant adjutant-general, and directed him to take a
squad of cavalry, and ride cautiously out to the first bend
in the road, and communicate with our pickets.

" Palmer was a noble fellow, — young, handsome, a
perfect gentleman, a graceful rider, a gallant soldier.
He was the pride of the brigade. Forgetful of the caution given him, with the impetuosity characteristic of
youth, he dashed forward at a full gallop, with sabre
drawn. He came to the first bend in the road, and
(fatal mistake) kept on. He came to the second bend,
and, as he turned it, directly across the road was a company of rebel infantry drawn up to receive him. They
fired. One ball crashed through that handsome face
into his brain, while another tore the arm that bore aloft
his trusty blade.

" The shots were heard at the battery ; and in a moment Palmer's riderless horse, bleeding from a wound in
its neck, galloped from the woods, followed by the squad
of cavalry, who told to the general the untimely fate of
his aide.

" ' Boys,' said the general to the veterans who clus-
tered around to hear the story, ' Lieut. Palmer's body
lies out in that road.' Not a word more needed saying.
Quickly the men fell in, and a general advance of the
line was made to secure it.

" Whilst the cavalrymen were telling the story, a negro-
servant of Lieut. Palmer's was standing by. Unnoticed,
he left the group ; down that road, the Williamsburg

Turnpike, he went. He passed our picket-line, and alone and unattended he walked along that avenue of death to so many, not knowing what moment he would be laid low by a rebel bullet, or be made a prisoner to undergo that still worse death, a life of slavery. Upon the advance of our line, that faithful servant was found by the side of his dead master, — faithful in life, and faithful amid all the horrors of the battle-field, even in the jaws of death.

"None but those who knew the locality — the gallant men that make up Hooker's division — can appreciate the heroism that possessed that contraband. That road was lined with sharpshooters. A wounded man once lay in it three days, neither party daring to rescue him. The act of that heroic, unknown (I regret that I cannot recall his name) but faithful contraband, was one of the most daring of the war, and prompted by none other than the noblest feelings known to the human breast." — *New-York Independent.*

"IN CAMP, BERMUDA HUNDRED, VA., May 26, 1864.

"The chivalry of Fitzhugh Lee, and his cavalry division, was badly worsted in the contest last Tuesday with negro troops composing the garrison at Wilson's Landing. Chivalry made a gallant fight, however. The battle began at half-past twelve, P.M., and ended at six o'clock; when chivalry retired, disgusted and defeated. Lee's men dismounted far in the rear, and fought as infantry. They drove in the pickets and skirmishers to the intrenchments, and several times made valiant charges upon our works. To make an assault, it was necessary to come across an 'open' in front of our position, up to the very edge of a deep and impassable ravine. The rebels, with deafening yells, made furious onsets; but the negroes did not flinch, and the mad assailants, discomfited, turned to cover with shrunken ranks. The rebel fighting was very wicked. It showed that Lee's heart was bent on taking the negroes at any cost. Assaults on the centre having failed, the rebels tried first the left and then the right flank, with no greater success. When the battle was over, our loss footed up one man killed outright, twenty wounded, and two missing. Nineteen rebels were prisoners in our hands. Lee's losses must have been very heavy. The proof thereof was left on the ground. Twenty-five rebel bodies lay in the woods unburied; and pools of blood unmistakably told of other victims taken away. The estimate, from all the evidence carefully considered, puts the enemy's casualties at two hundred. Among the corpses Lee left on the field was that of Major Breckinridge, of the Second Virginia Cavalry.

"There is no hesitation here in acknowledging the soldierly qualities which the colored men engaged in this fight have exhibited. Even the officers who have hitherto felt no confidence in them are compelled to express themselves mistaken. Gen. Wild, commanding the post, says that the troops stood up to their work like veterans."—*Correspondence of the New-York Times.*

"The conduct of the colored troops, by the way, in the actions of the last few days, is described as superb. An Ohio soldier said to me to-day, 'I never saw men fight with such desperate gallantry as those negroes did. They advanced as grim and stern as death; and, when within reach of the enemy, struck about them with a pitiless vigor that was almost fearful.' Another soldier said to me, 'These negroes never shrink nor hold back, no matter what the order. Through scorching heat and pelting storms, if the order comes, they march with prompt, ready feet.' Such praise is great praise, and it is deserved. The negroes here who have been slaves are loyal to a man, and, on our occupation of Fredericksburg, pointed out the prominent secessionists, who were at once seized by our cavalry, and put in safe quarters. In a talk with a group of these faithful fellows, I discovered in them all a perfect understanding of the issues of the conflict, and a grand determination to prove themselves worthy of the place and privileges to which they are to be exalted." — *New-York Herald.*

"CARROLLTON, LA., June 2, 1864.

"I am writing in the camp of the Twelfth Connecticut Regiment, and about here are encamped the Nineteenth Army Corps, under marching-orders for Morganza, near the mouth of the Red River. In this tent sits a man, — unfortunate because black, — once a slave, but free now, a member of the grand army of the United States, who is courageous, and who will wield a sword or thrust a bayonet as vigorously as any, because he has suffered so bitterly at the hands of those who would crush his race. His crime was remonstrating with his master for beating his wife. When our men found him, he was sitting on the floor, two long chains passing over his shoulders, and fastened to a staple; and over him stood four soldiers with muskets to prevent his escape. He is not only faithful; but he is gentlemanly, intelligent, and interesting in conversation and appearance. His brave heart is full of patriotism, and he is willing to serve or die for his country." — *Springfield Republican.*

An instance of the daring of negroes in that section is told by a Lake Providence (Louisiana) correspondent of "The Philadelphia Inquirer:" —

"Recently a black man, after several days' urgent request for a musket and rounds of ammunition, succeeded in securing his wish. He set out in the night, and by morning reached the vicinity of a rebel guard. He crept cautiously forward, but was seen and watched. Suddenly the sharp crack of rifles brought him to his feet. Before him were three rebel soldiers. He instantly brought his musket to his shoulder, and fired. One rebel fell dead. The negro, by the time the bewilderment of the other two had passed off, was upon them with uplifted musket, threatening them with its immediate descent, unless they surrendered at once. They acquiesced in a hurry. Leaving the dead rebel to the dogs, with the other two in tow, the negro returned to our lines, and delivered them to the authorities. Since this exploit, the negro has made himself useful in scouting and bringing in information."

A correspondent of "The Cleveland Leader," writing from the headquarters of the Fifty-ninth United-States Infantry (colored) at Memphis, under date of June 15, gives a detailed and graphic account of the brave fighting of the colored troops in Gen. Sturgis's command, fully confirming previous accounts. The following is the material part of the statement: —

"About sunrise, June 11, the enemy advanced on the town of Ripley, and threatened our right, intending to cut us off from the Salem Road. Again the colored troops were the only ones that could be brought into line; the Fifty-ninth being on the right, and the Fifty-fifth on the left, holding the streets. At this time, the men had not more than ten rounds of ammunition, and the enemy were crowding closer and still closer, when the Fifty-ninth were ordered to charge on them, which they did in good style, while singing, —

'We'll rally round the flag, boys.'

"This charge drove the enemy back, so that both regiments retreated to a pine-grove about two hundred yards distant.

"By this time, all the white troops, except one squadron of cavalry, that formed in the rear, were on the road to Salem; and, when this brigade came up, they, too, wheeled and left, and in less than ten minutes this now little band of colored troops found themselves flanked. They then divided themselves into three squads, and charged the enemy's lines; one squad taking the old Corinth Road, then a by-road, to the left. After a few miles, they came to a road leading to Grand Junction. After some skirmishing, they arrived, with the loss of one killed and one wounded.

"Another and the largest squad covered the retreat of the white troops, completely defending them by picking up the ammunition thrown away by them, and with it repelling the numerous assaults made by the rebel cavalry, until they reached Collierville, a distance of sixty miles. When the command reached Dan's Mills, the enemy attempted to cut it off by a charge; but the colored boys in the rear formed, and repelled the attack, allowing the whole command to pass safely on, when they tore up the bridge. Passing on to an open country, the officers halted, and re-organized the brigade into an effective force. They then moved forward until about four, P.M. ; when some Indian flank skirmishers discovered the enemy, who came up to the left, and in the rear, and halted. Soon a portion advanced, when a company faced about and fired, emptying three saddles. From this time until dark, the skirmishing was constant.

" A corporal in Company C, Fifty-ninth, was ordered to surrender. He let his would-be captor come close to him ; when he struck him with the butt of his gun.

" While the regiment was fighting in a ditch, and the order came to retreat, the color-bearer threw out the flag, designing to jump out and get it ; but the rebels rushed for it, and in the struggle one of the boys knocked down with his gun the reb who had the flag, caught it, and ran.

" A rebel, with an oath, ordered one of our men to surrender. He, thinking the reb's gun was loaded, dropped his gun ; but, on seeing the reb commence loading, our colored soldier jumped for his gun, and with it struck his captor dead.

" Capt. H., being surrounded by about a dozen rebels, was seen by one of his men, who called several of his companions : they rushed forward and fired, killing several of the enemy, and rescued their captain.

" A rebel came up to one, and said, 'Come, my good fellow, go with me and wait on me.' In an instant, the boy shot his would-be master dead.

" Once when the men charged on the enemy, they rushed forth with the cry, Remember Fort Pillow.' The rebs called back, and said, ' Lee's men killed no prisoners.'

" One man in a charge threw his antagonist to the ground, and pinned him fast ; and, as he attempted to withdraw his bayonet, it came off his gun, and, as he was very busy just then, he left him transfixed to mother-earth.

"One man killed a rebel by striking him with the butt of his gun, which he broke; but, being unwilling to stop his work, he loaded and fired three times before he could get a better gun: the first time, not being cautious, the rebound of his gun badly cut his lip.

"When the troops were in the ditch, three rebels came to one man, and ordered him to surrender. His gun being loaded, he shot one, and bayoneted another; and, forgetting he could bayonet the third, he turned the butt of his gun, and knocked him down."

Great were the sufferings which the colored people had to endure for their fidelity to liberty and the Union during the Rebellion. Space will allow me to give but one or two instances.

"On Monday, Feb. 21, a band of guerillas, commanded by Col. Moore, of Louisiana, made a bold dash upon our lines at Waterproof, La., opening with four pieces of artillery upon Fort Anderson. Capt. Johnson, of the gunboat 'No. 9,' was on hand, and, after two hours' vigorous shelling, the enemy abandoned the attack.

"Our loss was three killed. Two colored soldiers, members of the Eleventh Louisiana Volunteers, were captured, and afterwards brutally murdered, with an old slave known by the sobriquet of 'Uncle Peter.' The bodies of the two soldiers were discovered the next day riddled with bullets. Old Uncle Peter had been of great service to our Government in piloting our officers to localities where large quantities of cotton belonging to the rebel Government were concealed. After capturing this old man, the assassins compelled him to kneel, with his hands behind his back, in presence of some fifty slaves on one of the adjoining plantations; and two Minie-balls pierced his body. They then intimidated the slaves by threatening to treat all negroes in a similar manner whom they caught aiding the Yankees.

"Through the instrumentality of this faithful old man, Capt. Anderson had secured four hundred bales of fine cotton marked 'Confederate States of America,' together with a hundred and fifty fine horses, and a number of mules. The value of the cotton alone was a hundred thousand dollais. Among the prisoners captured by our forces was Lieut. Austin, adjutant-general on Gen. Harris's staff, with his fine horses and costly equipments. Capt. Anderson succeeded in capturing the murderer of old Uncle Peter, and, having plenty of slaves to testify who were obliged to witness the infamous crime, he ordered the guilty wretch to be shot; and in a few hours the villain paid the penalty of his dastard crime. Another one of the guerillas engaged in this outrage is now in our hands, under guard at this place; and it seems like an act of great injustice to our brave soldiers, that such outlaws should be treated as prisoners of war.

"After shooting these three defenceless men, the chivalrous knights robbed old Uncle Peter of a thousand dollars in treasury notes, and completely stripped the two colored soldiers of all their outer clothing and their boots. We hear Northern copperheads, who have never been south of Mason and Dixon's Line, constantly prating about the unconstitutionality of arming the slaves of rebels; and often these prejudiced people accuse the negro troops of cowardice. After the bloody proof at Milliken's Bend, Port Hudson, and at Fort Wagner in front of Charleston, it would seem that nothing more was needed to substantiate the resolution and undaunted courage of the slave when arrayed against his master, fighting for the freedom of his race. The following incident speaks for itself: —

"In the attack on Fort Anderson, Sergt. Robert Thompson exhibited traits of courage worthy of record. A party of eight guerillas surrounded Sergt. Thompson of Company I, Eleventh Louisiana, and Corp. Robinson of the same regiment. The two prisoners were threatened with torture and death, and were finally placed in charge of three guerillas, while the balance of their party were harassing our troops. Seeing a revolver in the sergeant's belt, they ordered him to give it up. As he fumbled around his belt, he touched the corporal with his elbow as a signal to be ready. Drawing it slowly from his belt, he cocked it, and, ere the rebel could give the alarm, he fell a corpse from his horse. At the same time, Corp. Robinson shot another; and the third guerilla, without waiting for further instructions, put the spurs to his horse, and in a few seconds was out of sight. The two brave men are now on duty ready for another guerilla visit."—*Correspondence of The Tribune.*

Kindness to Union men and all Northerners was a leading trait in the character of the colored people of the South throughout the war. James Henri Brown, special correspondent of "The New-York Tribune," in his very interesting work, "Four years in Secessia," says, "The negro who had guided us to the railway had told us of another of his color to whom we could apply for shelter and food at the terminus of our second stage. We could not find him until nearly dawn; and, when we did, he directed us to a large barn filled with corn-husks. Into that we crept with our dripping garments, and lay there for fifteen hours, until we could again venture forth. Floundering about in the husks, we lost our haversacks, pipes, and a hat. About nine o'clock, we procured a hearty supper from the generous negro, who even gave me his hat, — an appropriate presentation, as one of my companions remarked, by an 'intelligent contraband' to the reliable gentleman of 'The New-York Tribune.' The negro did picket-duty while we hastily ate our meal, and stood by his blazing fire. The old African and his wife gave us 'God bless you, massa!' with trembling voice and moistened eyes, as we parted from them with grateful hearts. 'God bless negroes!' say I, with earnest lips. During our entire captivity, and after our escape, they were ever our firm, brave, unflinching friends. We never made an appeal to them they did not answer. They never hesitated to do us a service at the risk even of life ; and, under the most trying circumstances, revealed a devotion and a spirit of self-sacrifice that were heroic.

"The magic word 'Yankee,' opened all their hearts, and elicited the loftiest virtues. They were ignorant, oppressed, enslaved ; but they always cherished a simple and beautiful faith in the cause of the Union, and its ultimate triumph, and never abandoned or turned aside from a man who sought food or shelter on his way to freedom."

"On the march of Grant's army from Spottsylvania to the North Anna, at intervals of every few miles, families of negroes were gathered along the roadside, exchanging words of salutation to our soldiers as they passed, and grinning all over their faces. 'Massa's gone away, gemmen,' was the answer in almost all cases where the query in relation to their master's whereabouts was raised. ' Specs he gwan to Richmon'. Dun know. He went away in a right smart hurry last night: dat's all I knows.' A sight of the fine, athletic, plump appearance of some of these negroes, of both sexes and all ages, would have driven a negro-trader crazy, especially when he became convinced of the fact that, according to the terms of President Lincoln's proclamation, these negroes are free the moment the lines of the Union army closed in upon them. It was a pleasing spectacle, and commingled with not a little pathos, to hear the benedictions which the aged and infirm negroes poured out upon our soldiers as they marched by. ' I'se been waitin' for you,' said an old negro, whose eyesight was almost entirely gone, and whose head was covered with the frosts of some eighty-five winters. ' Ah! I'se been waitin' for you gemmen some time. I knew you was comin', kase I heerd massa and missus often talkin' about you ; ' and then the old hero chuckled, and almost ground his ivories out of his head. "

No heroism surpasses that of the poor slave-boy Sam, on board the gunboat " Pawnee," who, while passing shell from the magazine, had both legs shot away by a ball from the rebel guns; but, still holding the shell, cried out at the top of his voice, " Pass up de shell, boys. Nebber mine me: my time is up." The greatest fidelity of the white man to the Union finds its parallel in the nameless negro, who, when his master sent him out to saddle his horse, mounted the animal, rode in haste to the Federal lines, and pointed out the road of safety to the harassed, retreating Army of the Potomac ; then, returning for his wife and children, was caught by the rebels, and shot. When the rebels made their raid into the State of Pennsylvania, and the governor called the peo-

ple to arms for defence, it is a well-known fact that a
company of colored men from Philadelphia were the first
to report at Harrisburg for service.   These men were
among the most substantial of the colored citizens in
point of wealth and moral culture.   Yet these patriotic
individuals, together with all of their class, are disfranchised in that State.

In the engagement on James Island between the Fifty-
fourth Massachusetts and the rebels, the latter surrounded three companies of the former, which were on
picket-duty, and ordered them to surrender ; the colored
troops replied by making the best possible use of their
muskets.   In the fight, Sergt. Wilson, of the Fifty-fourth
Massachusetts, fought bravely, having fired his last cart-
ridge, used the butt of his gun upon his enemies, and,
even after being severely wounded, still struggled against
the foe with his unloaded weapon.   The enemy, seeing
this, called repeatedly to the negro to surrender; but
Wilson refused, and fought till he was shot dead.

CHAPTER XL.

FALL OF THE CONFEDERACY, AND DEATH OF PRESIDENT LINCOLN.

Flight of Jeff. Davis from Richmond. — Visit of President Lincoln to the Rebel Capital. — Welcome by the Blacks. — Surrender of Gen. Lee. — Death of Abraham Lincoln. — The Nation in Tears.

JEFFERSON DAVIS and his cabinet had hastily quitted Richmond, on Sunday, the third day of April, 1865; the Union troops had taken possession the day following; and Abraham Lincoln, President of the United States, and the best-hated man by the rebels, entered the city a short time after. For the following account of the President's visit, I am indebted to a correspondent of "The Boston Journal:" —

"I was standing upon the bank of the river, viewing the scene of desolation, when a boat, pulled by twelve sailors, came up stream. It contained President Lincoln and his son, Admiral Porter, Capt. Penrose of the army, Capt. A. H. Adams of the navy, Lieut. W. W. Clements of the signal corps. Somehow the negroes on the bank of the river ascertained that the tall man wearing the black hat was President Lincoln. There was a sudden shout. An officer who had just picked up fifty negroes to do work on the dock found himself alone. They left work, and crowded round the President. As he approached, I said to a colored woman, —

"'There is the man who made you free.'

" ' What, massa ? '

" ' That is President Lincoln.'

" ' Dat President Linkum ? '

" ' Yes.'

" She gazed at him a moment, clapped her hands, and jumped straight up and down, shouting, ' Glory, glory, glory ! ' till her voice was lost in a universal cheer.

" There was no carriage near ; so the President, leading his son, walked three-quarters of a mile up to Gen. Weitzel's headquarters, — Jeff. Davis's mansion. What a spectacle it was ! Such a hurly-burly, such wild, indescribable, ecstatic joy I never witnessed. A colored man acted as guide. Six sailors, wearing their round blue caps and short jackets and bagging pants, with navy carbines, were the advance-guard. Then came the President and Admiral Porter, flanked by the officers accompanying him, and the correspondent of ' The Journal ; ' then six more sailors with carbines, — twenty of us all told, — amid a surging mass of men, women, and children, black, white, and yellow, running, shouting, dancing, swinging their caps, bonnets, and handkerchiefs. The soldiers saw him, and swelled the crowd, cheering in wild enthusiasm. All could see him, he was so tall, so conspicuous.

" One colored woman, standing in a doorway as the president passed along the sidewalk, shouted, ' Thank you, dear Jesus, for this ! thank you, Jesus ! ' Another standing by her side was clapping her hands, and shouting, ' Bless de Lord ! '

" A colored woman snatched her bonnet from her head, and whirled it in the air, screaming with all her might, ' God bless you, Massa Linkum ! '

" A few white women looking out from the houses

waved their handkerchiefs. One lady in a large and elegant building looked a while, and turned away her head as if it was a disgusting sight.

" President Lincoln walked in silence, acknowledging the salutes of officers and soldiers, and of the citizens, black and white. It was the man of the people among the people. It was the great deliverer meeting the delivered. Yesterday morning the majority of the thousands who crowded the streets and hindered our advance were slaves: now they were free, and beholding him who had given them their liberty."

On the 9th of the same month, Gen. Lee, with his whole army, surrendered to Gen. Grant; and thus fell the Southern Confederacy, the enemy of the negro and of Republican government. The people of the North, already tired of the war, at once gave themselves up to rejoicing all over the free States.

But the time of merry-making was doomed to be short; for slavery, the cause of the Rebellion, was dying hard. The tyrants of the South, so long accustomed to rule, were now determined to ruin. Slavery must have its victim. If it could not conquer, it must at least die an honorable death; and nothing could give it more satisfaction than to commit some great crime in its last struggles.

Therefore the death of Abraham Lincoln by the hand of an assassin was but the work of slavery. It murdered Lovejoy at Alton, it slowly assassinated Torrey in a Maryland prison, it struck down Sumner in the Senate,[1] it had taken the lives, by starvation, of hundreds at Anderson, Richmond, and Salisbury ; why spare the great liberator ?

President Lincoln fell a sacrifice to his country's sal-

vation as absolutely and palpably, as though he had been
struck down while leading an assault on the ramparts of
Petersburg.   The wretch who killed him was impelled
by no private malice, but imagined himself an avenger
of that downcast idol, which, disliking to be known
simply as slavery, styles itself "The South." He was
murdered, not that slavery might live; but that it might
bring down its most conspicuous enemy in its fall.

The tears of four millions of slaves whom he had liberated, five hundred thousand free blacks whose future
condition he had made better, and the twenty millions
of whites in the free States, stricken as they never
had been before by the death of a single individual,
followed his body to the grave.   No nation ever mourned
more sincerely the loss of its head than did the people
of the United States that of President Lincoln.   We all
love his memory still.

> "His name is not a sculptured thing, where old Renown has reared
>   Her marble in the wilderness, by smoke of battle seared;
>   But graven on life-leaping hearts, where *Freedom's* banners wave,
>   It gleams to bid the tyrant back, and *loose the fettered slave.*"

Faults he had; but we forget them all in his death.
It seemed to us that God had raised this man up to do a
great work; and when he had finished his mission,
flushed with success over the enemies of his country,
while the peals of exultation for the accomplishment of
the noble deed were yet ringing in his ears, and while
our hearts were palpitating more generously for him, he
permitted him to fall, that we should be humbled, and
learn our own weakness, and be taught to put more dependence in the ruler of the universe than in man.

" So sleep the good, who sink to rest
By all their country's wishes blest.
When Spring with dewy fingers cold
Returns to deck their hallowed mould,
She there shall dress a sweeter sod
Than Fancy's feet have ever trod :
By forms unseen, their dirge is sung ;
By fairy hands, their knell is rung ;
There Honor comes, a pilgrim gray,
To bless the turf that wraps their clay ;
And Freedom shall a while repair,
To dwell a weeping hermit there."

CHAPTER XLI.

PRESIDENT ANDREW JOHNSON.

Origin of Andrew Johnson. — His Speeches in Tennessee. — The Negro's Moses. — The Deceived Brahmin. — The Comparison. — Interview with Southerners. — Northern Delegation. — Delegation of Colored Men. — Their Appeal.

SPRINGING from the highest circle of the lowest class of whites of the South, gradually rising, coming up over a tailor's board, and all the obstacles that slaveholding society places between an humbly-born man and social and political elevation, Andrew Johnson entered upon his presidential duties, at the death of Mr. Lincoln, with the hearty good feeling of the American people. True, he had taken a glass too much on the day of his inauguration as vice-president, and the nation had not forgotten it; yet there were many palliating circumstances to be offered. The weather was cold, his ride from Tennessee had been long and fatiguing, he had met with a host of friends, who, like himself, were not afraid of the "critter." And, after all, who amongst that vast concourse of politicians, on that fourth day of March, had not taken a "Tom and Jerry," a "whiskey punch," a "brandy smash," or a "cocktail"? Again: the people had been robbed of their idol, and suddenly plunged into grief, and felt like looking up the commendable acts of the new President, rather than finding fault, and were desirous to see how

328

far he was capable of filling the gap so recently made vacant.

They remembered that when the secessionists were withdrawing from Congress, in 1860, Mr. Johnson said, "If I were president, I would try them for treason, and, if convicted, I would hang them." This was mark number one in his favor. They had not forgotten his address to the Tennessee Convention, which, in the preceding January, had, by an almost unanimous vote, declared slavery in that State forever abolished.

This speech was made on the 14th of January, and is very uncompromising and eloquent. "Yesterday," said he to the Convention, "you broke the tyrant's rod, and set the captive free. (Loud applause.) Yes, gentlemen, yesterday you sounded the death-knell of negro aristocracy, and performed the funeral obsequies of that thing called slavery. . . . I feel that God smiles on what you have done. Oh, how it contrasts with the shrieks and cries and wailings which the institution of slavery has brought on the land!"

And his speech to the colored people of Nashville in the preceding October was exceedingly touching, by reason of its tender, heartfelt compassion for all the degradation, insult, and cruelty which had been heaped upon that poor and unoffending people so long. Its scorn and sarcasm were terrible as he arraigned the "master" class for their long career of lust, tyranny, and crime. He hoped a Moses would arise to lead this persecuted people to their promised land of freedom. "You are our Moses," shouted first one, and then a great multitude of voices. But the speaker went on, "God, no doubt, has prepared, somewhere, an instrument for the great work he designs to perform in behalf of this outraged people; and in due time your leader will come forth, — your Moses will be revealed to you." "We want no Moses but you!" again shouted the crowd. "Well, then," replied Mr. Johnson, "humble and unworthy as I am, if no better shall be found, I will indeed be your Moses, and lead you through the Red Sea of war and bondage to a fairer future of liberty and peace."

These were brave words in behalf of the rights of man, and weighed heavily in Mr. Johnson's favor. Also in his first public words, after taking the oath as President of the United States, Mr. Johnson referred to *the past* of his life as an indication of his course and policy in the future, rather than to make any verbal declarations now; thereby manifesting an honorable willingness to be judged by his acts, and a consciousness that the record was one which he need not be ashamed to own.

What better words or greater promises could be demanded? And, moreover, the American people are admirers of self-made men. Indeed, it is the foundation of true republican principles; and those who come to the surface by their own genius or energies are sure to be well received by the masses. But was Andrew Johnson a genius? was he shrewd? was he smart? If not, how could he have attained to such a high position in his own State? Were the people there all fools, that they should send a mountebank to the United-States Senate? Or were they, as well as the National-Republican Convention that nominated him in 1864 for the Vice-Presidency, deceived?

Macaulay, in his Criticism on the Poems of Robert Montgomery, says, "A pious Brahmin, it is written, made a vow, that, on a certain day, he would sacrifice a

sheep; and on the appointed morning he went forth to
buy one. There lived in his neighborhood three rogues,
who knew his vow, and laid a scheme for profiting by
it. The first met him, and said, ' O Brahmin! wilt thou
buy a sheep? I have one fit for sacrifice.' — ' It is for
that very purpose,' said the holy man, 'that I came
forth this day.' Then the impostor opened a bag, and
brought out of it an unclean beast, — an ugly dog, lame
and blind. Thereon the Brahmin cried out, ' Wretch,
who touchest things impure, and utterest things untrue,
callest thou that cur a sheep?' — ' Truly,' answered
the other, ' it is a sheep of the finest fleece, and of the
sweetest flesh. O Brahmin! it will be an offering most ac-
ceptable to the gods!' — ' Friend,' said the Brahmin,
' either thou or I must be blind.' Just then, one of the
accomplices came up. 'Praised be the gods,' said this
second rogue, ' that I have been saved the trouble of
going to the market for a sheep! This is such a sheep
as I wanted. For how much wilt thou sell it?' When
the Brahmin heard this, his mind waved to and fro, like
one swinging in the air at a holy festival. ' Sir,' said
he to the new-comer, ' take heed what thou dost. This
is no sheep, but an unclean cur.' — ' O Brahmin!' said
the new-comer, ' thou art drunk or mad.' At this time,
the third confederate drew near. ' Let us ask this
man,' said the Brahmin, ' what the creature is; and I
will stand by what he shall say.' To this the others
agreed; and the Brahmin called out, ' O stranger! what
dost thou call this beast?' — ' Surely, O Brahmin!'
said the knave, ' it is a fine sheep.' Then the Brahmin
said, ' Surely the gods have taken away my senses!'
and he asked pardon of him who carried the dog, and
bought it for a measure of rice and a pot of ghee; and

offered it up to the gods, who, being wroth at this unclean sacrifice, smote him with a sore disease in all his
joints."

The poor Brahmin was never more thoroughly imposed upon in receiving the dog for a sheep than were
the American people in accepting Andrew Johnson as a
statesman, or even as a friend of liberty and republican
institutions. That he hated the slaveocracy, there is
not the slightest doubt; for they were far above him,
and all his efforts to be recognized by them as an equal
had failed.

But did he like the negro any better than the master?
It is said, that while in his apprenticeship, on one occasion, young Johnson was passing along the street with a
pair of pants upon his arm, when a well-dressed free negro accidentally ran against him, pushing the tailor into a
ditch; whereupon, the latter threw a handful of mud
at the black man, soiling his clothes very much. The
negro turned, and indignantly said, "You better mind
what you 'bout, you low white clodhopper, poor white
trash!" This retort of the negro no doubt touched a
tender chord; for it reminded the rising young man of
the "pit from whence he was digged," and it is said
he hated the race ever after. *But it must be acknowledged* that Mr. Johnson is a big man in little things;
that he showed some shrewdness in taking advantage
of the Union feeling, and especially the antislavery sentiment, of the North, in wiggling himself into the Republican party by his bunkum speeches. After all, what is
the real character of the man?

"Great Judas of the nineteenth century,
 Foul political traitor of the age,
 Persistent speechmaker, covered with falsity,

Come, sit now for your portrait. I will paint
As others see you, — men who love their God,
And hate not even you, aye you, attaint
With love of self, and power that's outlawed.
Behold the picture ! See a drunken man
Whose age brings nothing but increase of sin, —
A deceptive ' policy,' a hateful plan
To deceive the people, and re-enslave the sons of Ham !
Now see it stretching out a slimy palm,
And striking hands with rebels. Nay, nay !
It grasps Columbia by the throat and arm,
And seeks to give her to that beast of prey."

Intensely in love with himself, egotistical, without
dignity, tyrannical, ungrateful, and fond of flattery,
Mr. Johnson was entirely unprepared to successfully
resist the overtures of the slaveholding aristocracy,
by whom he had so long wished to be recognized. It
was some weeks after the death of the good President,
that a committee of these Southerners visited the
White House. They found Mr. Johnson alone ; for
they had asked for an audience, which had been readily
granted. Humbly they came, the lords of the lash, the
men who, five years before, would not have shaken
hands with him with a pair of tongs ten feet long.
Many of them the President had seen on former occasions : all of them he knew by reputation. As they
stood before him, he viewed them from head to feet, and
felt an inward triumph. He could scarcely realize the
fact, and asked himself, " Is it possible ? have I my old
enemies before me, seeking favors ? " Yes : it was so ;
and they had no wish to conceal the fact. The chairman of the committee, a man of years, one whose very
look showed that he was not without influence among
those who knew him, addressing the Chief Magistrate,
said, " Mr. President, we come as a committee to rep-

resent to you the condition of the South, and its wants. We fear that your Excellency has had things misrepresented to you by the Radicals; and knowing you to be a man of justice, a statesman of unsullied reputation, one who to-day occupies the proudest position of any man in the world, we come to lay our wants before you. We have, in the past, been your political opponents. In the future, we shall be your friends; because we now see that you were right, and we were wrong. We ask, nay, we beg you to permit us to reconstruct the Southern States. Our people, South, are loyal to a man, and wish to return at once to their relations in the General Government. We look upon you, Mr. President, as the embodiment of the truly chivalrous Southerner, — one who, born and bred in the South, understands her people : to you we appeal for justice; for we are sure that your impulses are pure. Your future, Mr. President, is to be a brilliant one. At the next presidential election, the South will be a unit for the man who saves her from the hands of these Yankees, who now, under the protection of the Freedman's Bureau, are making themselves rich. We shall stand by the man that saves us; and you are that man. Your genius, your sagacity, and your unequalled statesmanship, mark you out as the father of his country. Without casting a single ungenerous reflection upon the great name of George Washington, allow me to say what I am sure the rest of the delegation will join me in, and that is, that, a hundred years to come, the name of Andrew Johnson will be the brightest in American history."

Several times during the delivery of the above speech, the President was seen to wipe his eyes, for he was indeed moved to tears. At its conclusion, he said, " Gentlemen, your chairmân has perfectly overwhelmed me. I was not, I confess, prepared for these kind words, this cordial support, of the people of the South. Your professions of loyalty, which I feel to be genuine, and your promises of future aid, unman me. I thought you were my enemies, and it is to enemies that I love to give battle. As to my friends, they can always govern me. I will lay your case before the cabinet." — " We do not appeal to your cabinet," continued the chairman, " it is to you, Mr. President, that we come. Were you a common man, we should expect you to ask advice of your cabinet; but we regard you as master, and your secretaries as your servants. You are capable of acting without consulting them: we think you the Andrew Jackson of to-day. Presidents, sir, are regarded as mere tools. We hope you, like Jackson, will prove an exception. We, the people of the South, are willing to let you do precisely as you please; and still we will support you. We are proud to acknowledge you as our leader. All we ask is, that we shall be permitted to organize our State Governments, elect our senators and representatives, and return at once into the Union; and this, Mr. President, lies entirely with you, unless you acknowledge yourself to be in leading-strings, which we know is not so; for Andrew Johnson can never play second fiddle to men or parties." These last remarks affected Mr. Johnson very much, which he in vain attempted to conceal. " Gentlemen," replied the President, " I confess that your chairman, has, in his remarks, made an impression on my mind that I little dreamed of when you entered. I admit that I am not pleased with the manner in which the Radicals are acting." — "Allow me," said the chairman, interrupting the President, " to say a word or two that I had forgotten. "Proceed," said the Chief Magistrate. "You are not appreciated," continued the chairman, "by the Radicals. They speak of you sneeringly as the 'accidental President,' just as if you were not the choice of the people. The people of the North would never elect you again. No man, except Mr. Lincoln, has ever been elected a second time to the presidency, from the free States. They have so many peddling politicians, like so many hungry wolves, seeking office, that they are always crying, 'Rotation, rotation.' But, with us of the South, it is different. When we find a man with genius, talent, a statesman, we hold on to him, and keep him in office. You, Mr. President, can carry all the Southern, and enough of the Northern States to elect you to another term."—"Yes," responded one of the committee, "to two terms more." Mr. Johnson, with suppressed emotion, said, "I will at once lay down a policy, which, I think, will satisfy the entire people of the South; but, but—I said that treason should be made odious, and traitors should be punished: what can I do so as not to stultify myself?"

"I see it as clear as day, Mr. President," said the chairman. "You have already made treason odious by those eloquent speeches which you have delivered at various times on the Rebellion; and now you can punish traitors by giving them office. St. Paul said, 'If thine enemy hunger, feed him; if he thirst, give him drink: for in so doing, thou shalt heap coals of fire on his head.' Now, many of the Southerners are your old enemies; and they are hungry for office, and thirst for the good liquor they used to get in the congressional saloons." "I am satisfied," said the President, "that I can restore the Southern States to their relations to the Union, and let all who held office before the war, resume their positions again. — " Yes," remarked a member of the committee ; "and you can build up a new party of your own, that shall take the place of the Democratic party, which is already dead." — " Very true," replied the President, " there is both room and need of another political party. You may rest assured, gentlemen, that you will be re-instated in your former positions." The committee withdrew. " My policy" was commenced. The Republicans did not like it ; and a committee was sent to the White House, composed of some of the leading men of the North, the chairman of which was a man some six feet in height, stout, and well made ; features coarse ; full head of hair, touched with the frost of over fifty winters ; dressed in a gray suit, light felt hat. [1] The committee, on entering, found the President seated, with his feet under the table. He did not rise to welcome the delegation, but seemed to push his feet still farther under the table, for fear that they might think he was going to rise. The chairman, whom I have already described, said in a rather strong voice, " Mr. President, we have called to ask you to use your official power to protect the Union men of the South, white and black, from the murderous feeling of the rebels.

" As faithful friends, and supporters of your Administration, we most respectfully petition you to suspend for the present your policy towards the rebel States. We should not present this prayer if we were not painfully convinced that, thus far, it has failed to obtain any reasonable guarantees for that security in the future which is essential to peace and reconciliation. To our minds, it abandons the freedmen to the control of their ancient masters, and leaves the national debt exposed to repudiation by returning rebels. The Declaration of Independence asserts the equality of all men, and that rightful government can be founded only on the consent of the governed. We see small chance of peace unless these great principles are practically established. Without this, the house will continue divided against itself."

" Gentlemen," replied the President, " I will take your request into consideration, and give it that attention that it demands." The committee left, satisfied that Mr. Johnson was a changed man. Soon after, the President was called upon by another delegation, a committee of colored men, consisting of Frederick Douglass, William Whipper, George T. Downing, and L. H. Douglass.[2] The negro race was singularly fortunate in having these gentlemen to represent them; for they are not only amongst the ablest of their class, but are men of culture, and all of them writers and speakers of distinguished ability. The delegation, on entering, found the President seated, with his feet under the table, and his hands in his breeches pockets, and looking a little sour. Mr. Downing, the delegate from New England, first addressed the Chief Magistrate; and his finely chosen-words, and well-rounded periods, no doubt made the President not a little uneasy, for he looked daggers at the speaker. The reflection of Downing's highly cultivated mind, as seen through his admirable address, doubtless reminded the President of his own inferiority, and made him still more petulant; for, when he replied to the delegate, he said, —

" I am free to say to you that I do not like to be arraigned by some who can get up handsomely-rounded periods, and deal in rhetoric, and talk about abstract ideas of liberty, who never perilled life, liberty, or property. This kind of theoretical, hollow, unpractical friendship, amounts to very little."

After Downing, came the strong words of Douglass. Of this speaker, the President had heard much, and appeared to eye him from head to feet; took his hands out of his pockets; and rested his elbows upon the table. Douglass, no doubt, reminded him of the well-dressed free negro, who, nearly forty years before, had pushed him into the ditch ; and this recollection brought up, also, that hateful tailor's bench, and, still back of that, his low origin.

Mr. Douglass also reminded the President of his promise to be the negro's Moses. This last remark was cruel in the speaker, for it carried Mr. Johnson back to the days when he was carrying out that deceptive policy by which he secured the nomination on the ticket with Mr. Lincoln ; and he appeared much irritated at the remark. His whole reply to the delegation was weak, unfair, and without the slightest atom of logic. Mr. Downing addressed the President as follows : —

" We present ourselves to your Excellency to make known, with pleasure, the respect which we are glad to cherish for you, — a respect which is your due as our Chief Magistrate. It is our desire that you should know that we come, feeling that we are friends meeting friends. We may, however, have manifested our friendship by not coming to further tax your already much-burdened and valuable time ; but we have another object in calling. We are in a passage to equality before the law. God hath made it by opening a Red Sea. We would have your assistance through the same. We come to you in the name of the United States, and are delegated to come by some who have unjustly worn iron manacles

on their bodies ; by some whose minds have been mana-
cled by class legislation in States called free. The colored
people of the States of Illinois, Wisconsin, Alabama, Mississippi, Florida, South Carolina, North Carolina, Virginia,
Maryland, Pennsylvania, New York, the New-England
States, and the District of Columbia, have specially
delegated us to come. Our coming is a marked circumstance. We are not satisfied. with an amendment pro-
hibiting slavery ; but we wish that amendment enforced
with appropriate legislation. This is our desire. We
ask for it intelligently, with the knowledge and conviction that the fathers of the Revolution intended freedom
for every American; that they should be protected in
their rights as citizens, and be equal before the law.
We are Americans, — native-born Americans. We are
citizens. We are glad to have it known to the world
that we bear no doubtful record on this point. On this
fact, and with confidence in the triumph of justice, we
base our hope. We see no recognition of color or race
in the organic law of the land. It knows no privileged
class, and therefore we cherish the hope that we may be
fully enfranchised, not only here in this district, but
throughout the land. We respectfully submit, that rendering any thing less than this will be rendering to us
less than our just due ; that granting any thing less than
our full rights will be a disregard of our just rights, —
of due respect for our feelings. If the powers that be
do so, it will be used as a license, as it were, or an apology, for any community or individual, so disposed, to
outrage our rights and feelings. It has been shown in
the present war that the Government may justly reach
its strong arm into States, and demand from them —
from those who owe it — their allegiance, assistance, and

support. May it not reach out a like arm to secure and protect its subjects upon whom it has a claim ? "

Following Mr. Downing, Mr. Frederick Douglass advanced, and addressed the President, saying, —

" Mr. President, we are not here to enlighten you, sir, as to your duties as the Chief Magistrate of this republic, but to show our respect, and to present in brief the claims of our race to your favorable consideration. In the order of divine Providence, you are placed in a position where you have the power to save or destroy us, to bless or blast us, — I mean our whole race. Your noble and humane predecessor placed in our hands the sword, to assist in saving the nation ; and we do hope that you, his able successor, will favorably regard the placing in our hands the ballot with which to save ourselves. We shall submit no argument on that point. The fact that we are the subjects of government, and subject to taxation, subject to volunteer in the service of the country, subject to being drafted, subject to bear the burdens of the State, makes it not improper that we should ask to share in the privileges of this condition. I have no speech to make on this occasion. I simply submit these observations as a limited expression of the views and feelings of the delegation with which I have come."

I omit Mr. Johnson's long and untruthful speech, and give the reply of the delegation, which he would not listen to : —

" Mr. President, in consideration of a delicate sense of propriety, as well as your own repeated intimation of indisposition to discuss or to listen to a reply to the views and opinions you were pleased to express to us in your elaborate speech to-day, we

would respectfully take this method of reply thereto.

"Believing, as we do, that the views and opinions expressed in that address are entirely unsound, and preju-
dicial to the highest interests of our race, as well as of
our country, we cannot do otherwise than expose the
same, and, so far as may be in our power, arrest their
dangerous influence.

"It is not necessary at this time to call attention to
more than two or three features of your remarkable
address.

"The first point to which we feel especially bound to
take exception is your attempt to found a policy opposed to our enfranchisement, upon the alleged ground
of an existing hostility on the part of the former slaves
towards the poor white people of the South.

"We admit the existence of this hostility, and hold that
it is entirely reciprocal.

"But you obviously commit an error by drawing an
argument from an incident of a state of slavery, and
making it a basis for a policy adapted to a state of freedom.

"The hostility between the whites and blacks of the
South is easily explained. It has its root and sap in the
relation of slavery, and was incited on both sides by
the cunning of the slave-masters. These masters secured their ascendency over both the poor whites and
the blacks by putting enmity between them. They
divided both to conquer each.

"There was no earthly reason why the blacks should
not hate and dread the poor whites when in a state of
slavery; for it was from this class that their masters
received their slave-catchers, slave-drivers, and over-

seers. They were the men called in upon all occasions
by the masters when any fiendish outrage was to be
committed upon the slave.

" Now, sir, you cannot but perceive that, the cause of
this hatred removed, the effect must be removed also.
Slavery is abolished. The cause of antagonism is removed; and you must see that it is altogether illogical —
' putting new wine into old bottles, mending new garments with old clothes ' — to legislate from slave-holding
and slave-driving premises for a people whom you have
repeatedly declared your purpose to maintain in freedom.
Besides, even if it were true, as you allege, that the
hostility of the blacks toward the poor whites must necessarily be the same in a state of freedom as in a state of
slavery, in the name of Heaven, we reverently ask, how
can you, in view of your professed desire to promote
the welfare of the black man, deprive him of all means
of defence, and clothe him whom you regard as his
enemy in the panoply of political power?

" Can it be that you would recommend a policy which
would arm the strong and cast down the defenceless?
Can you, by any possibility of reasoning, regard this as
just, fair, or wise?

" Experience proves that those are oftenest abused
who can be abused with the greatest impunity. Men are
whipped oftenest who are whipped easiest. Peace between races is not to be secured by degrading one race,
and exalting another; by giving power to one race, and
withholding it from another : but by maintaining a state
of equal justice between all parties, — first pure, then
peaceable.

" On the colonization theory that you were pleased to
broach, very much could be said. It is impossible to

suppose, in view of the usefulness of the black man in time of peace as a laborer in the South, and in time of war as a soldier at the North, and the growing respect for his rights among the people, and his increasing adaptation to a high state of civilization in this his native land, that there can ever come a time when he can be removed from this country without a terrible shock to its prosperity and peace.

" Besides, the worst enemy of the nation could not cast upon its fair name a greater infamy than to suppose that negroes could be tolerated among them in a state of the most degrading slavery and oppression, and must be cast away and driven into exile for no other cause than having been freed from their chains."

The most unhandsome and untruthful remarks of the President to the delegation are those in which he charges the slave-masters and the slave with combining to keep the poor whites in degradation.

The construction which he put upon his promise to the blacks of Tennessee — to be the " Moses to lead the black race through the Red Sea of bondage " to — expatriation — was mean in the extreme, and shows a mind whose moral degradation is without its parallel.

CHAPTER XLII.

HAUGHTY and scornful as ever; regarding themselves as overpowered, but not conquered; openly regretting their failure to establish a Southern Confederacy; backed up by President Johnson in their rebellious course, — the Southerners appear determined to reduce the blacks to a state of serfdom if they cannot have them as slaves. The new labor-laws of all the Southern States place the entire colored population as much in the hands of the whites as they were in the palmiest day of chattel slavery, if we except the buying and selling. The negro *whipping-post*, which the laws of war swept away, has, under Andrew Johnson's reconstruction policy, been again re-instated throughout the South. The Freedmen's Bureau is as powerless to-day to protect the emancipated blacks in their rights as was the Hon. Samuel Hoar to remain in South Carolina against the will of the slave-holders of the days of Calhoun and of McDuffie. Where the old masters cannot control their former slaves, they do not hesitate to shoot them down in open day, as the following will show: —

A Texas correspondent writes to "The New-York Evening Post" (he dare not allow his name and residence to be printed) as follows: —

"Every day I hear of murders of freedmen. Since five o'clock this afternoon, four new ones have been reported here. The disloyal press suppress the mention of such occurrences.

"Should there be another outbreak in Texas, very many Union men, as well as a large proportion of freedmen, would at once be massacred in order to bring about such another reign of terror as would make the South a unit. . . .

"Three freedmen were murdered in or near the line of an adjoining county a few days ago. The wagon which one of them was driving was robbed of all the fine goods it contained. The other two freedmen were shot by the same man, who is believed to be their former owner. The head of one of them was cut off, and they were left unburied. No investigation has been, or probably will be, made into these murders. If any Union man were to move in the matter, it would be at the peril of his life.

"The brave and loyal man who told me of these murders was applied to by a freedman, a kinsman of one of the murdered, for advice. The freedman was told to go to Austin, and report the facts to the agent of the Freedmen's Bureau; but he appears not to have arrived. Like the freedman despatched by the chief justice of Refugio County, with a letter setting forth the disorders in that county, he may have been shot on the road.

"My informant, seeing that I set about writing down the facts as to these murders just as he stated them, said to me, 'Do not make my name public, for it is all I can do to hold my own in — county just now;' and added, 'I keep no money in my house but a few dollars for current expenses. I can take care of myself in the daytime, but I do not feel safe at night.'"

On the 2d of April, 1866, a Mr. Quisenbery was tried at the Circuit Court for the County of Louisa, Va., for the murder of Washington Green. Green was the former slave of Quisenbery, had worked for said Quisenbery from the fall of Richmond, about the 3d of April, 1865, until about the 1st of October, 1865, when Quisenbery told him, the said Washington Green, that he had better go and get work somewhere else; that he would not pay him for any thing that he had done. Washington Green went to work for a lady to get some shingles for her, and Quisenbery made a contract with this lady, that she should pay him, for Green's getting the shingles, by thrashing out his, Quisenbery's, wheat. It did not satisfy Washington Green, that Quisenbery should not only refuse to pay him for the work which he had already done for him, but that he should also collect what he had earned by hard working for this lady. Green went to Quisenbery, and asked him for the amount of getting the shingles for this lady. Quisenbery said, "Washington, this is three times that you have been after me for that money; I am now going to my hog-pen, and I warn you not to follow me." He repeated that warning three times. He then went to the hog-pen, got over the fence, stooped down to throw out some corn that the hogs had not eaten. He looked up, and saw Washington Green at or near the fence, and said, "I thought I warned you not to follow me," and pulled out his knife, and stabbed Green in the throat, and killed him instantly. This is the evidence and confession of Quisenbery, who was tried, and the jury found a verdict of *not guilty*, without scarcely leaving the jury-box; and Quisenbery was declared guiltless of any crime amid the plaudits of the people.

At Jacksonville, Fla., on the 20th of June last, a freed-man complained before Col. Hart, that his last employer would not pay him. The black man afterwards went to the pine-woods, chopping logs. While absent, the man of whom he had complained got a woman to go to the freedman's wife, and get into a difficulty with her ; where-upon the freedman's wife was arrested, tried, found guilty, and fined fifty dollars, being unable to pay which, she was *put up at auction*, and sold to the person who would take her for the shortest time, and pay fine and costs. The *shortest time* was *four years !* Under another law of the State, the children were *bound out till they should become of age!*

A free colored man named Jordan opened, by permis-sion of the commandant of the post at Columbia, Tenn., a school for the blacks. The school went on smoothly till Monday, the 11th instant, when two soldiers of the Eighth Tennessee Cavalry went into the school, and broke it up ; but the teacher, being so advised, resumed his la-bor the next day. But, on the 14th, Messrs. Datty, Por-ter, White, and others, including soldiers of the Eighth Tennessee, the party headed by White the city constable, proceeded to the schoolroom, seized the teacher, and brought him under guard to the court-house, where he received a mock trial. When being asked for his au-thority for teaching a school, Mr. Jordan replied, that Lieut.-Col. Brown and Major Sawyer were his authority, and wished they would bring Major Sawyer in. One of the men went out, but was absent only for a moment, when he came in, stating that Major Sawyer could not be found; whereupon Mr. Andrews ordered that the teacher be given twenty-five lashes. And they were administered, the man receiving the scourge like a martyr, telling his persecutors that he was willing to suffer for the right; and that Christ had received the same punishment for the same purpose ; and he thought, if he could teach the children to read the Bible so that they might learn of heaven, he was doing a good work.   To this, a soldier of the Eighth Tennessee said, " If you want to go to heaven you must pray : you can't get there by teaching the niggers.   We can't go to school, and I'll be damned if niggers shall."

Volumes might be written, recounting the shameful outrages committed at the South since the surrender of Lee.   Not satisfied with murders of an individual character, the Southerners have, of late, gone into it more, extensively.   The first of these took place at Memphis, Tenn., May 4, 1866.[1]   A correspondent of Hon. W. D. Kelley, of Philadelphia, said, —

" I have been an eye-witness to such sights as should cause the age in which we live to blush.   Negro men have been shot down in cold blood on the streets ; barbers, at their chairs and in their own shops ; draymen on their drays, while attempting to earn an honest living ; hotel-waiters, while in the discharge of their duties ; hackmen, while driving female teachers of negro children to their schools ; laborers, while handling cotton on the wharves, &c.   All the negro schoolhouses, and all the negro churches, and many of the houses of the negroes, have been burned, this too, under the immediate auspices of the city police and the mayor : in fact, most of these outrages were committed by the police themselves, — *all Irish, and all rebels, and mostly drunk.*   This is not the half: I have no heart to recount the outrages I have *seen.*   The most prominent citizens stand on the streets, and see negroes hunted down and shot, and *laugh* at it as a good joke. Attempts have been made to fire every Government building, and fire has been set to many of the abodes and business-places of Union people.

"There is no doubt but that there is a *secret* organization sworn to purge the city of all Northern men who are not *rebels*, all negro teachers, all Yankee enterprise, and return the city 'to the good old days of Southern rule and chivalry.'

"When the miscreants had fired Collins's chapel (a large frame church, corner of Washington and Orleans Streets, which would now cost fully ten thousand dollars, to rebuild), they stood around the fire which lighted the midnight sky, and made the night hideous with their hellish cheers for 'Andy Johnson' and a 'white man's government!' And the supporters of the President, aside from being midnight burners of churches and schoolhouses, robbed women and children, and men, — sparing none on account of age, sex, physical disabilities, or innocence of crime, — even burning women and children alive.

"The board of aldermen had their usual meetings last night. Their proceedings show no reference to the riot. No rewards have been offered for the apprehension of the murderous assassins, thieves, and house-burners."

Next came, on a still larger scale, the rebel riot at New Orleans. The Military Commission appointed to investigate the cause of the riot charge it upon Mayor Monroe, Lieut.-Gov. Voorhies, and the rebel press of the city. The Commission speak of the murders as follows : —

"They can only say that the work of massacre was pursued with a cowardly ferocity unsurpassed in the annals of crime. Escaping negroes were mercilessly pur-

sued, shot, stabbed, and beaten to death by the mob and
police.   Wounded men on the ground begging for mercy
were savagely despatched by mob, police, firemen, and, incredible as it may seem, in two instances by women;
but, in two or three most honorable and exceptionable
cases, white men and members of the Convention were
protected by members of the police, both against the
mob, and against other policemen.   The chief of police,
by great exertions, defended in this manner Gov. Hahn.

"After the attack had commenced, the police appeared
to be under no control as such; but acted as and with
the mob.   Their cheers and waving of hats as they
threw the mangled Dostie, then supposed a *corpse, like a
dead dog into the cart, sufficiently show their unison of
feeling with their allies.*"

Nothing, we take it, is more apparent from the array
of evidence presented in this Report than that the New-
Orleans riot was a preconcerted, deliberate, cold-blooded
attempt to massacre the Unionists, white and black, of
that city.[2]   The design can be traced like the development of a tragedy.   Mayor Monroe is busy for a long
time in advance in stirring up the passions of the mob
by stigmatizing the members of the Convention as outlaws and revolutionists, threatening them with whole-
sale arrest, and preparing his police for action.   He might
have ascertained that the members had resolved to peacefully submit the legality of their course to the proper
tribunals; but he had bloodier ends in view.   He knew
that the excitement he had fanned would surely lead to
an outburst of violence, unless restrained by two forces
alone, — his police and the United-States troops.   To
keep the latter away, Mayor Monroe suppresses all re-
quisition for them until it is too late; and then tries to

cover up his conduct with downright falsehood and per-
jury. His police, instead of being brought forward
openly, so that they would have to take sides for the
preservation of order, are concealed in hiding-places till
the collision occurs ; when they rush forth as allies of the
mob, murdering negroes in cold blood ; firing repeatedly
into the Convention, even after a white flag is raised ;
shooting and barbarously maltreating the wounded ; and
perpetrating such feats of cowardly brutality and ferocity as were never before seen in this country, except in
the congenial affairs of Memphis and Fort Pillow.

Nothing goes so far towards reconciling one to what
is called the "total-depravity" theory, as the contem-
plation of those scenes of blood. They carry us back to
the crimes and cruelty of the Massacre of St. Bartholo-
mew. Mayor Monroe acts the part of the Duke of Guise ;
Lieut.-Gov. Voorhies, that of the Duke of Alva ; while
President Johnson acts the part of Charles IX., who, on
approaching the burning corpse of Admiral Coligny, exclaimed, "The smell of a dead enemy is always good."

During the mob, the appearance of rebel organizations
on the ground with marks and badges, and scores of similar incidents, show that the plot was as deliberate as it
was infernal.

Again : a dispassionate consideration of the facts detailed by the Commission will lead to the conclusion that
the underlying cause of the New-Orleans massacre was
the old virus of slavery, still existing in the passions of
Southern society, and likely to issue forth in violence
whenever it shall be favored by similar circumstances.
The members of the Louisiana Convention were entirely
harmless, no matter how obnoxious or how indiscreet
they were. Even if they were not disposed to submit

their pretensions to a legal test, — as they were, — there would have been no difficulty in making their peaceable arrest on the occurrence of their first overt act; but the mob of New Orleans, who, by the acquiescence of the better classes, or else in defiance of them through their great numerical preponderance, elect and control the city authorities, were determined to permit no such result of the controversy. The Convention claimed to exercise free speech; they would have none of that Northern innovation: it was composed of Union men; and they should be made to feel their place in " reconstructed " New Orleans: worse than all, they had for their allies and supporters *colored* Unionists; and *they* should be made such an example of as should deter any more such movements at the South. It was a bloody crusade against the men and the principles that had triumphed in the Government of this country. Well do this Commission say, that, but for martial law and the United-States troops, " fire and bloodshed would have raged throughout the night in all negro quarters of the city, and that the lives and property of Unionists and Northern men would have been at the mercy of the mob."

Finally: the Report throws an impressive light upon President Johnson's connection with the New-Orleans massacre. He had already, in a manner, inculpated himself in his speech at St. Louis. He there suppresses all the facts found by the Commission, and stigmatizes the members of the Convention as " traitors," engaged, under the instigation of Congress, in getting up a " rebellion," and therefore responsible for all the bloodshed that occurred. That is precisely the pretence of Mayor Monroe and his mob. Well might the President, therefore, play into their hands. Gen. Baird, from official experience, has been taught not to interfere with Mayor Monroe. When he telegraphs to Washington for orders, he gets no answer: the other side telegraph, and receive replies that encourage them in their course. Gen. Sheridan, like a true soldier, telegraphs the facts, with indignant comments; and his despatches are garbled for public effect. Of all the murderers on that dreadful day, not one has been called to account; nor has any one of them received therefor the least censure of the Government at Washington.

The appointment, since the riot, of Adams, one of the most notorious of the rioters, as sergeant in the police force, by Mayor Monroe, confirms the fact of his guilt in the massacre. The blood of the martyrs Dostie and Horton cries to Heaven for justice for the Union men of the South, white and black. The mob, composed of ex-rebel soldiers and citizens, that broke up the colored camp-meeting near Baltimore, Md., a few weeks after the New-Orleans riot, was only a part of the programme concocted by the men engaged in carrying out the reconstruction policy of Andrew Johnson.

CHAPTER XLIII.

PROTECTION FOR THE COLORED PEOPLE.

Protection for the Colored People South. — The Civil Rights Bill. — Liberty without the Ballot no Boon. — Impartial Suffrage. — Test Oaths not to be depended upon.

In attempting to form a Southern Confederacy, with slavery as its corner-stone, by breaking up the Union, and repudiating the Constitution, the people of the South compelled the National Government to abolish chattel slavery in self-defence. The protection, defence, and support which self-interest induced the master to extend to the slave have been taken away by the emancipation of the latter. This, taken in connection with the fact that the negroes, by assisting the Federal authorities to put down the Rebellion, gained the hatred of their old masters, placed the blacks throughout the South in a very bad position. Now, what shall be done to protect these people from the abuse of their former oppressors? The Civil Rights Bill passed by Congress is almost a dead letter, and many of the rebel judges declare it unconstitutional.[1] The States having relapsed into the hands of the late slave-holders, and they becoming the executioners of the law, the blacks cannot look for justice at their hands. The negro must be placed in a position to protect himself. How shall that be done? We answer, the only thing to save him is the ballot. Liberty without equality is no boon. Talk not of civil

without political emancipation! It is the technical plead
ing of the lawyer: it is not the enlarged view of the
statesman. If a man has no vote for the men and the
measures which tax himself, his family, and his property,
and all which determine his reputation, that man is still
a slave.

We are told — what seems to be the common idea —
that the elective franchise is not a *right*, but a *privilege*.
But is this true? We used to think so; that is, we as-
sented to it before we gave the subject any special
thought: but we do not think so now. We maintain, that
in a government like ours, a republican government, or
government of *the people*, the elective franchise, as it is
called, is not a mere privilege, but an actual and absolute
right, — a right belonging, of right, to every free man who
has not forfeited that right by crime. We in this country
enjoy what is properly called self-government, and self-
government necessarily implies the *right to vote*, — the
right to *help to govern*, and to make the laws; and this,
in a government like ours, a government of the people,
can only be done by or through the elective franchise.
We maintain that in self-government, or government of
the people, every man who is a free man and citizen has
a right to assist and take part in that government.
This right inheres and belongs to every man alike, to you
and me, and every other man, — no matter what the color
of his skin, — if he be a free man and citizen, and helps
to support the government by paying taxes: it is one of
the fundamental principles of self-government and of a
democratic or republican government. But the elective
franchise, the right to choose and elect the men who are
to fill the offices, and make the laws and execute them,
lies at the very bottom of such government. It is the

first principle and starting-point, and is as much implied in the very name and idea of self-government, or *government of the people*, as any other principle, right, or idea pertaining to such a government.   Does any one doubt this ?   Let him ask himself what constitutes a republican government, or government of the people, and what is implied by such a government, and he will soon see, that without the elective franchise, or right to choose rulers and law-makers, there can be no such government.   It will not do, therefore, to call this right a privilege.   If it is but a privilege, all may be deprived of its exercise. What sort of a republican or self government would that be in which none of the people were allowed to vote ? But if it is but a privilege, and granted to but a class or part, it may be restricted to a still smaller part, and finally allowed to none !

Any proposal to submit the question of the political or civil rights of the negroes to the arbitrament of the whites is as unjust and as absurd as to submit the question of the political rights of the whites to the arbitrament of the negroes, with this difference, — that the negroes are loyal everywhere, and the great body of the whites disloyal everywhere.

A white loyalist of the South, one who remained loyal during the whole of the Rebellion, says, —

"To permit the whites to disfranchise the negroes is to permit those who have been our enemies to ostracize our friends.   The negroes are the only persons in those States who have not been in arms against us.   They have not been in arms against us.   They have always and everywhere been friendly, and not hostile, to us. They alone have a deep interest in the continued supremacy of the United States ; for their freedom depends on it.   On them alone can we depend to suppress a new insurrection.   They alone will be inclined to vote for the friends of the Government in all the Southern States.   They alone have sheltered, fed, and pioneered our starved and hunted brethren through the swamps and woods of the South, in their flight from those who now aspire to rule them.

"The *shame and folly of deserting the negroes* are equalled by the *wisdom of recognizing and protecting their power.*   They will form a clear and controlling majority against the united white vote in South Carolina, Mississippi, and Louisiana.   With a very small accession from the loyal whites, they will form a majority in Alabama, Georgia, and Virginia.   Unaided in all those States, they will be a majority in many congressional and legislative districts; and that alone suffices to break the terrible and menacing unity of the Southern vote in Congress."

It is said that the slaves are too ignorant to exercise the elective franchise judiciously.   To this we reply, they are as intelligent as the average of "poor whites," and were intelligent enough to be Unionists during the great struggle, when the Federal Government needed friends.   In a conflict with the spirit of rebellion, the blacks can always be depended upon, the whites cannot; and, for its own security against future outbreaks, the National Government should see that the negro is placed where he can help himself, and assist it.

The ballot will secure for the colored people respect; that respect will be a protection for their schools; and, through education and the elective franchise, the negro is to rise to a common level of humanity in the Southern States.

But little aid can be expected for the freedmen from the Freedmen's Bureau ; for its officers, if not Southern men, will soon become upon intimate terms with the former slave-holders, and the Bureau will be converted into a power of oppression, instead of a protection.

The anti-Union whites know full well the great influence of the ballot, and therefore are afraid to give it to the blacks. The franchise will be of more service to this despised race than a standing army in the South. The ballot will be his standing army. The poet has truly said, —

> " There is a weapon surer yet,
>   And better, than the bayonet;
> A weapon that comes down as still
>   As snow-flakes fall upon the sod,
> And executes a freeman's will
>   As lightning does the will of God;
> A weapon that no bolts nor locks
>   Can bar. It is the ballot-box."

Even " The New-York Herald," some time ago, went so far as to say, —

" We would give the suffrage at once to four classes of Southern negroes. First, and emphatically, to every negro who has borne arms in the cause of the United States ; second, to every negro who owns real estate ; third, to every negro who can read and write ; and, fourth, to every negro that had belonged to any religious organization or church for five years before the war. These points would cover every one that ought to vote ; and they would insure in every negro voter a spirit of manhood as well as discipline, some practical shrewdness, intellectual development, and moral consciousness and culture."

Impartial suffrage is what we demand for the colored people of the Southern States. No matter whether the basis be a property or an educational qualification, let it be impartial: upon this depends the future happiness of all classes at the South. Test-oaths, or promises to support the laws, mean nothing with those who have come up through the school of slavery.

"As for oaths, the rebels, whose whole career has been a violation of the solemn obligations of which oaths are merely the sign, care no more for them than did the rattlesnake to which our soldiers in West Virginia once administered the oath of allegiance. Impartial suffrage affords the only sure and permanent means of combating the rebel element in the Southern States."

CHAPTER XLIV.

CASTE.

Slavery the Foundation of Caste. — Black its Preference. — The General Wish for Black Hair and Eyes. — No Hatred to Color. — The White Slave. — A Mistake. — Stole his Thunder. — The Burman. — Pew for Sale.

CASTE is usually found to exist in communities or countries among majorities, and against minorities. The basis of it is owing to some supposed inferiority or degradation attached to the hated ones. However, nothing is more foolish than this prejudice. But the silliest of all caste is that which is founded on *color ;* for those who entertain it have not a single logical reason to offer in its defence.

The fact is, slavery has been the cause of all the prejudice against the negro. Wherever the blacks are ill treated on account of their color, it is because of their identity with a race that has long worn the chain of slavery. Is there any thing in black, that it should be hated ? If so, why do we see so much black in common use as clothing among all classes ? Indeed, black is preferred to either white or colors. How often the young man speaks in ecstasies of the black eyes and black hair of his lady-love! Look at the hundreds of advertised hair-dyes, used for the purpose of changing nature ! See men with their gray beards dyed black; women with those beautiful black locks, which, but yes-

terday, were as white as the driven snow! Not only
this, but even those with light or red whiskers run to
the dye-kettle, steal a color which nature has refused
them, and, an hour after, curse the negro for a complexion that is not stolen. If black is so hateful, why
do not gentlemen have their boots whitewashed? If the
slaves of the South had been white, the same prejudice
would have existed against them. . Look at the "poor
white trash," as the lower class of whites in the Southern States are termed.

Henry Clay would much rather have spent an evening
with his servant Charles than to have made a companion of one of his poor white neighbors. It is the condition, not the color, that is so hateful.

"When the Britons first became known to the Tyrian
mariners," says Macaulay, "they were little superior to
the Sandwich Islanders." Cæsar, writing home from
Britain, said, "They are the most ignorant people I ever
conquered." Many of the Britons, after their conquest
by the Romans, were sent as slaves to Rome. Cicero,
writing to his friend Atticus, advised him not to buy
slaves from England; "because," said he, "they cannot
be taught to read, and are the ugliest and most stupid
race I ever saw." These writers created a prejudice
against the Britons, which caused them to be sold very
cheap in Rome, where they were seen for years with
brass collars on, containing their owner's name. The
prejudice against the American negro is not worse to-
day than that which existed against the Britons. But, as
soon as the condition of the poor, ill-treated, and enslaved Britons was changed, the caste disappears.[1]

Twenty-five years ago, a slave escaped from Tennessee, and came to Buffalo, N.Y. He was as fair as the

majority of whites, and, having been a house-servant, his manners and language were not bad. His name was Green. It was said that he had helped himself to some of his master's funds before leaving. For more than a month he had boarded at the American, the finest hotel in the city, where he sat at table with the boarders, and occupied the parlors in common with the rest of the inmates.

Mr. Green passed for a Southern gentleman, sported a gold watch, smoked his Havanas, and rode out occasionally. He was soon a favorite, especially with the daughters of Col. D——. Unfortunately for Mr. Green, one day, as he was taking his seat at the dinner-table, he found himself in front of one of his master's neighbors, who recognized him. The Southerner sent for the landlord, with whom he had a few moments' conversation, after which mine host approached the boarder, and said, "We don't allow niggers at the table here : get up. You must wait till the servants eat." Mr. Green was driven from the table, not on account of his color, but his condition. Under the old reign of slavery, it not unfrequently occurred that the master's acknowledged sons or daughters were of a much darker complexion than some of the slave children.

On one occasion, after my old master had returned home from the Legislature (of which he was a member), he had many new visitors. One of these, a Major Moore, called in my master's absence. The major had never been to our place before, and therefore we were all strangers to him. The servant showed the visitor into the parlor, and the mistress soon after came in, and to whom the major introduced himself. I was at that time about ten years old, and was as white as most white boys. Whenever visitors came to the house, it was my part of the programme to dress myself in a neat suit, kept for such times, and go into the room, and stand behind the lady's chair. As I entered the room on this occasion, I had to pass near by the major to reach the mistress. As I passed him, mistaking me for the son, he put out his hand, and said, " How do you do, bub ? " And, before any answer could be given, he continued, " Madam, I would have known your son if I had met him in Mexico; for he looks so much like his papa." The lady's face reddened up, and she replied, " That's one of the niggers, sir ; " and told me to go to the kitchen.

On my master's return home, I heard him and the major talking the matter over in the absence of the mistress. " I came near playing the devil here to-day, colonel," said the major. — " In what way ? " inquired the former. "It is always my custom," said the latter, " to make fond of the children where I visit; for it pleases the mammas. So, to-day, one of your little niggers came into the room, and I spoke to him, reminding the madam how much he resembled you." — " Ha, ha, ha ! " exclaimed the colonel, and continued, "you did not miss it much by calling him my son. Ha, ha, ha ! "

An incident of a rather amusing character took place on Cayuga Lake some years ago. I had but recently returned from England, where I had never been unpleasantly reminded of my color, when I was called to visit the pretty little city of Ithaca. On my return, I came down the lake in the steamer which leaves early in the morning. When the bell rang for breakfast, I went to the table, where I found some twenty or thirty persons. I had scarcely taken my seat, when a rather snobby-appearing man, of dark complexion, looking as if a South-

Carolina or Georgia sun had tanned him, began rubbing his hands, and, turning up his nose, called the steward, and said to him, " Is it the custom on this boat to put niggers at the table with white people? " The servant stood for a moment, as if uncertain what reply to make, when the passenger continued, " Go tell the captain that I want him." Away went the steward. I had been too often insulted on account of my connection with the slave, not to know for what the captain was wanted. However, as I was hungry, I commenced helping myself to what I saw before me, yet keeping an eye to the door, through which the captain was soon to make his appearance. As the steward returned, and I heard the heavy boots of the commander on the stairs, a happy thought struck me; and I eagerly watched for the coming-in of the officer.

A moment more, and a strong voice called out, " Who wants me? "

I answered at once, " I, sir."

" What do you wish? " asked the captain.

" I want you to take this man from the table," said I.

At this unexpected turn of the affair, the whole cabin broke out into roars of laughter; while my rival on the opposite side of the table seemed bursting with rage. The captain, who had joined in the merriment, said, —

" Why do you want him taken from the table? "

" Is it your custom, captain," said I, " to let niggers sit at table with white folks on your boat? "

This question, together with the fact that the other passenger had sent for the officer, and that I had " stolen his thunder," appeared to please the company very much, who gave themselves up to laughter; while the Southern-looking man left the cabin with the exclamation, " *Damn fools!* "

Nothing is more ridiculous than the legal decision in the States of Ohio and Michigan, that a man containing not more than one-sixteenth of African blood in his veins shall be considered a white man, and, upon the above basis, shall enjoy the elective franchise.

We know of a family in Cincinnati, with three brothers, the youngest of whom is very fair, and who, under the above rule, is a voter; while the other two brothers are too dark to exercise the suffrage. Now, it so happens that the voting brother is ignorant and shiftless, while the others are splendid scholars. Where there is a great difference in the complexion of the husband and wife, there is generally a much greater difference in the color of the children; and this picking out the sons, on account of their fair complexion, seems cruel in the extreme, as it creates a jealous feeling in the family. While visiting my friend William Still, Esq., in Philadelphia, some time since, I was much amused at seeing his little daughter, a child of eight or nine years, and her cousin, entering the omnibus which passed the door, going towards their school.[2] Colored persons were not allowed to ride in those conveyances; and one of the girls, being very fair, would pay the fare for both; while the dark-complexioned one would keep her face veiled. Thus the two children daily passed unmolested from their homes to the school, and returned. I was informed that once while I was there the veil unfortunately was lifted, the dark face seen, and the child turned out of the coach. How foolish that one's ride on a stormy day should depend entirely on a black veil !

"Colorphobia, which has hitherto been directed against 'American citizens of African descent,' has broken out in a new direction. Mong Chan Loo is a Burman who recently graduated at Lewisburg University, Penn., and has since been studying medicine, preparatory to returning to Asia as a missionary. He is quite dark, but has straight hair, and is a gentlemen of much cultivation. The other day, he took passage on the Muskingum-river packet, " J. H. Bert," and, when the supper-bell rang, was about to seat himself at the table. The captain prevented him, informing him that, by the rules of the boat, colored persons must eat separately from the whites. He grew indignant at this, refused to eat on the boat at all, and, on arriving at Marietta, sued the owners of the boat for five thousand dollars damages for ' mental and bodily anguish suffered.' The case is a novel one ; and its decision will perhaps involve the question, whether Africans alone, or Asiatics, and, perhaps, all dark-complexioned people, are included in the designation ' colored.' If the more sweeping definition prevails, brunettes will have to be provided with legally-attested pedigrees to secure for themselves seats at the first table and other Caucasian privileges." — *Cincinnati Gazette.*

" The Dunkards, a peculiar religious society, numerous in some of the Western States, at their recent annual meeting discussed the question, ' Shall we receive colored persons into the church? and shall we salute them with the holy kiss ?' It was decided that they should be received into the church, but that all the members were to be left to their own choice and taste in regard to saluting their colored brethren, with the understanding, however, that all who refused to do so were to be regarded as weak."

In the year 1844, I visited a town in the State of

Ohio, where a radical abolitionist informed me that he owned a pew in the village church, but had not attended worship there for years, owing to the proslavery character of the preacher.

"Why don't you sell your pew?" I inquired.

"I offered to sell it, last week, to a man, for ten dollars' worth of manure for my garden," said he; "but the farmer, who happens to be one of the pillars of the church, wants it for five dollars."

"What did it cost?" I inquired.

"Fifty dollars," was the reply.

"Are they very proslavery, the congregation?" I asked.

"Yes: they hate a black man worse than *pizen*," said he.

"Have you any colored family in your neighborhood?" I inquired.

"We have," said he, "a family about four miles from here."

"Are they very black?" I asked.

"Yes: as black as tar," said he.

"Now," said I, "my friend, I can put you in the way of selling your pew, and for its worth, or near what it cost you."

"If you can, I'll give you half I get," he replied.

"Get that colored family, every one of them, take them to church, don't miss a single Sunday; and, my word for it, in less than four weeks, they, the church-folks, will make you an offer," said I.

An arrangement was made with Mr. Spencer, the black man, by which himself, wife, and two sons, were to attend church four successive Sabbaths; for which, they were to receive in payment a hog. The following

Sunday, Mason's pew was the centre of attraction. From the moment that the Spencer Family arrived at the church, till the close of the afternoon service, the eyes of the entire congregation were turned towards " the niggers." Early on Monday, Mr. Mason was called upon by the " pillar," who said, " I've concluded to give you ten dollars' worth of manure for your pew, Mr. Mason."

" I can't sell it for that," was the reply. " I ask fifty dollars for my pew ; and I guess Mr. Spencer will take it, if he likes the preaching," continued the abolitionist.

" What ! " said the " pillar," "does that nigger want the pew ? "

" He'll take it if the preaching suits him," returned Mason.

The churchman left with a flea in his ear. The second Sunday, the blacks were all on hand to hear the lining of the first hymn. The news of the pew being occupied by the negroes on the previous occasion had spread far and wide, and an increase of audience was the result. The clergyman preached a real negro-hating sermon, apparently prepared for the express purpose of driving the blacks away. However, this failed ; for the obnoxious persons were present in the afternoon. Mr. Mason was called upon on Monday by another weighty member, who inquired if the pew was for sale, and its price.

" Fifty dollars," was the reply.

" I'll give you twenty-five dollars," said the member."

" Fifty dollars, and nothing less," was Mason's answer.

The weighty member left, without purchasing the pew. Being on a lecturing tour in the vicinity, I ran into town, occasionally, to see how the matter progressed; for I had an eye to one-half of the proceeds of the sale of the pew.

During the week, Spencer came, complained of the preaching, saying that his wife could not and would not stand it, and would refuse to attend again; whereupon, I went over, through a dreary rain, and promised the wife a shilling calico-dress if she would fulfil the agreement. This overcame her objections. I also arranged that two colored children of another family, near by, should be borrowed for the coming Sunday. Mason was asked how the Spencers liked the preaching. He replied that the blacks were well pleased, and especially with the last sermon, alluding to the negro-hating discourse.

The following Sunday found Mason's pew filled to overflowing; for the two additional ones had left no space unoccupied. That Sunday did the work completely; for the two borrowed boys added interest to the scene by taking different courses. One was tumbling about over the laps of the older persons in the pew, attracting rather more attention than was due him, and occasionally asking for " bed and butter ; " while the smaller one slept, and snored loud enough to be heard several pews away. On Monday morning following, Mr. Mason was called upon. The pew was sold for fifty dollars cash. I received my portion of the funds, and gave Spencer's wife the calico gown. Mason called in the few hated radicals, and we had a general good time.

During the same lecturing tour, I was called to visit the village of Republic, some thirty miles from Sandusky.

On taking a seat in one of the cars where other passengers had seated themselves, I was ordered out, with the remark, that "Niggers ain't allowed in here." Refusing to leave the car, two athletic men, employed by the road, came in at the bidding of the conductor, and, taking me by the collar, dragged me out.

"Where shall I ride?" I asked. "Where you please; but not in these cars," was the reply. Under ordinary circumstances, I would have declined going by the train. But I had an appointment, and must go. As the signal for starting was given, I reluctantly mounted a flour-barrel in the open freight-car attached to the train, and away we went through the woods.

From my position, I had a very good view of the passengers in the nearest car, and must confess that they did not appear to be the most refined individuals. The majority looked like farmers. There were some drovers, one of whom, with his dog at his feet, sat at the end window : the animal occasionally got upon the seat by the side of its master, when the latter would take him by the ears, and pull him off. The drover seemed to say to me, as he eyed me sitting on the barrel in the hot sun, "You can't come where my dog is." At the first stopping-place, a dozen or more laboring-men, employed in repairing the road, got on the train with their pick-axes and shovels. They, too, took seats in a passenger-car. I had a copy of Pope's poems, and was trying to read "The Essay on Man;" but almost failed, on account of the severity of the sun. However, a gentleman in the car, seeing my condition, took pity on me, and, at the next stopping-place, kindly lent me his umbrella; which was no sooner hoisted than it drew the attention of the drover at one of the end windows, and some of the Irishmen at the other, who set up a jolly laugh at my expense. Up to this time, the conductor had not called on me for my ticket; but, as the train was nearing the place of my destination, he climbed upon the car, came to me, and, holding out his hand, said, "I'll take your ticket, sir."—"I have none," said I. "Then, I'll take your fare," continued he, still holding out his hand. "How much is it?" I inquired. "A dollar and a quarter," he replied. "How much do you charge those in the passenger-car?" — "The same," was the response. "Do you think that I will pay as much as those having comfortable seats? No, sir. I shall do no such thing," said I. "Then," said the conductor, "you must get off."—"Stop your train, and I'll get off," I replied. "Do you think I'll stop these cars for you?" "Well," said I, "you can do as you please. I will not pay full fare, and ride on a flour-barrel in the hot sun." — "Since you make so much fuss about it, give me a dollar, and you may go," said the conductor. "I'll do no such thing," I replied. "Why? Don't you wish to pay your fare?" asked he. "Yes," I replied. "I will pay what's right; but I'll not pay you a dollar for riding on a flour-barrel in the hot sun." — "Then, since you feel so terribly bad about it, give me seventy-five cents, and I'll say no more about it," said the officer. "No, sir: I shall not do it," said I. "What do you mean to pay?" asked he. "How much do you charge per hundred for freight?" I asked. "Twenty-five cents per hundred," answered the conductor. "Then I'll pay thirty-seven and a-half cents," said I; "for I weigh one hundred and fifty pounds." The astonished man eyed me from head to feet; while the drover and the Irish laborers, who were piled up at each window of the passenger-car, appeared not a little amused at what they supposed to be a muss between the conductor and me.

Finally, the officer took a blank account out of his pocket, and said, " Give me thirty-seven and a-half cents, and I'll set you down as freight." I paid over the money, and saw myself duly put among the other goóds in the freight-car.

A New-York journal is responsible for the following : —

"It is not many months since a colored man came to this city from abroad. A New-York merchant had been in business connection with him for several years ; and from that business connection had realized a fortune, and felt that he must treat him kindly. When Sunday came, he invited him to go to church with him. He went ; and the merchant took him into his own pew, near the pulpit, in a fashionable church. There was a prominent member of the church near the merchant, who saw this with great amazement. He could not be mistaken : it was a genuine " nigger," and not a counterfeit. Midway in his sermon, the minister discovered him, and was so confused by it, that he lost his place, and almost broke down.

After service, the man who sat near the merchant went to him, and in great indignation asked, —

" What does this mean ? "

" What does what mean ?"

" That you should bring a nigger into this church ? "

" It is my pew."

" Your pew, is it ? And, because it is your pew, you must insult the whole congregation ! "

" He is intelligent and well educated," answered the merchant.

" What do I care for that ? He is a nigger ! "

" But he is a friend of mine."

"What of that? Must you therefore insult the whole congregation?"

"But he is a Christian, and belongs to the same denomination."

"What do I care for that? Let him worship with his nigger Christians."

"But he is worth five million dollars," said the merchant.

"Worth what?"

"Worth five million dollars."

"For God's sake introduce me to him," was the reply."

CHAPTER XLV.

SIXTH REGIMENT UNITED—STATES VOLUNTEERS.

Organization of the Regiment. — Assigned to Hard Work. — Brought under Fire. — Its Bravery. — Battle before Richmond. — Gallantry of the Sixth. — Officers' Testimony.

THE following sketch of the Sixth Regiment United-States colored troops was kindly furnished by a gentleman of Philadelphia, but came too late to appear in its proper place.

The Sixth Regiment United-States colored troops was the second which was organized at Camp William Penn, near Philadelphia, by Lieut.-Col. Louis Wagner, of the Eighty-eighth Pennsylvania Volunteers. The regiment left Philadelphia on the 14th of October, 1863, with nearly eight hundred men, and a full complement of officers, a large majority of whom had been in active service in the field.

The regiment reported to Major-Gen. B. F. Butler, at Fortress Monroe, and were assigned to duty at Yorktown, Va., and became part of the brigade (afterwards so favorably known), under the command of Col. S. A. Duncan, Fourth United-States colored troops. Here they labored upon the fortifications, and became thoroughly disciplined under the tuition of their colonel, John W. Ames, formerly captain of the Eleventh Infantry, United-States Army, ably seconded by Lieut.-Col. Royce and Major Kiddoo. During the winter, the regiment took a prominent part in the several raids made in the direction of Richmond, and exhibited qualities that elicited the praise of their officers, and showed that they could be fully relied upon in more dangerous work.

The regiment was ordered to Camp Hamilton, Virginia, in May, 1864; where a division of colored troops was formed, and placed under the command of Brig.-Gen. Hinks. In the expedition made up the James River the same month, under Gen. Butler, this division took part. The white troops were landed at Bermuda Hundreds. Three regiments of colored men were posted at various points along the river. Duncan's brigade landed at City Point, where they immediately commenced fortifications. The Sixth and Fourth Regiments were soon after removed to Spring Hill, within five miles of Petersburg. Here they labored night and day upon those earthworks, which were soon to be the scene of action which was to become historical. The Sixth was in a short time left alone, by the removal of the Fourth Regiment to another point.

On the 29th of May, the rebel forces made an assault on the picket-line, the enemy soon after attacking in strong force, but were unable to drive back the picket-line any considerable distance. The Fourth Regiment was ordered to the assistance of the Sixth; but our forces were entirely too weak to make it feasible or prudent to attack the enemy, who withdrew during the night, having accomplished nothing.

This was the first experience of the men under actual fire, and they behaved finely. When the outer works around Petersburg were attacked, June 15, Duncan's brigade met the rebels, and did good service, driving the enemy before him. We had a number killed and wounded in this engagement. The rebels sought shelter in their main works, which were of the most formidable character. These defences had been erected by the labor of slaves, detailed for the purpose. Our forces followed them to their stronghold. The white troops occupied the right; and in order to attract the attention of the enemy, while these troops were manœuvring for a favorable attacking position, the colored soldiers were subject to a most galling fire for several hours, losing a number of officers and men. Towards night, the fight commenced in earnest by the troops on the right, who quickly cleared their portion of the line : this was followed by the immediate advance of the colored troops, the Fourth, Fifth, Sixth, and Twenty-second Regiments. In a very short time, the rebels were driven from the whole line ; these regiments capturing seven pieces of artillery, and a number of prisoners. For their gallantry in this action, the colored troops received a highly complimentary notice from Gen. W. H. Smith, in General Orders.

A few hours after entering the rebel works, our soldiers were gladdened by a sight of the veterans of the Army of the Potomac, who that night relieved our men at the front. A glance at the strong works gave the new-comers a better opinion of the fighting qualities of the negroes than they had calculated upon ; and a good feeling was at once established, that rapidly dispelled most of the prejudices then existing against the blacks ; and from that time to the close of the war the negro soldier stood high with the white troops.

After spending some time at the Bermuda Hundreds, the Sixth Regiment was ordered to Dutch Gap, Va., where, on the 16th of August, they assisted in driving the rebels from Signal Hill ; Gen. Butler, in person, leading our troops. The Sixth Regiment contributed its share towards completing Butler's famous canal, during which time they were often very much annoyed by the rebel shells thrown amongst them. The conduct of the men throughout these trying scenes reflected great credit upon them. On the 29th of September, the regiment occupied the advance in the demonstration made by Butler that day upon Richmond. The first line of battle was formed by the Fourth and Sixth Regiments: the latter entered the fight with three hundred and fifteen men, including nineteen officers.

The enemy were driven back from within two miles of Deep Bottom, to their works at New-Market Heights: the Sixth was compelled to cross a small creek, and then an open field. They were met by a fearful fire from the rebel works, men fell by scores: still the regiment went forward. The color-bearers, one after another, were killed or wounded, until the entire color-guard were swept from the field. Two hundred and nine men, and fourteen officers, were killed and wounded. Few fields of battle showed greater slaughter than this; and in no conflict did both officers and men prove themselves more brave. Capts. York and Sheldon and Lieut. Meyer were killed close to the rebel works. Lieuts. Pratt, Landon, and McEvoy subsequently died of the wounds received. Lieut. Charles Fields, Company A, was killed on the skirmish line: this left the company in charge of the first sergeant, Richard Carter, of Philadelphia, who kept it in its advanced position throughout the day, commanding with courage and great ability, attracting marked attention for his officer-like bearing. During the battle many instances of unsurpassed bravery were shown by the common soldier, which proved that these heroic men were fighting for the freedom of their race, and the restoration of a Union that should protect man in his liberty without regard to color.   No regiment did more towards extinguishing prejudice against the negro than the patriotic Sixth.

> " And thus are Afric's injured sons
> The oppressor's scorn abating,
> And to the world's admiring gaze
> Their manhood vindicating."

The writer regrets that he cannot remember all those whose good conduct in this our last battle deserves honorable mention.   It may not, however, be invidious to mention the names remembered.   These are, Sergt.- Major Hawkins, Sergt. Jackson, Company B (since deceased) ; Sergts. Ellesberry, Kelley, Terry, and Carter.   All of these, as well as a number of others, were capable of filling positions as commissioned officers.

Several of the enlisted men received medals for gallantry, and were mentioned in General Orders by Major- Gen. Butler.   The works which the Sixth Regiment attempted to take at such fearful cost of life were in a short time taken at the point of the bayonet by another brigade of colored troops.   Had these latter been present to aid in the first attack, it would have saved many valuable lives ; for the force was entirely too weak for the object.   When the Sixth Regiment was finally paid off at Philadelphia, at the close of the Rebellion, the officers held a farewell meeting at the Continental Hotel; and the following resolutions were adopted as expressive of their appreciation of the conduct of the troops under their command : —

" 1. *Resolved*, That, in our intercourse with them during the past two years, they have shown themselves to be brave, reliable, and efficient as soldiers ; patient to en dure, and prompt to execute.

" 2. That, being satisfied with their conduct in the high position of soldiers of the United States, we see no reason why they should not be fully recognized as equals, honorable and responsible citizens of the same."

From the commencement of the enlistment of colored troops, to the close of the war, there were engaged in active service one hundred and sixty-nine thousand six hundred and twenty-four colored men.

NOTES

Chapter I

1. More than two-thirds of this chapter is a verbatim compilation of eight passages from Livermore's *An Historical Research*. Brown's original writing in the chapter consists of the first two and a half pages and a few paragraphs which link the quoted passages.

2. As in the first paragraph of the Preface to his *Clotel* and in the second paragraph of its Chapter XXI, Brown wrote here 1620 for 1619, the year generally given in American history as that in which Negro slavery was introduced into colonial America, the place being Jamestown, Virginia.

Chapter II

1. With the exception of the first two paragraphs, this chapter is essentially the same as the sketch of Denmark Vesey in the several editions of Brown's *The Black Man: His Antecedents, His Genius, and His Achievements* (New York and Boston, 1863 and 1865), pp. 142-148. The time of Vesey's abortive insurrection was not 1812, as Brown said in the second paragraph that it was, but June, 1822.

Chapters III and IV

1. Brown published under the heading "Celebrated Colored Americans" an article entitled "Nat Turner"

and one entitled "Madison Washington" in *The Pine and Palm* (Boston and New York) respectively for August 3 and 17, 1861. These articles were reprinted with only minor changes in the several editions of *The Black Man,* whence they were reprinted as Chapters III and IV in *The Negro in the American Rebellion.* In this work the article on Nat Turner was reduced to one-half of its original length, and the first and the last three paragraphs of the one on Madison Washington were added.

For an account of Brown's sources for these articles, see William Edward Farrison's *William Wells Brown: Author and Reformer* (Chicago: The University of Chicago Press, 1969), pp. 338-340.

2. The customary present tense in the first three sentences in this paragraph should have been changed to the past tense, since slavery had been abolished before *The Negro in the American Rebellion* was published.

Chapter VI

1. Brown's reference here is to James Redpath's *The Public Life of Captain John Brown* (Boston, 1860).

Chapter VII

1. This paragraph is an adaptation of the first two paragraphs in the sketch of Captain Cailloux in the second and later editions of *The Black Man* (1863 and 1865), pp. 297-298.

2. The meeting referred to here was held on April 23, 1861, in the wake of the fall of Fort Sumter and Lincoln's call for 75,000 volunteers. For a full account

of it, see William Edward Farrison, *op. cit.*, pp. 331-333.

Chapter IX

1. Wendell Phillips delivered his famous lecture entitled *Toussaint L'Ouverture* first in the fall of 1861 in New York and next in Boston. One purpose of the lecture was to create sentiment in favor of the enlistment of Negroes in the Union army. Warren Choate Shaw, *History of American Oratory* (Indianapolis, 1928), pp. 352-355.

2. This account of James Lawson was taken from his sketch in the second and later editions of *The Black Man*, pp. 291-297.

Chapter XI

1. There were reports of Tillman's heroic deed in the *New York Herald* and the *New York Daily Tribune* for July 22, 1861.

2. The name "George Green" in the subtitle of this chapter is incorrect. The Negro steward who was instrumental in the liberation of the *Enchantress* was Jacob Garrick. There was a report of his feat in the *New York Daily Tribune* for August 1, 1861.

3. Accounts of Smalls's exploit were given in the *New York Commercial Advertiser*, in the *New York Herald* for May 18, 1862, and in an editorial in the *New York Daily Tribune* for May 20. In a sketch of Smalls in the several editions of *The Black Man*, Brown had quoted from only the first and third of these accounts.

Chapter XIII

1. For a brief account of Gordon's case, see Helen Tunnicliff Catterall (Editor), *Judicial Cases Concerning American Slavery and the Negro* (Washington, D. C.), IV (1936), 408 and 409.

Chapter XV

1. This is one of the oldest and most popular Negro spirituals. The stanzas Brown gave are different from those found in the most familiar versions of it, but the chorus is essentially the same. In spite of its age and popularity, this spiritual was not included in either of the pioneering collections of Negro spirituals, namely, Thomas Wentworth Higginson, "Negro Spirituals," *The Atlantic Monthly,* June, 1867; and William Francis Allen, Charles Pickard Ware, and Lucy McKim Garrison, *Slave Songs of the United States* (New York, 1867). Brown's book was off the press before either of these collections was published.

2. Mrs. Frances E. W. Harper (1825-1811) was an anti-slavery lecturer with whom Brown shared many platforms. She was also a prolific poet, writer of prose stories, temperance worker, and lyceum lecturer. William Still, *The Underground Rail Road* (Philadelphia, 1872), pp. 755-780. Benjamin Brawley, *Early Negro American Writers* (Chapel Hill, N. C., 1935, and Freeport, N. Y., 1968), pp. 290-298.

Chapter XX

1. The Reverend Leonard A. Grimes, who had spent two years in a prison in Richmond for helping fugitive slaves to escape from Virginia, was a prominent Ne-

gro abolitionist and for many years the pastor of Twelfth Baptist Church in Boston. There are sketches of his life in the several editions of Brown's *The Black Man* and *The Rising Son* (Boston, 1874 *et seq.*) and William J. Simmons's *Men of Mark: Eminent, Progressive and Rising* (Cleveland, 1887).

2. Since the Negro population of Massachusetts was too small to supply a complement of enlistees for a regiment, agents authorized by the governor of the state had recruited enlistees wherever they could find them. Brown, who was one of the agents, had recruited not only in Massachusetts but also in New York, New Jersey, and Pennsylvania.

Chapter XXIII

1. This chapter is mainly a combination and adaptation of the sketches of Captains André Cailloux and Joseph Howard from the second and later editions of Brown's *The Black Man*. Both of the newspapers from which Brown quoted the laudatory passages at the end of the chapter erroneously referred only to the Second Regiment Louisiana Native Guards as participants in the battle of Port Hudson instead of the First Regiment. In the quotations Brown replaced "Second" with "First" but did not inform his readers of his correction. In this chapter, as in *The Black Man* and elsewhere, he consistently misspelled Cailloux's surname.

Chapter XXVII

1. Most probably Brown's authority for this story was James Redpath's *The Public Life of Captain John Brown* (Boston, 1860), pp. 396-397. In 1882 John Avis,

the jailer who had accompanied John Brown from the prison to the scaffold, declared the story "wholly incorrect." Oswald Garrison Villard, *John Brown, 1800-1859: A Biography Fifty Years After* (Boston and New York, 1910), pp. 670-677.

2. This poem entitled "Col. Robert G. Shaw" was published in *The Liberator* for March 24, 1865, p. 48, with the following prefatory note: "An esteemed friend encloses, for the *Liberator,* the following expressive poem, written by a young lady in Florence, Italy." Brown's version differs from that in *The Liberator* only in minor instances of capitalization, the use of italics, and punctuation.

3. Mrs. Lydia Maria Child included this poem in her *The Freedmen's Book* (Boston, 1865), pp. 268-269, and named Eliza B. Sedgwick as its author. Brown's version is the same as the one in that volume with the exception of unimportant differences in punctuation.

Chapter XXVIII

1. This poem entitled "The Slave-Martyr" was reprinted in *The Anglo-African* (New York) for June 13, 1863, and in *The Liberator* for July 10, in both instances from *The American Baptist.* It was written by Miss E. W. (according to *The Anglo-African*) or E. B. (according to *The Liberator*) Brown.

Chapter XXXVI

1. In the first sentence of this chapter, 1832 was erroneously written for 1852, and Drayton for Dayton.
From the beginning through the sentence "So, sir,

for once, you have a man standing before you without
a name" (p. 288), this chapter is a repetition of the
sketch entitled "A Man Without a Name" in the several editions of *The Black Man*. With variations in
some details and the addition of others, notably that
of the beating of the overseer, this is essentially an
account of Brown's own life principally in Saint Louis
to the time of his escape from slavery in January,
1834.

The remainder of the chapter, which relates "a
thrilling incident of the war," is an imaginary story.
Doubtless the fortuitous meeting of George Loomis,
formerly William, and his mother was basically the
kind of incident that happened many times during and
after the war, but not to Brown and his mother. Brown
was never a soldier, nor did he see his mother, sister,
or brothers after 1833. Before the end of that year all
of them had been sold and resold and taken from Saint
Louis to the deep South and lost in the inferno of
slavery there. The mother's identification of William
by his scars reminds one of the old nurse Eurycleia's
identification of Odysseus by the same means in
Homer's *The Odyssey*, Book XIX. Brown had long
since read Homer.

Chapter XL

1. Because he persisted in his right, in accordance
with the principles of freedom of speech and the press,
to publish an antislavery newspaper in Alton, Illinois,
the Reverend Elijah P. Lovejoy was murdered there
on November 7, 1837. For helping fugitive slaves to
escape, the Reverend Charles T. Torrey was impris-

oned in a Maryland penitentiary, where he died in May, 1846. In a speech in the United States Senate on May 19-20, 1856, Charles Sumner castigated Senator Butler of South Carolina and other proslavery leaders. Two days later he was brutally assaulted by Preston Smith Brooks, a relative of Butler, in the Senate chamber in the United States Capitol. Joseph C. Lovejoy and Owen Lovejoy, *Memoir of the Rev. Elijah P. Lovejoy,* With an Introduction by John Quincy Adams (New York, 1838) 382 pp. Samuel J. May, *Some Recollections of Our Antislavery Conflict* (Boston, 1869), pp. 221-230. Henry Wilson, *History of the Rise and Fall of the Slave Power in America* II (Boston, 1874), 74-80 and 478-495. Archibald H. Grimké, *Charles Sumner: The Scholar in Politics* (American Reformers Series, New York and London, 1892), pp. 278-288.

Chapter XLI

1. Presumably the group Brown had in mind here were members of the Committee of Fifteen—nine members of the House of Representatives and six senators—which constituted the Joint Congressional Committee on Reconstruction. This committee was formed soon after the Thirty-ninth Congress convened in December, 1865.

(2) The committee of Negroes consisted of the four persons Brown mentioned plus seven others. L. H. Douglass was Frederick Douglass's son Lewis. The committee met with President Johnson on February 7, 1866. [Frederick Douglass,] *Life and Times of Frederick Douglass, Written by Himself,* With an In-

troduction by George L. Ruffin, New Revised Edition
(Boston, 1895), pp. 466-469.

Chapter XLII

1. The period of the Memphis riot seems to have
been April 30-May 2, 1866. John Hope Franklin, *Reconstruction: After the Civil War* (Chicago, 1961),
pp. 62-63.

2. The New Orleans riot, or "massacre," of July 30,
1836, was the work of opponents of the constitutional
convention which had been called for that date. W. E.
Burghardt Du Bois, *Black Reconstruction* (New York,
1935), pp. 464-465.

Chapter XLIII

1. The reference here is to the Civil Rights Bill
which was passed by Congress in April, 1866, over
President Johnson's veto.

Chapter XLIV

1. Brown repeated this paragraph in part from the
several editions of *The Black Man,* pp. 33 and 34.

2. William Still (1821-1902) was the author of *The
Underground Rail Road* (Philadelphia, 1872). There
are sketches of his life in William J. Simmons's *Men of
Mark: Eminent, Progressive and Rising* (Cleveland,
1887) and the *Dictionary of American Biography.*